WRITING THROUGH ANCIENT HISTORY
Level 2
"Cursive Models"

A Charlotte Mason Writing Program
"Gentle and Complete"

Historical Narratives, Primary Source Documents, Poetry, and Cultural Tales

BOOKS PUBLISHED BY BROOKDALE HOUSE:

The Writing Through Ancient History books
Writing Through Ancient History Level 1 Cursive Models
Writing Through Ancient History Level 1 Manuscript Models
Writing Through Ancient History Level 2 Cursive Models
Writing Through Ancient History Level 2 Manuscript Models

The Writing Through Medieval History books
Writing Through Medieval History Level 1 Cursive Models
Writing Through Medieval History Level 1 Manuscript Models
Writing Through Medieval History Level 2 Cursive Models
Writing Through Medieval History Level 2 Manuscript Models

The Writing Through Early Modern History Books
Writing Through Early Modern History Level 1 Cursive Models
Writing Through Early Modern History Level 1 Manuscript Models
Writing Through Early Modern History Level 2 Cursive Models
Writing Through Early Modern History Level 2 Manuscript Models

The Writing Through Modern History Books
Writing Through Modern History Level 1 Cursive Models
Writing Through Modern History Level 1 Manuscript Models
Writing Through Modern History Level 2 Cursive Models
Writing Through Modern History Level 2 Manuscript Models

The Fun Spanish Level 1

Sheldon's Primary Language Lessons
(Introductory grammar workbook for elementary students)

The Westminster Shorter Catechism Copybook
(Available in the following font styles: traditional, modern, italic, and vertical, both print and cursive)

The Geography Drawing Series
Drawing Around the World: Europe
Drawing Around the World: USA

Easy Narrative Writing

ISBN: 978-1-64281-033-2

© Copyright 2015. Kimberly Garcia. Published by Brookdale House. Brookdale House grants permission to photocopy pages for use within a single family. All other rights reserved. For permission to make copies, written or otherwise, except for the use within one immediate family, please contact the author at www.brookdalehouse.com or Kimberly@brookdalehouse.com .

Table of Contents

Introduction	v
Definitions—Narration, Copywork, Studied Dictation	vii
Scheduling	x

Chapter I — Historical Narratives

The Goddess of the Silkworm	c. 2640 BC	I-3
Early Inhabitants of Greece	c. 20th century BC	I-7
The Story of Joseph and His Coat of Many Colors	17th Century BC	I-11
The Story of the Grapes from Canaan	15th Century BC	I-16
The Story of Gideon and His Three Hundred Soldiers	13th Century BC	I-21
The Story of Samson, the Strong Man	12th Century BC	I-28
Ruth	12th Century BC	I-36
The Story of the Fight with the Giant	c. 1037 BC – c. 967 BC	I-43
The Story of the Cave of Adullam	c. 1037 BC – c. 967 BC	I-48
The Blind Poet	c. 800 BC – 701 BC	I-52
Death of Romulus	c. 771 BC – c. 717 BC	I-56
Laws of Lycurgus	700 BC – 630 BC	I-60
The Laws of Solon	638 BC–558 BC	I-64
The Story of the Fiery Furnace	c 630 BC – 562 BC	I-69
Aesop	620 BC – 560 BC	I-75
Death of Pericles	495 BC – 429 BC	I-80
The Philosopher Socrates	c. 469 BC – 399 BC	I-84
Accusation of Socrates	c. 469 BC – 399 BC	I-88
Pythagoras	c. 428 BC – 348 BC	I-93
Birth of Alexander	356 BC – 323 BC	I-99
Alexander and Diogenes	356 BC – 323 BC	I-104
A Roman's Honor	249 BC	I-109
The Story of the Empty Tomb	c. 4 BC – 33 AD	I-114
The Wild Caligula	12 AD – 41 AD	I-120
Nero's First Crimes	37 AD – 68 AD	I-125
The Christians Persecuted	37 AD – 68 AD	I-130
The Siege of Jerusalem	9 AD – 79 AD	I-135
A Prophecy Fulfilled	c. 272 AD – 337 AD	I-140

Chapter II* — Primary Source Documents

The Babylonian Story of the Deluge	c. 2600 BC	II-3
The Code of Laws (excerpt) by Hammurabi	c.1760 BC	II-9
The Babylonian Legends of the Creation	? 18th century BC	II-14
The Shih King or Book of Poetry (excerpt)	c. 1763 BC – c. 1123 BC	II-19
The Literature of the Ancient Egyptians (excerpt)	1479 BC to 1425 BC	II-24
David and Goliath **	c. 1037 BC – c. 967 BC	II-28
Works And Days (excerpt) by Hesiod	700 BC	II-32
Apocryphal Life of Esop, the Fabulist ** (excerpt)	620 BC – 560 BC	II-35
The Tao Teh King, Tao and its Characteristics (excerpt)	c. 6th century BC	II-40
The Sayings of Confucius (excerpt)	551 BC – 479 BC	II-46
An Account of Egypt (excerpt), by Herodotus	c. 484 BC–c. 425 BC	II-50

*Note: While some stories may be legends, the dates indicate the estimated lifespan of the main character.
**Note: The date of the story reflects the approximate time in which the main character lived although the written story was dated later.

The Apology (excerpt), by Xenophon about Socrates	c. 431 BC – c. 350 BC	II-54
The Categories (excerpt), by Aristotle	384 BC – 322 BC	II-59
On Old Age (excerpt), by Marcus Tullius Cicero	106 BC – 43 BC	II-63
The Crucifixion of Christ	c. 4 BC to 33 AD	II-67
Marcus Aurelius Antoninus (excerpt), Roman Emperor and philosopher	121 AD – 180 AD	II-72
The Nicene Creed, the second Ecumenical Council	381 AD	II-76

Chapter III[+]   Poetry from/about ancient times

Age, by Anacreon	c. 570 BC – 480 BC	III-3
The Boaster, Aesop	620 BC – 560 BC	III-6
The Cloud Chorus (excerpt), by Aristophanes	c. 456 BC – c. 386 BC	III-9
The Destruction of Sennacherib	705-681 BC	III-12
Horatius (excerpt)	c. 6th Century BC	III-15
Hymn to the Nile, Egypt	c. 2100 BC	III-19
Moderation, by Horace	65 BC – 8 BC	III-22
The Mouse and the Lion, Aesop	620 BC – 560 BC	III-25
Night, by Alcman	c. 7th Century BC	III-28
The People Who Are Really Happy, Jesus Christ	c. 4 BC to 33 AD	III-31
Psalms 23 and 121, by King David	c. 1037 BC – 967 BC	III-34
The Two Paths, Proverbs	c. 1000 BC – 931 BC	III-37
The Vision of Belshazzar, Lord Byron	died 539 BC	III-40

Chapter IV[++]   Cultural Tales

The Deluge of Ogyges[+++]	Greek myth	IV-3
Story of Deucalion	Greek myth	IV-7
The Enchanted Waterfall	Tale of Japan	IV-11
The Escape from the Burning City	Roman myth	IV-16
The Clever Trick	Roman myth	IV-21
The Boards are Eaten	Roman myth	IV-26
The Wolf and the Twins	Roman myth	IV-57
Romulus Rebuilds Rome	Roman myth	IV-62
The Golden Nugget	Tale of China	IV-30
The Lion and the Goat	Tale of India	IV-35
The Penny-Wise Monkey	Jataka tale	IV-39
The Story of the Shipwrecked Sailor	Egyptian tale	IV-43
The Tale of Ivan	Celtic tale	IV-48
The Two Melons	Tale of China	IV-53

Appendix

Oral narration questions	2
Grammar Guide	3
Models from Chapter I Historical Narratives	6
Models from Chapter II Text Excerpt from Primary Source Documents	16
Models from Chapter III Poetry from Ancient History	22
Models from Chapter IV Folktales from Various Cultures	28
Models from *The King James Bible*, alternative models	33

+Note: Chapter III is in alphabetical order. Search for the time period or topic that will best fit your history schedule.
++Note: The publication dates for Chapter IV are not included. These are very old tales with many variations published at various times.
+++Note: The tales grouped by culture are in choronological order rather than alphabetical.

Introduction

Writing Through Ancient History **Layout**

Writing Through Ancient History is a writing program that teaches grammar, spelling, and history—all at once. This volume covers ancient history, from creation myths to 400 AD—the first year of a 4-year cycle.

Writing Through Ancient History, L2 teaches writing the Charlotte Mason way for upper grammar stage students, third through fifth grade. It is divided into four chapters: short stories, text excerpts from primary source documents, poetry, and cultural tales. For Chapter I, short stories that give insight into people, places, and events during ancient times have been selected. Chapter II contains excerpts from primary source documents including, but not limited to, ancient codes, biblical passages, and ancient philosophy. Chapter III contains poetry from and about ancient times. Chapter IV contains folk tales.

In all four chapters, the reading selection is followed by a practice model, which is used for copywork and dictation. There are more than 60 selections included in *Writing Through Ancient History*. **Note: Some of the copywork and dictation passages are about ancient religions and pagan gods. If you do not want your student to copy those passages, see page 31 of the Appendix for substitute models which are from the bible.**

To coordinate *Writing Through Ancient History* with your history topics, refer to the Table of Contents, which also serves as a timeline. Use the timeline provided to determine which selection would be the best fit for that week's history lesson. Historical narratives will primarily come from Chapters I and IV. Feel free to move around the book.

In the Appendix, you will find two models for each reading selection. The first model is the same as the copywork model which followed the reading selection. The second model, which is in italics, is also from the reading selection. It has been added for use by those that like to use a separate model for dictation.

Because *Writing Through Ancient History* was written for grades 3–5, some selections will be too long for some students. Simply reduce any of the models by drawing a line through the unneeded portion. Sometimes you will have to break the model in the middle of a sentence. In that case, stop at a semi-colon (;) or coordinating conjunction (", and" ", or" ", but" ", nor" ", for" ", so" ", yet") to make the selection shorter. Semi-colons and coordinating conjunctions are used to separate main clauses—those with a subject and a predicate. If you must break the model into a shorter sentence, modify the new selection by adding a period at the end and ensure that you have a grammatically correct model. Explain to your student the use of semi-colons and coordinating conjunctions and why the change is being made. This is an excellent opportunity to reinforce and explain the grammar rules involved.

Note: Some of the works included were taken from the public domain; many have been edited for Writing Through Ancient History.

Note: Although titles of books and ships would normally be italicized in texts, they are underlined to teach children that these names are underlined in handwritten works.

All of the principles in *Writing Through Ancient History* are based on the work of Ms. Charlotte Mason. She advocated that children of the grammar or elementary stage practice narration, copywork, and dictation as their primary method of learning to write. But because Ms. Mason's methods have been interpreted differently over the years, I have included alternative suggestions on how to implement *Writing Through Ancient History*. So to begin using *Writing Through Ancient History* as your child's writing program, please read all of the introduction, pages v–ix, before your student begins.

Reading Levels

Chapters II and III contain excerpts from historical documents and history relevant poetry that may be well above the reading level of some grammar and even logic stage students. I recommend that these advanced selections be read to your student. If you would like to stretch your student, ask him to read all or part of the selection back to you. These reading selections offer great opportunity to cover new vocabulary as well as new ideas.

Appendix "Models Only"

The Appendix lists all of the models by chapter. The first model is in normal typeface while the second model is italicized. Only the first model follows the reading selections. The second models were added to give the students a different model for dictation. For the sake of organization, the Appendix contains a copy of the models to assist the instructor with copywork and studied dictation.

Getting Started

On the following page, I have covered each area of the program: Narration, Copywork, and Dictation. I have also provided a guide suggesting how to incorporate grammar into the program. Please read these in their entirety.

Correcting Work

Correcting writing, whether written summations, copywork, or dictation, is always difficult. Ms. Mason advised teachers and parents to correct the student's writings occasionally. This makes perfect sense when realizing that Ms. Mason's methods did not require the need for extensive corrections. She consistently emphasized that work be done correctly the first time. She believed that a student should not be allowed to visually dwell on incorrect work. When a child made a mistake during dictation, Ms. Mason had stamps or pieces of paper available to cover the mistakes so that the mistakes were not reinforced visually.

When a child made a mistake during narrations, she withheld correcting him. I believe that she used the time after the oral narration was finished to discuss the material that had been narrated.

When corrections are needed, it is good to practice the principle of praise before correcting children. Find out what is right with what they've done. Be impressed. Focus on their effort. Build them up. Ephesians 5:29 of the King James Bible says—

Let no corrupt communication
proceed out of your mouth, but
that which is good to the use of edifying,
that it may minister grace
unto the hearers.

The hearers are our students—our children. And the words we say will either minister grace or condemnation. We must encourage them and free them from the fear of our frustrations and negative feedback as we correct them.

Definitions

Personal Narrations – the act of retelling

Ms. Mason believed narrations should be done immediately after the story was read to the student or by the student. Narrations are very simple, yet very effective in teaching writing. The act of narrating helps children to internalize the content of the reading material they have been exposed to and allows them to make it their own. In order to narrate, students must listen carefully, dissect the information, and then express that same information in their own words. It is a powerful tool, but very simple to put into practice.

Oral narrations Read all or part of the story only once before requiring the student to narrate! It will require him to pay attention. Simply ask your student to tell you what he has just heard or read.

If your student has trouble with this process, show him how to narrate by demonstrating the process for him. **Read a selection yourself and then narrate it to him. Ask him to imitate you.** If he continues to draw a blank, use the list of questions below to prompt him. (See the removable list of narration questions in the Appendix, page 2, for daily use. The Appendix also contains questions for poetry and primary source documents.)

Besides all of the previously mentioned benefits, oral narrations teach students to digest information, dissect it, and reorganize it into their own words while thinking on their feet. This practice helps students to develop the art of public speaking. This formal process will force them to express their ideas without a written plan. It strengthens the mind. And over time, their speech will become fluent and natural. (I sometimes have my children stand as they narrate. It makes the process more formal.)

If your student has difficulty with narrations, ask some or all of the following questions:

1. Who was the main character?
2. What was the character like?
3. Where was the character?
4. What time was it in the story?
5. Who else was in the story?
6. Does the main character have an enemy?
   (The enemy may be another character, himself, or nature.)
7. Did the main character have a problem? If not, what did the character want?
8. What does the main character do? What does he say? If there are others, what do they do?
9. Why does the character do what he does?
10. What happens to the character as he tries to solve his problem?
11. Is there a moral to the story? If so, what was it?
12. What happens at the end of the story? Or how does the main character finally solve his problem?

Written Summations Around the age of 10, students were required by Ms. Mason to write down their narrations for themselves. Many students can do this earlier. Written summations will allow your student to develop this skill. If your student is able, have him write as much as he can, as perfectly as he can, even around the age of 8.

At the end of each oral narration, ask your child to summarize the reading selection by identifying the beginning, the middle, and the end. He should be able to do this in about three to six sentences. Younger students will sometimes begin each sentence with "First,..." or "At the beginning,..." This is okay. But once the student masters the summation, ask him to summarize without these types of words. Tell him to begin with the subject or the time.

Ex: When Louisa May Alcott was a young girl, she was very happy because she spent her time playing with her sisters and writing in her diary.

The benefits of written summations are manifold. They will help your student to think linearly from the beginning of the reading selection to the end. They also provide the right amount of content for the reluctant writer. Additionally, the act of summarizing teaches students to identify the main thread or central idea of a passage. (Even though your child begins to write his written summations, have him continue his oral narrations without limit. These will help him to internalize and learn the historical content of the stories in *Writing Through Ancient History* as well as develop his public speaking skills.)

Copywork and Grammar—copying a passage exactly as written

As your child copies the model before him, stay near so that you are able to correct any problems immediately.

Before your child begins, discuss the model with him. Point out the grammatical elements that he is learning. Have your child identify the part of speech in the model and circle it with a colored pencil. See page 3 of the Appendix for a grammar guide. (Spend approximately one month on each new part of speech.) When using the grammar guide, continue to review by including all previously learned work in the current lesson. For the second month, he is to identify both nouns and verbs. The third—nouns, verbs, and pronouns.

Ms. Mason recommended the formal study of grammar at about 4th or 5th grade. If you opt to add a formal program for your upper grammar stage student, that would be worthwhile. If you do so, you may omit the grammar study in this program.

Grammar
If you would prefer that your student study grammar with his copywork, see the grammar guide in the Appendix page 3. It focuses on the 8 parts of speech, as well as fundamental punctuation. The process involves the student identifying the parts of speech and color-coding the copywork selections according to the guide. The process is cumulative in that students should roll the new grammar concept in with the old. By of the end of the year, students should be identifying all eight parts of speech in their copywork.

Studied Dictation—the act of writing from an oral reading

Once again, Ms. Mason's ideas are simple, yet effective. The goal in dictation is to teach your child to write correctly and from memory the sentences or clauses he has just heard. Ms. Mason let the child study the dictation for a few minutes. She wrote down any unknown or difficult for him on a board. She then erased the board and read each passage only once. From this one reading, the child wrote; however, if the child made a mistake, she covered the mistake instantly so that the student was not allowed to visualize and internalize it.

For the child who has never done dictation, start by reading as many times as necessary so that your child memorizes the sentences. Work down to one reading per 2 or 3 sentences or main clauses. This is an advanced skill and may require time to achieve. Be patient, but consistent. (If needed, allow your student to repeat the model back to you before he writes. Some students may need this reinforcement; others may not.)

After you write the model on the whiteboard, discuss it, in depth, with your student. An example of the process follows.

MODEL

"Mary, did you spill the ink on the carpet?" asked Tom.
"No, Tom," answered Mary. "Did you, Will?"
"I did not, Mary, but I know who did," said Will.
"Who was it, Will?"
Will did not answer in words. He pointed a finger at Fido, and guilty little Fido crept under the sofa.

QUESTIONS TO ASK:

1. What are the names of the people in this story? How does each name begin?
   The names of people always begin with capital letters.
2. Study this model, telling what words begin with capitals and why; which words are indented and why; what marks of punctuation are used and why.

FIRST PARAGRAPH

3. Why is Mary indented in this paragraph.
4. Why is Mary capitalized? Why are the names capitalized?
5. Why is there a comma to separate "Mary" from the rest of the sentence?
6. Why are there quotation marks around certain words?
7. Why does the quoted sentence end with a question mark?
8. Why do some sentences end with a period?

SECOND PARAGRAPH

9. Where does the second paragraph begin?
10. The paragraph begins with someone speaking. How do we know this?
11. Why is the word no capitalized?
12. Why is there a comma after no?
13. Why is there a comma after Tom? After you?
14. Why is there a period after Mary and a question after Will.

DO THIS WITH EACH PARAGRAPH

If there are any questions that your student cannot answer, tell him the answers. Discuss the grammar with him, and work with him until he can narrate why the model is punctuated the way it is.

Do the same with spelling. Identify the words that your student doesn't know and discuss why that word is spelled the way it is.

To see an example of studied dictation, visit the youtube video at the link below:
https://www.youtube.com/watch?v=xoTACGomwsw

or search "Studied Dictation Demonstration" on youtube.
There I demonstrate this dictation process.

Scheduling Information

Listed below is a recommendation for the use of *Writing Through Ancient History*; however, this is **only a recommendation** and should be adjusted for your student's individual needs. **Further explanations and alternate methods** are included on the next page. Please feel free to adjust these methods to make writing as painless as possible for your student. Every child is different.

One Suggested Schedule:

Day 1   **Reading, Oral Narrations, and Written Summations**
From the Table of Contents, choose a story from Chapters I or IV.
Either you or your student should read the story selection once.
First, have the student orally narrate the story back to you.
(If he has difficulty, use the narration questions listed in the Appendix.)
Second, ask the student to summarize the story in about three sentences to six sentences. If he is able, have him write one or more sentences from his summation. Write for him, if needed. **(For more on narrations, see page vii.)**

Day 2   **Copywork and Grammar** Complete Model Practice 1 from Day 1's reading selection. Discuss/explain the grammar and punctuation in the model. Do a color-coded grammar study.
(For more on copywork and grammar, see page viii.)

Day 3   **Studied Dictation** Complete Model Practice 2, using the additional model located in the Appendix, also from Day 1's reading selection. Follow the guidelines for studied dictation on page viii. Neatly write the italic model provided in the Appendix for your student on a separate paper or white board. Allow the student to study the model before writing. Erase the model and dictate.

Day 4   **Oral narrations and Copywork**
From the Table of Contents, choose a selection from Chapters II or III.
Read all **or part** of the primary source document to your student. He may read the poem himself. If so, teach him to read with expression.
Discuss the complicated ideas in the document. Have your student narrate what he has learned. Complete Model Practice 1 using the copywork model.

Day 5   **Studied Dictation** Complete Model Practice 2, also from Day 4's reading selection. Follow the guidelines for studied dictation on page viii. Neatly write the Italic model provided in the Appendix for your student on a separate piece of paper or a white board. Allow the student to study the model before writing. Erase the model and dictate.

If the models are too long

If the models are too long for your student, reduce them. Third graders, or even older reluctant writers, should not be forced to do more than they are able. See the bolded paragraph on page v for guidelines on reducing the models.

If your child isn't ready for dictation

Replace the dictation with copywork of the same model, or write the dictation model from the Appendix into the model practice 2 area. Have your student copy your written model in the model practice 3 area.

Optional Schedules

Charlotte Mason's Methods

Ms. Mason used narration, copywork, and dictation simultaneously throughout a young child's education. Narrations were done immediately after he had listened to or read the selection. Copywork was done from well-written sentences. And while many don't believe copywork to be valuable once a student learns to write from dictation, Ms. Mason believed that copywork was extremely valuable for many years alongside dictation. Dictation was a separate part of the process, mostly for the purpose of teaching spelling.

Ms. Mason allowed students to look at the dictation passages and study them before the student began writing. This process was helpful because it allowed the student to visualize how the passage should look. It taught him to study with intention. It taught him to focus on the words. After the passage was read once, the student wrote the passage from memory. This method improved a child's spelling and his grasp of correct punctuation as well.

But not everyone who follows Ms. Mason's methods follows each area of narration, copywork, and dictation in the same way. Below are some ways to incorporate some or all of these ideas into your child's learning adventure.

Different Copywork Passages Daily

Simply use *Writing Through Ancient History* as written, covering two stories per week. **Day 1**, pick a selection from Chapters I or IV. Read and have the student do an oral narration and a written summation. **Day 2**, do copywork and a color-coded grammar study of the model. **Day 3,** the teacher should write all or part of the italicized model from the Appendix onto the Model Practice 2 area, in ink. The student should copy the model and then do a color-coded grammar study of the model in the Model Practice 2 area. **Day 4**, pick a selection from Chapters II or III, a primary source selection or poetry selection. Do oral narration, copywork, and a color-coded grammar study of the model. **Day 5,** the teacher should write the italicized model from the Appendix onto the Model Practice 2 area, in ink. The student should copy the model and do a color-coded grammar study of the model in the Model Practice 2 area. This will provide your student with four different copywork selections each week from two different sources.

Copywork as Dictation

Day 1, pick a selection from Chapters I or IV. Read and have the student do an oral narration and a written summation. **Day 2**, do copywork and a color-coded grammar study of the model. **Day 3,** do studied dictation of the same model. Have your student write in the Model Practice 2 area. **Day 4**, pick a selection from Chapters II or III, a primary source selection or poetry selection. Do an oral narration, copywork and a color-coded grammar study of the model. **Day 5,** do studied dictation of yesterday's copywork. Have your student write in the Model Practice 2 area.

Copywork and Dictation

Follow the suggested schedule on page x.

Reminders and Helps

- Use *Writing Through Ancient History* in the best way possible to serve your student's needs. Adapt any area, as necessary.
- Help students with spelling, as necessary. Set your student up for success.
- In the case of dialogue, remind your student that each time a different character is speaking, a new paragraph is started via indentions. When they first encounter this, show them an example before requiring them to do this.
- If the size of the selection is too large, **simply reduce it and require less.**
- Set your student up for success. He shouldn't be expected to know what he has not yet been taught.
- To sum up Charlotte Mason's methods:

Quality over quantity.
Accuracy over speed.
Ideas over drill.
Perfection over mediocrity.

Added Note on Paragraphing
For full-length written narrations (not summations, but the whole story)

You may want your student to occasionally write his narrations in place of the summation. Ms. Mason had children begin writing their narrations around the age of 10. This is equivalent to fourth or fifth grade, and it is a good time for most students. To make the transition to written narrations, have your student orally narrate first, then ask him to write down his narration. Eventually he won't need the oral narration.

In the actual writing of the narration, the difficult elements for most students will be punctuation, grammar, spelling, and paragraph breaks. Through the copywork and dictation, students actively learn correct punctuation, grammar, and spelling. And although they make mistakes, with practice in these areas, they will improve.

Paragraph breaks, however, are not often taught—in any curriculum. Many students intuitively learn when to begin a new paragraph because they read well-written literature. But this isn't always enough.

Paragraphing is easy to learn. Each time the who, what, when, where, why, or how of the story changes, a new paragraph is begun. Look at the following story—

The Penny-Wise Monkey
re-told by Ellen C. Babbitt
from <u>More Jataka Tales</u>

  Once upon a time the king of a large and rich country gathered together his army to take a faraway little country. The king and his soldiers marched all morning long and then went into camp in the forest.
(who=king and soldiers, what=march and went, when=once upon a time, where=camp in forest, why=to take a country)

  When they fed the horses, they gave them some peas to eat. One of the Monkeys living in the forest saw the peas and jumped down to get some of them. He filled his mouth and hands with them, and up into the tree he went again, and sat down to eat the peas.

(New paragraph, a change in the what, what=gave the horses peas, change in the when, when=feeding the horses, the monkey is introduced)

As he sat there eating the peas, one pea fell from his hand to the ground. At once, the greedy Monkey dropped all the peas he had in his hands and ran down to hunt for the lost pea. But he could not find that one pea. He climbed up into his tree again and sat still looking very glum. "To get more, I threw away what I had," he said to himself.
(New paragraph, a change in the who, the story is now focused on the monkey and not the king, who=monkey)

The king had watched the Monkey, and he said to himself, "I will not be like this foolish Monkey, who lost much to gain a little. I will go back to my own country and enjoy what I now have."
(New paragraph, a change in the who, who=the king, the story is now focused on the king again)

So he and his men marched back home.
(New paragraph, a change in the what, what=marched back home)

Note: Also, when writing dialogue in a conversation, a new paragraph is started each time a different character is speaking.

Bonus Materials

To get additional educational resources, free and almost free, sign up for our newsletter at

www.brookdalehouse.com

or

scan:

CHAPTER I

Historical Narratives Covering Ancient History

The Goddess of the Silkworm

c. 2640 BC
from A Child's World Reader
by Hetty Browne, Sarah Withers, and W K. Tate

Hoangti was the emperor of China. He had a beautiful wife whose name was Si-ling. The emperor and his wife loved their people and always thought of their happiness.

In those days, the Chinese people wore clothes made of skins. By and by animals grew scarce, and the people did not know what they should wear. The emperor and empress tried in vain to find some other way of clothing them.

One morning Hoangti and his wife were in the beautiful palace garden. They walked up and down, up and down, talking of their people.

Suddenly the emperor said, "Look at those worms on the mulberry trees, Si-ling. They seem to be spinning."

Si-ling looked, and sure enough, the worms were spinning. A long thread was coming from the mouth of each, and each little worm was winding this thread around its body.

Si-ling and the emperor stood still and watched the worms. "How wonderful!" said Si-ling.

The next morning Hoangti and the empress walked under the trees again. They found some worms still winding thread. Others had already spun their cocoons and were fast asleep. In a few days, all of the worms had spun cocoons.

"This is indeed a wonderful, wonderful thing!" said Si-ling. "Why, each worm has a thread on its body long enough to make a house for itself!"

Si-ling thought of this day after day. One morning as she and the emperor walked under the trees, she said, "I believe I could find a way to weave those long threads into cloth."

"But how could you unwind the threads?" asked the emperor.

"I'll find a way," Si-ling said. And she did; but she had to try many, many times.

She put the cocoons in a hot place, and the little sleepers soon died. Then the cocoons were thrown into boiling water to make the threads soft. After that the long threads could be easily unwound.

Now Si-ling had to think of something else; she had to find a way to weave the threads into cloth. After many trials, she made a loom—the first that was ever made. She taught others to weave, and soon hundreds of people were making cloth from the threads of the silkworm.

The people ever afterward called Si-ling "The Goddess of the Silkworm." And whenever the emperor walked with her in the garden, they liked to watch the silkworms spinning threads for the good of their people.

Written Summation

"This is indeed a wonderful, wonderful thing!" said Si-ling. "Why, the worms have threads on their bodies. Each worm has a thread long enough to make a house for itself!"

Model Practice 1 (adapted from the original)

Model Practice 2

Model Practice 3

Early Inhabitants of Greece

c. 20th century BC
from The Story of the Greeks
by H. A. Guerber

Although Greece (or Hellas) is only half as large as the state of New York, it holds a very important place in the history of the world. It is situated in the southern part of Europe, cut off from the rest of the continent by a chain of high mountains which form a great wall on the north. It is surrounded on nearly all sides by the blue waters of the Mediterranean Sea, which stretch so far inland that it is said no part of the country is forty miles from the sea, or ten miles from the hills. Thus shut in by sea and mountains, it forms a little territory by itself, and it was the home of a noted people.

The history of Greece goes back to the time when people did not know how to write, and kept no record of what was happening around them. For a long while, the stories told by parents to their children were the only information which could be had about the country and its former inhabitants; and these stories, slightly changed by every new teller, grew more and more extraordinary as time passed. At last, they were so changed that no one could tell where the truth ended and fancy began.

The beginning of Greek history is therefore like a fairy tale; and while much of it cannot, of course, be true, it is the only information we have about the early Greeks. It is these strange fireside stories, which used to amuse Greek children so many years ago, that you are first going to hear.

About two thousand years before the birth of Christ, in the days when Isaac wanted to go down into Egypt, Greece was inhabited by a savage race of men called the Pelasgians. They lived in the forests or in caves hollowed out of the mountainside and hunted wild beasts with great clubs and stone-tipped arrows and spears. They were so rude and wild that they ate nothing but raw meat, berries, and the roots which they dug up with sharp stones or even with their hands.

For clothing, the Pelasgians used the skins of the beasts they had killed; and to protect themselves against other savages, they gathered together in families or tribes, each having a chief who led in war and in the chase.

There were other far more civilized nations in those days. Among these were the Egyptians who lived in Africa. They had long known the use of fire, had good tools, and were much further advanced than the Pelasgians. They had learned not only to build houses, but to erect the most wonderful monuments in the world—the Pyramids, of which you have no doubt heard.

In Egypt, there were at that time a number of learned men. They were acquainted with many of the arts and sciences and recorded all they knew in a peculiar writing of their own invention. Their neighbors, the Phœnicians whose land also bordered on the Mediterranean Sea, were quite civilized too; and as both of these nations had ships, they soon began to sail all around that great inland sea.

As they had no compass, the Egyptian and Phœnician sailors did not venture out of sight of land. They first sailed along the shore and then to the islands which they could see far out on the blue waters.

When they had come to one island, they could see another still farther on; for, as you will see on any map, the Mediterranean Sea, between Greece and Asia, is dotted with islands which look like stepping-stones going from one coast to the other.

Advancing thus carefully, the Egyptians and Phœnicians finally came to Greece, where they made settlements, and began to teach the Pelasgians many useful and important things.

Written Summation

About two thousand years before the birth of Christ, Greece was inhabited by a savage race of men called the Pelasgians. They lived in the forests or in caves hollowed out of the mountainside and hunted wild beasts with great clubs and stone-tipped arrows and spears. They were so rude and wild that they ate nothing but raw meat, berries, and roots.

Model Practice 1

Model Practice 2

Model Practice 3

The Story of Joseph and His Coat of Many Colors

c. 1650 BC-1540 BC
from The Wonder Book of Bible Stories
by Logan Marshall

After Jacob came back to the land of Canaan with his eleven sons, another son was born to him, the second child of his wife Rachel, whom Jacob loved so well. But soon after the baby came, his mother Rachel died, and Jacob was filled with sorrow. Even to this day, you can see the place where Rachel was buried, on the road between Jerusalem and Bethlehem. Jacob named the child whom Rachel left, Benjamin; and now Jacob had twelve sons. Most of them were grown-up men; but Joseph was a boy seventeen years old, and his brother Benjamin was almost a baby.

Of all his children, Jacob loved Joseph the best, because he was Rachel's child; because he was so much younger than most of his brothers; and because he was good and faithful and thoughtful. Jacob gave to Joseph a robe or coat of bright colors, made somewhat like a long cloak with wide sleeves. This was a special mark of Jacob's favor to Joseph, and it made his older brothers envious of him.

Then, too, Joseph did what was right, while his older brothers often did very wrong acts, of which Joseph sometimes told their father; and this made them very angry at Joseph. But they hated him still more because of two strange dreams he had and of which he told them.

He said one day, "Listen to this dream that I have dreamed. I dreamed that we were out in the field binding sheaves, when suddenly my sheaf stood up, and all your sheaves came around it and bowed down to my sheaf!"

And they said scornfully, "Do you suppose that the dream means that you will some time rule over us, and that we shall bow down to you?"

Then, a few days after, Joseph said, "I have dreamed again. This time, I saw in my dream the sun and the moon and eleven stars all come and bow to me!"

And his father said to him, "I do not like you to dream such dreams. Shall I and your mother and your brothers come and bow down before you as if you were a king?"

His brothers hated Joseph and would not speak kindly to him; but his father thought much of what Joseph had said.

At one time, Joseph's ten brothers were taking care of the flock in the fields near Shechem, which was nearly fifty miles from Hebron, where Jacob's tents were spread. And Jacob wished to send a message to his sons, and he called Joseph and said to him:

"Your brothers are near Shechem with the flock. I wish that you would go to them and take a message and find if they are well and if the flocks are doing well; and bring me word from them."

That was quite an errand—for a boy to go alone over the country and find his way for fifty miles and then walk home again. But Joseph was a boy who could take care of himself and could be trusted; so he went forth on his journey, walking northward over the mountains past Bethlehem and Jerusalem and Bethel—though we are not sure those cities were then built, except Jerusalem, which was already a strong city.

When Joseph reached Shechem, he could not find his brothers, for they had taken their flocks to another place. A man met Joseph wandering in the field and asked him, "Whom are you seeking?"

Joseph said, "I am looking for my brothers, the sons of Jacob. Can you tell me where I will find them?"

And the man said, "They are at Dothan; for I heard them say that they were going there."

Then Joseph walked over the hills to Dothan, which was fifteen miles further. And his brothers saw him afar off coming toward them. They knew him by his bright garment; and one said to another: "Look, that dreamer is coming! Come, let us kill him and throw his body into a pit and tell his father that some wild beast has eaten him; and then we will see what becomes of his dreams."

One of his brothers, whose name was Reuben, felt more kindly toward Joseph than the others. He said:

"Let us not kill him, but let us throw him into this pit in the wilderness and leave him there to die."

But Reuben intended, after they had gone away, to lift Joseph out of the pit and take him home to his father. The brothers did as Reuben told them; they threw Joseph into the pit, which was empty. He cried and begged them to save him, but they would not. They calmly sat down to eat their dinner on the grass, while their brother was calling to them from the pit.

After the dinner, Reuben chanced to go to another part of the field; so that he was not at hand when a company of men passed by with their camels, going from Gilead, on the east of the river Jordan, to Egypt, to sell spices and fragrant gum from trees to the Egyptians.

Then Judah, another of Joseph's brothers, sáid, "What good will it do us to kill our brother? Would it not be better for us to sell him to these men and let them carry him away? After all, he is our brother, and we would better not kill him."

His brothers agreed with him, so they stopped the men who were passing and drew up Joseph from the pit. For twenty pieces of silver, they sold Joseph to these men; and they took him away with them down to Egypt.

After a while, Reuben came to the pit, where they had left Joseph and looked into it; but Joseph was not there. Then Reuben was in great trouble; and he came back to his brothers, saying: "The boy is not there! What shall I do?"

Then his brothers told Reuben what they had done; and they all agreed together to deceive their father. They killed one of the goats and dipped Joseph's coat in its blood; and they brought it to their father, and they said to him: "We found this coat out in the wilderness. Look at it, father, and tell us if you think it was the coat of your son."

And Jacob knew it at once. He said: "It is my son's coat. Some wild beast has eaten him. There is no doubt that Joseph has been torn in pieces!"

And Jacob's heart was broken over the loss of Joseph, all the more because he had sent Joseph alone on the journey through the wilderness. They tried to comfort him, but he would not be comforted. He said: "I will go down to the grave mourning for my poor lost son."

So the old man sorrowed for his son Joseph; and all the time his wicked brothers knew that Joseph was not dead; but they would not tell their father the dreadful deed they had done to their brother in selling him as a slave.

Written Summation

Of all his children, Jacob loved Joseph the best. Jacob gave to Joseph a robe or coat of bright colors, made somewhat like a long cloak with wide sleeves. This was a special mark of Jacob's favor to Joseph, and it made his older brothers envious of him.

Model Practice 1

Model Practice 2

Model Practice 3

The Story of the Grapes from Canaan

15th century BC
from The Wonder Book of Bible Stories
by Logan Marshall

The Israelites stayed in their camp before Mount Sinai almost a year, while they were building the Tabernacle and learning God's laws given through Moses. At last, the cloud over the Tabernacle rose up, and the people knew that this was the sign for them to move. They took down the Tabernacle and their own tents, and journeyed toward the land of Canaan for many days.

At last, they came to a place just on the border between the desert and Canaan, called Kadesh, or Kadesh-barnea. Here they stopped to rest, for there were many springs of water and some grass for their cattle. While they were waiting at Kadesh-barnea and were expecting soon to march into the land which was to be their home, God told Moses to send onward some men who should walk through the land and look at it, and then come back and tell what they had found; what kind of a land it was, and what fruits grew in it, and what people were living in it. The Israelites could more easily win the land if these men, after walking through it, could act as their guides and point out the best places in it and the best plans of making war upon it.

So Moses chose out some men of high rank among the people, one ruler from each tribe, twelve men in all. One of these was Joshua, who was the helper of Moses in caring for the people, and another was Caleb, who belonged to the tribe of Judah. These twelve men went out and walked over the mountains of Canaan and looked at the cities and saw the fields. In one place, just before they came back to the camp, they cut down a cluster of ripe grapes which was so large that two men carried it between them, hanging from a staff. They named the place where they found this bunch of grapes Eshcol, a word which means "a cluster." These twelve men were called "spies," because they went "to spy out the land"; and after forty days, they came back to the camp, and this was what they said:

"We walked all over the land and found it a rich land. There is grass for all our flocks, and fields where we can raise grain, and trees bearing fruits, and streams running down the sides of the hills. But we found that the people who live there are very strong and are men of war. They have cities with walls that reach almost up to the sky; and some of the men are giants, so tall that we felt that we were like grasshoppers beside them."

One of the spies, who was Caleb, said, "All that is true, yet we need not be afraid to go up and take the land. It is a good land, well worth fighting for; God is on our side, and he will help us to overcome those people."

But all the other spies, except Joshua, said, "No, there is no use in trying to make war upon such strong people. We can never take those walled cities, and we dare not fight those tall giants."

And the people, who had journeyed all the way through the wilderness to find this very land, were so frightened by the words of the ten spies that now, on the very border of Canaan, they dared not enter it. They forgot that God had led them out of Egypt, that he had kept them in the dangers of the desert, that he had given them water out of the rock, and bread from the sky, and his law from the mountain.

All that night, after the spies had brought back their report, the people were so frightened that they could not sleep. They cried out against Moses, and blamed him for bringing them out of the land of Egypt. They forgot all their troubles in Egypt, their toil and their slavery, and resolved to go back to that land. They said:

"Let us choose a ruler in place of Moses, who has brought us into all these evils, and let us turn back to the land of Egypt!"

But Caleb and Joshua, two of the spies, said, "Why should we fear? The land of Canaan is a good land; it is rich with milk and honey. If God is our friend and is with us, we can easily conquer the people who live there. Above all things, let us not rebel against the Lord, or disobey him, and make him our enemy."

But the people were so angry with Caleb and Joshua that they were ready to stone them and kill them. Then suddenly the people saw a strange sight. The glory of the Lord, which stayed in the Holy of Holies, the inner room of the Tabernacle, now flashed out, and shone from the door of the Tabernacle.

And the Lord, out of this glory, spoke to Moses, and said, "How long will this people disobey me and despise me? They shall not go into the good land that I have promised them. Not one of them shall enter in, except Caleb and Joshua, who have been faithful to me. All the people who are twenty years old and over it shall die in the desert; but their little children shall grow up in the wilderness, and when they become men, they shall enter in and own the land that I promised to their fathers. You people are not worthy of the land that I have been keeping for you. Now turn back into the desert and stay there until you die. After you are dead, Joshua shall lead your children into the land of Canaan. And because Caleb showed another spirit and was true to me, and followed my will fully, Caleb shall live to go into the land, and shall have his choice of a home there. To-morrow, turn back into the desert by the way of the Red Sea."

And God told Moses that for every day that the spies had spent in Canaan, looking at the land, the people should spend a year in the wilderness; so that they should live in the desert forty years, instead of going at once into the promised land.

When Moses told all God's words to the people, they felt worse than before. They changed their minds as suddenly as they had made up their minds.

"No," they all said, "we will not go back to the wilderness; we will go straight into the land, and see if we are able to take it, as Joshua and Caleb have said."

"You must not go into the land," said Moses.

But the people would not obey. They marched up the mountain and tried to march at once into the land. But they were without leaders and without order—a mob of men, untrained and in confusion. And the people in that part of the land, the Canaanites and the Amorites, came down upon them and killed many of them and drove them away. Then, discouraged and beaten, they obeyed the Lord and Moses, and went once more into the desert.

And in the desert of Paran, on the south of the land of Canaan, the children of Israel stayed nearly forty years; and all because they would not trust in the Lord.

Written Summation

But all the other spies, except Joshua, said, "No, there is no use in trying to make war upon such strong people. We can never take those walled cities, and we dare not fight those tall giants."

Model Practice 1

Model Practice 2

Model Practice 3

The Story of Gideon and His Three Hundred Soldiers

13th century BC
from The Wonder Book of Bible Stories
by Logan Marshall

At last, the people of Israel came into the promised land, but they did evil in the sight of the Lord in worshipping Baal; and the Lord left them to suffer for their sins. Once the Midianites, living near the desert on the east of Israel, came against the tribes. The two tribes that suffered the hardest fate were Ephraim, and the part of Manasseh on the west of Jordan. For seven years, the Midianites swept over their land every year, just at the time of harvest, and carried away all the crops of grain, until the Israelites had no food for themselves, and none for their sheep and cattle. The Midianites brought also their own flocks and camels without number, which ate all the grass of the field.

The people of Israel were driven away from their villages and their farms, and were compelled to hide in the caves of the mountains. And if any Israelite could raise any grain, he buried it in pits covered with earth, or in empty winepresses, where the Midianites could not find it.

One day, a man named Gideon was threshing out wheat in a hidden place, when he saw an angel sitting under an oak tree. The angel said to him: "You are a brave man, Gideon, and the Lord is with you. Go out boldly, and save your people from the power of the Midianites." Gideon answered the angel:

"O, Lord, how can I save Israel? Mine is a poor family in Manasseh, and I am the least in my father's house."

And the Lord said to him: "Surely I will be with you, and I will help you drive out the Midianites."

Gideon felt that it was the Lord who was talking with him, in the form of an angel. He brought an offering, and laid it on a rock before the angel. Then the angel touched the offering with his staff. At once, a fire leaped up and burned the offering; and then the angel vanished from his sight. Gideon was afraid when he saw this; but the Lord said to him: "Peace be unto you, Gideon, do not fear, for I am with you."

On the spot where the Lord appeared to Gideon, under an oak tree, near the village of Ophrah, in the tribe-land of Manasseh, Gideon built an altar and called it by a name which means: "The Lord is peace." This altar was standing long afterward in that place.

Then the Lord told Gideon that before setting his people free from the Midianites, he must first set them free from the service of Baal and Asherah, the two idols most worshipped among them. Near the house of Gideon's own father stood an altar to Baal, and the image of Asherah.

On that night, Gideon went out with ten men, and threw down the image of Baal, and cut in pieces the wooden image of Asherah, and destroyed the altar before these idols. And in its place, he built an altar to the God of Israel; and on it laid the broken pieces of the idols for wood, and with them offered a young ox as a burnt offering.

On the next morning, when the people of the village went out to worship their idols, they found them cut in pieces, the altar taken away; in its place an altar of the Lord, and on it the pieces of the Asherah were burning as wood under a sacrifice to the Lord. The people looked at the broken and burning idols; and they said: "Who has done this?"

Some one said: "Gideon, the son of Joash, did this last night."

Then they came to Joash, Gideon's father, and said:

"We are going to kill your son because he has destroyed the image of Baal, who is our god."

And Joash, Gideon's father, said, "If Baal is a god, he can take care of himself and punish the man who has destroyed his image. Why should you help Baal? Let Baal help himself."

And when they saw that Baal could not harm the man who had broken down his altar and his image, the people turned from Baal, back to their own Lord God.

Gideon sent messengers through all Manasseh on the west of Jordan, and the tribes near on the north; and the men of the tribes gathered around him, with a few swords and spears, but very few, for the Israelites were not ready for war. They met beside a great spring on Mount Gilboa, called "the fountain of Harod." Mount Gilboa is one of the three mountains on the east of the plain of Esdraelon, or the plain of Jezreel, where once there had been a great battle. On the plain, stretching up the side of another of these mountains, called "the Hill of Moreh," was the camp of a vast Midianite army. For as soon as the Midianites heard that Gideon had undertaken to set his people free, they came against him with a mighty host.

Gideon was a man of faith. He wished to be sure that God was leading him, and he prayed to God and said:

"O Lord God, give me some sign that thou wilt save Israel through me. Here is a fleece of wool on this threshing floor. If tomorrow morning the fleece is wet with dew, while the grass around it is dry, then I shall know that thou art with me; and that thou wilt give me victory over the Midianites."

Very early the next morning, Gideon came to look at the fleece. He found it wringing wet with dew, while all around the grass was dry. But Gideon was not yet satisfied. He said to the Lord:

"O Lord, be not angry with me; but give me just one more sign. Tomorrow morning let the fleece be dry, and let the dew fall all around it, and then I will doubt no more."

The next morning, Gideon found the grass and the bushes wet with dew, while the fleece of wool was dry. And Gideon was now sure that God had called him, and that God would give him victory over the enemies of Israel.

The Lord said to Gideon: "Your army is too large. If Israel should win the victory, they would say, 'we won it by our own might.' Send home all those who are afraid to fight."

For many of the people were frightened, as they looked at the host of their enemies, and the Lord knew that these men would only hinder the rest in the battle. So Gideon sent word through the camp:

"Whoever is afraid of the enemy may go home." And twenty-two thousand people went away, leaving only ten thousand in Gideon's army. But the army was stronger though it was smaller, for the cowards had gone, and only the brave men were left.

But the Lord said to Gideon: "The people are yet too many. You need only a few of the bravest and best men to fight in this battle. Bring the men down the mountain, past the water, and I will show you there how to find the men whom you need."

In the morning, Gideon, by God's command, called his ten thousand men out, and made them march down the hill, just as though they were going to attack the enemy.

And as they were beside the water, he noticed how they drank, and set them apart in two companies, according to their way of drinking.

When they came to the water, most of the men threw aside their shields and spears, and knelt down and scooped up a draft of the water with both hands together like a cup. These men Gideon commanded to stand in one company.

There were a few men who did not stop to take a large draft of water. Holding spear and shield in the right hand, to be ready for the enemy if one should suddenly appear, they merely caught up a handful of the water in passing and marched on, lapping up the water from one hand. God said to Gideon:

"Set by themselves these men who lapped up each a handful of water. These are the men whom I have chosen to set Israel free."

Gideon counted these men, and found that there were only three hundred of them, while all the rest bowed down on their faces to drink. The difference between them was that the three hundred were earnest men, of one purpose; not turning aside from their aim even to drink, as the others did. Then, too, they were watchful men, always ready to meet their enemies.

So Gideon, at God's command, sent back to the camp on Mount Gilboa all the rest of his army, nearly ten thousand men, keeping with himself only his little band of three hundred.

Gideon's plan did not need a large army; but it needed a few careful, bold men, who should do exactly as their leader commanded them. He gave to each man a lamp, a pitcher, and a trumpet, and told the men just what was to be done with them. The lamp was lighted, but was placed inside the pitcher, so that it could not be seen. He divided his men into three companies, and very quietly led them down the mountain in the middle of the night, and arranged them all in order around the camp of the Midianites.

Then at one moment, a great shout rang out in the darkness, "The sword of the Lord and of Gideon," and after it came a crash of breaking pitchers, and then a flash of light in every direction. The three hundred men had given the shout, and broken their pitchers, so that on every side lights were shining. The men blew their trumpets with a mighty noise; and the Midianites were roused from sleep, to see enemies all round them, lights beaming and swords flashing, while everywhere the sharp sound of the trumpets was heard.

They were filled with sudden terror, and thought only of escape, not of fighting. But wherever they turned, their enemies seemed to be standing with swords drawn. They trampled each other down to death, flying from the Israelites. Their own land was in the east, across the river Jordan, and they fled in that direction, down one of the valleys between the mountains.

Gideon had thought that the Midianites would turn toward their own land, if they should be beaten in the battle, and he had already planned to cut off their flight. The ten thousand men in the camp, he had placed on the sides of the valley leading to the Jordan. There they slew very many of the Midianites as they fled down the steep pass toward the river. And Gideon had also sent to the men of the tribe of Ephraim, who had thus far taken no part in the war, to hold the only place at the river where men could wade through the water. Those of the Midianites who had escaped from Gideon's men on either side of the valley were now met by the Ephraimites at the river, and many more of them were slain. Among the slain were two of the princes of the Midianites, named Oreb and Zeeb.

A part of the Midianite army was able to get across the river, and to continue its flight toward the desert; but Gideon and his brave three hundred men followed closely after them, fought another battle with them, destroyed them utterly, and took their two kings, Zebah and Zalmunna, whom he killed. After this great victory, the Israelites were freed forever from the Midianites. They never again ventured to leave their home in the desert to make war on the tribes of Israel.

After this, as long as Gideon lived, he ruled as Judge in Israel. The people wished him to make himself a king.

"Rule over us as king," they said, "and let your son be king after you, and his son king after him."

But Gideon said:

"No, you have a king already; for the Lord God is the King of Israel. No one but God shall be king over these tribes."

Of all the fifteen men who ruled as Judges of Israel, Gideon, the fifth Judge, was the greatest, in courage, in wisdom, and in faith in God.

Written Summation

And Joash, Gideon's father, said, "If Baal is a god, he can take care of himself and punish the man who has destroyed his image. Why should you help Baal? Let Baal help himself."

And when they saw that Baal could not harm the man who had broken down his altar and his image, the people turned from Baal, back to their own Lord God.

Model Practice 1

Model Practice 2

Model Practice 3

The Story of Samson, the Strong Man

12th century BC
from The Wonder Book of Bible Stories
by Logan Marshall

Now we are to learn of three judges who ruled Israel in turn. Their names were Ibzan, Elon, and Abdon. None of these were men of war, and in their days the land was quiet.

But the people of Israel again began to worship idols; and as a punishment God allowed them once more to pass under the power of their enemies. The seventh oppression, which now fell upon Israel, was by far the hardest, the longest and the most widely spread of any, for it was over all the tribes. It came from the Philistines, a strong and warlike people who lived on the west of Israel upon the plain beside the Great Sea. They worshipped an idol called Dagon, which was made in the form of a fish's head on a man's body.

These people, the Philistines, sent their armies up from the plain beside the sea to the mountains of Israel and overran all the land. They took away from the Israelites all their swords and spears, so that they could not fight; and they robbed their land of all the crops, so that the people suffered for want of food. And as before, the Israelites in their trouble, cried out to the Lord, and the Lord heard their prayer.

In the tribe land of Dan, which was next to the country of the Philistines, there was living a man named Manoah. One day an angel came to his wife and said:

"You shall have a son, and when he grows up he will begin to save Israel from the hand of the Philistines. But your son must never drink any wine or strong drink as long as he lives. And his hair must be allowed to grow long and must never be cut, for he shall be a Nazarite under a vow to the Lord."

When a child was given especially to God, or when a man gave himself to some work for God, he was forbidden to drink wine, and as a sign, his hair was left to grow long while the vow or promise to God was upon him. Such a person as this was called a Nazarite, a word which means "one who has a vow"; and Manoah's child was to be a Nazarite, and under a vow, as long as he lived.

The child was born and was named Samson. He grew up to become the strongest man of whom the Bible tells. Samson was no general, like Gideon or Jephthah, to call out his people and lead them in war. He did much to set his people free; but all that he did was by his own strength.

When Samson became a young man he went down to Timnath, in the land of the Philistines. There he saw a young Philistine woman whom he loved, and wished to have as his wife. His father and mother were not pleased that he should marry among the enemies of his own people. They did not know that God would make this marriage the means of bringing harm upon the Philistines and of helping the Israelites.

As Samson was going down to Timnath to see this young woman, a hungry lion came out of the mountain, roaring against him. Samson seized the lion, and tore him in pieces as easily as another man would have killed a little kid of the goats, and then went on his way. He made his visit and came home, but said nothing to any one about the lion.

After a time Samson went again to Timnath for his marriage with the Philistine woman. On his way he stopped to look at the dead lion; and in its body he found a swarm of bees, and honey which they had made. He took some of the honey and ate it as he walked, but told no one of it.

At the wedding-feast, which lasted a whole week, there were many Philistine young men, and they amused each other with questions and riddles.

"I will give you a riddle," said Samson. "If you answer it during the feast, I will give you thirty suits of clothing; and if you cannot answer it then you must give me the thirty suits of clothing."

"Let us hear your riddle," they said. And this was Samson's riddle:

"Out of the eater came forth meat, And out of the strong came forth sweetness."

They could not find the answer, though they tried to find it all that day and the two days that followed. And at last they came to Samson's wife and said to her:

"Coax your husband to tell you the answer. If you do not find it out, we will set your house on fire, and burn you and all your people."

And Samson's wife urged him to tell her the answer. She cried and pleaded with him and said:

"If you really loved me, you would not keep this a secret from me."

At last Samson yielded, and told his wife how he had killed the lion and afterward found the honey in its body. She told her people, and just before the end of the feast they came to Samson with the answer. They said:

"What is sweeter than honey? And what is stronger than a lion?" And Samson said to them:

"If you had not plowed with my heifer, you had not found out my riddle."

By his "heifer,"—which is a young cow,—of course Samson meant his wife. Then Samson was required to give them thirty suits of clothing. He went out among the Philistines, killed the first thirty men whom he found, took off their clothes, and gave them to the guests at the feast. But all this made Samson very angry. He left his wife and went home to his father's house. Then the parents of his wife gave her to another man.

But after a time Samson's anger passed away, and he went again to Timnath to see his wife. But her father said to him:

"You went away angry, and I supposed that you cared nothing for her. I gave her to another man, and now she is his wife. But here is her younger sister; you can have her for your wife, instead."

But Samson would not take his wife's sister. He went out very angry; determined to do harm to the Philistines, because they had cheated him. He caught all the wild foxes that he could find, until he had three hundred of them. Then he tied them together in pairs, by their tails; and between each pair of foxes he tied to their tails a piece of dry wood which he set on fire. These foxes with firebrands on their tails he turned loose among the fields of the Philistines when the grain was ripe. They ran wildly over the fields, set the grain on fire, and burned it; and with the grain the olive trees in the fields.

When the Philistines saw their harvests destroyed, they said, "Who has done this?"

And the people said, "Samson did this, because his wife was given by her father to another man."

The Philistines looked on Samson's father-in-law as the cause of their loss; and they came and set his home on fire, and burned the man and his daughter whom Samson had married. Then Samson came down again, and alone fought a company of Philistines, and killed them all, as a punishment for burning his wife.

After this Samson went to live in a hollow place in a split rock, called the rock of Etam. The Philistines came up in a great army, and overran the fields in the tribe land of Judah.

"Why do you come against us?" asked the men of Judah, "what do you want from us?"

"We have come," they said, "to bind Samson, and to deal with him as he has dealt with us."

The men of Judah said to Samson:

"Do you not know that the Philistines are ruling over us? Why do you make them angry by killing their people? You see that we suffer through your pranks. Now we must bind you and give you to the Philistines, or they will ruin us all."

And Samson said, "I will let you bind me, if you will promise not to kill me yourselves; but only to give me safely into the hands of the Philistines."

They made the promise; and Samson gave himself up to them, and allowed them to tie him up fast with new ropes. The Philistines shouted for joy as they saw their enemy brought to them, led in bonds by his own people. But as soon as Samson came among them, he burst the bonds as though they had been light strings; and picked up from the ground the jawbone of an ass, and struck right and left with it as with a sword. He killed almost a thousand of the Philistines with this strange weapon. Afterward he sang a song about it, thus:

"With the jawbone of an ass, heaps upon heaps, With the jawbone of an ass, have I slain a thousand men."

After this Samson went down to the chief city of the Philistines, which was named Gaza. It was a large city; and like all large cities, was surrounded with a high wall. When the men of Gaza found Samson in their city, they shut the gates, thinking that they could now hold him as a prisoner. But in the night Samson rose up, went to the gates, pulled their posts out of the ground, and put the gates with their posts upon his shoulder. He carried off the gates of the city and left them on the top of a hill not far from the city of Hebron.

After this Samson saw another woman among the Philistines, and he loved her. The name of this woman was Delilah. The rulers of the Philistines came to Delilah and said to her:

"Find out, if you can, what it is that makes Samson so strong, and tell us. If you help us to get control of him, so that we can have him in our power, we will give you a great sum of money."

And Delilah coaxed and pleaded with Samson to tell her what it was that made him so strong. Samson said to her, "If they will tie me with seven green twigs from a tree, then I shall not be strong any more."

They brought her seven green twigs, like those of a willow tree; and she bound Samson with them while he was asleep. Then she called out to him, "Wake up, Samson, the Philistines are coming against you!"

And Samson rose up and broke the twigs as easily as if they had been charred in the fire, and went away with ease.

And Delilah tried again to find his secret. She said:

"You are only making fun of me. Now tell me truly how you can be bound." And Samson said:

"Let them bind me with new ropes that have never been used before; and then I cannot get away."

While Samson was asleep again, Delilah bound him with new ropes. Then she called out as before:

"Get up, Samson, for the Philistines are coming!" And when Samson rose up, the ropes broke as if they were thread. And Delilah again urged him to tell her; and he said:

"You notice that my long hair is in seven locks. Weave it together in the loom, just as if it were the threads in a piece of cloth."

Then, while he was asleep, she wove his hair in the loom and fastened it with a large pin to the weaving frame. But when he awoke, he rose up and carried away the pin and the beam of the weaving frame; for he was as strong as before.

And Delilah, who was anxious to serve her people, said:

"Why do you tell me that you love me, as long as you deceive me and keep from me your secret?" And she pleaded with him day after day, until at last he yielded to her and told her the real secret of his strength. He said:

"I am a Nazarite, under a vow to the Lord, not to drink wine, and not to allow my hair to be cut. If I should let my hair be cut short, then the Lord would forsake me, and my strength would go from me, and I would be like other men."

Then Delilah knew that she had found the truth at last. She sent for the rulers of the Philistines, saying:

"Come up this once, and you shall have your enemy; for he has told me all that is in his heart."

Then while the Philistines were watching outside, Delilah let Samson go to sleep, with his head upon her knees. While he was sound asleep, they took a razor and shaved off all his hair. Then she called out as at other times.

"Rise up, Samson, the Philistines are upon you."

He awoke, and rose up, expecting to find himself strong as before; for he did not at first know that his long hair had been cut off. But the vow to the Lord was broken, and the Lord had left him. He was now as weak as other men, and helpless in the hands of his enemies. The Philistines easily made him their prisoner; and that he might never do them more harm, they put out his eyes. Then they chained him with fetters, and sent him to prison at Gaza. And in the prison they made Samson turn a heavy millstone to grind grain, just as though he were a beast of burden.

But while Samson was in prison, his hair grew long again; and with his hair his strength came back to him; for Samson renewed his vow to the Lord.

One day, a great feast was held by the Philistines in the temple of their fish-god, Dagon. For they said:

"Our god has given Samson, our enemy, into our hand. Let us be glad together and praise Dagon."

And the temple was thronged with people, and the roof over it was also crowded with more than three thousand men and women. They sent for Samson, to rejoice over him; and Samson was led into the court of the temple, before all the people, to amuse them. After a time, Samson said to the boy who was leading him:

"Take me up to the front of the temple, so that I may stand by one of the pillars, and lean against it."

And while Samson stood between the two pillars, he prayed:

"O Lord God, remember me, I pray thee, and give me strength, only this once, O God: and help me, that I may obtain vengeance upon the Philistines for my two eyes!"

Then he placed one arm around the pillar on one side, and the other arm around the pillar on the other side; and he said: "Let me die with the Philistines."

And he bowed forward with all his might, and pulled the pillars over with him, bringing down the roof and all upon it upon those that were under it. Samson himself was among the dead; but in his death, he killed more of the Philistines than he had killed during his life.

Then in the terror which came upon the Philistines the men of Samson's tribe came down and found his dead body, and buried it in their own land. After that, it was years before the Philistines tried again to rule over the Israelites.

Samson did much to set his people free; but he might have done much more, if he had led his people, instead of trusting alone to his own strength; and if he had lived more earnestly, and not done his deeds as though he was playing pranks. There were deep faults in Samson, but at the end, he sought God's help and found it, and God used Samson to set his people free.

Written Summation

As Samson was going down to Timnath to see this young woman, a hungry lion came out of the mountain, roaring against him. Samson seized the lion and tore him in pieces as easily as another man would have killed a little kid of the goats, and then went on his way. He made his visit and came home, but said nothing to any one about the lion.

Model Practice 1

Model Practice 2

Model Practice 3

Ruth

c. 500 BC
from <u>Journeys Through Bookland, Vol. 6</u>
by Charles H. Sylvester

Now it came to pass in the days when the judges ruled in Judah that there was a famine in the land, and a certain man of Bethlehem-Judah went to sojourn in the country of Moab—he and his wife and his two sons. Together they came into the land and continued there; but the man died, and the wife was left, and her two sons.

And they took them wives of the women of Moab; the name of the one was Orpah, and the name of the other was Ruth; and they dwelled there about ten years. Then the two sons died also both of them; and the woman, Naomi, their mother, alone was left of the family that came into Moab.

Then she arose with her daughters-in-law, that she might return from the country of Moab; for she had heard in the country of Moab how that the Lord had visited his people in giving them bread.

Wherefore she went forth out of the place where she was, and her two daughters-in-law with her; and they went on the way to return unto the land of Judah.

But Naomi said unto her two daughters-in-law, "Go, return each to her mother's house. The Lord deal kindly with you, as ye have dealt with the dead and with me. The Lord grant you that ye may find rest again, each in the house of her husband."

Then she kissed them; and they lifted up their voices and wept and said unto her, "Surely we will return with thee unto thy people."

Naomi said, "Turn again, my daughters, why will you go with me? Have I yet any more sons that may be your husbands? Nay, it grieveth me much for your sakes that the hand of the Lord is gone out against me. Turn again my daughters; go your way."

Again they lifted up their voice and wept, and Orpah kissed her mother-in-law, but Ruth clave unto her.

Naomi said, "Behold, thy sister-in-law is gone back unto her people, and unto her gods; return thou after thy sister-in-law."

And Ruth said, "Entreat me not to leave thee, or to return from following after thee: for whither thou goest, I will go; and where thou lodgest, I will lodge: thy people shall be my people, and thy God my God: where thou diest, will I die, and there will I be buried: the Lord do so to me, and more also, if ought but death part thee and me."

When Naomi saw that Ruth was steadfastly minded to go with her, then she left speaking unto her. So they two went until they came to Bethlehem.

There it came to pass that all the city was moved about them, and the people said, "Is this Naomi?"

"Call me not Naomi," she said unto them. "Call me Mara: for the Almighty hath dealt very bitterly with me. I went out full and the Lord hath brought me home again empty: why then call me Naomi, seeing the Lord hath testified against me, and the Almighty hath afflicted me?"

So Naomi returned, and Ruth the Moabitess, her daughter-in-law, with her, which returned out of the country of Moab; and they came to Bethlehem in the beginning of barley harvest.

Naomi had a kinsman of her husband's, a mighty man of wealth; and his name was Boaz.

And Ruth said unto Naomi, "Let me now go to the field and glean ears of corn after him in whose sight I shall find grace."

And Naomi answered, "Go, my daughter."

And she went, and came, and gleaned in the field after the reapers; and her hap was to light on a part of the field belonging unto Boaz.

And, behold, Boaz came from Bethlehem and said unto the reapers, "The Lord be with you." And the reapers answered him, "The Lord bless thee." Then said Boaz unto his servant that was set over the reapers, "Whose damsel is this?"

And the servant answered and said, "It is the Moabitish damsel that came back with Naomi out of the country of Moab. And she said, 'I pray you, let me glean and gather after the reapers among the sheaves.' So she came, and hath continued even from the morning until now, that she tarried a little in the house."

Boaz said unto Ruth, "Hearest thou not, my daughter? Go not to glean in another field, neither go from hence, but abide here fast by my maidens. Let thine eyes be on the field that they do reap, and go thou after them. Have I not charged the young men that they shall not touch thee? And when thou art with thirst, go unto the vessels, and drink of that which the young men have drawn."

Then she fell on her face and bowed herself to the ground, and said unto him, "Why have I found grace in thine eyes, that thou shouldest take knowledge of me, seeing I am a stranger?"

And Boaz answered and said unto her, "It hath fully been shewed me, all that thou hast done unto thy mother-in-law since the death of thine husband. And how thou hast left thy father and thy mother, and the land of thy nativity, and art come unto a people which thou knewest not heretofore. The Lord recompense thy work, and a full reward be given thee of the Lord God of Israel, under whose wings thou art come to trust."

Then she said, "Let me find favour in thy sight, my lord; for that thou hast comforted me, and for that thou hast spoken friendly unto thine handmaid, though I be not like unto one of thine handmaidens."

And Boaz said unto her, "At mealtime come thou hither and eat of the bread and dip thy morsel in the vinegar."

And she sat beside the reapers; and he reached her parched corn, and she did eat and was sufficed and left.

And when she was risen up to glean again, Boaz commanded his young men, saying, "Let her glean even among the sheaves and reproach her not. And let fall also some handfuls of purpose for her, and leave them that she may glean them, and rebuke her not."

So she gleaned in the field until even and beat out that she had gleaned; and it was about an ephah of barley. And she took it up and went into the city. And her mother-in-law saw what she had gleaned.

And her mother-in-law said unto her, "Where hast thou gleaned today? And where wroughtest thou? Blessed be he that did take knowledge of thee."

And she showed her mother-in-law with whom she had wrought, and said, "The man's name with whom I wrought today is Boaz."

And Naomi said unto her daughter-in-law, "Blessed be he of the Lord, who hath not left off his kindness to the living and to the dead." And Naomi said unto her, "The man is near of kin unto us, one of our next kinsmen."

And Ruth the Moabitess said, "He said unto me also, 'Thou shalt keep fast by my young men, until they have ended all my harvest.'"

And Naomi said unto Ruth, her daughter-in-law, "It is good, my daughter, that thou go out with his maidens, that they meet thee not in any other field."

So she kept fast by the maidens of Boaz to glean unto the end of barley harvest and of wheat harvest; and dwelt with her mother-in-law.

Then Naomi, her mother-in-law, said unto Ruth, "My daughter, shall I not seek rest for thee that it may be well with thee? And now is not Boaz of our kindred, with whose maidens thou wast? Behold he winnoweth barley tonight in the threshing floor. Wash thyself, therefore, and anoint thee, and put thy raiment upon thee and get thee down to the floor, and he will tell thee what to do."

And Ruth said, "All that thou sayest unto me, that will I do."

Therefore went she down unto the threshing floor and did according to all that her mother-in-law bade her. And Boaz saw her and loved her and asked her, "Who art thou?"

She answered, "I am Ruth, thy handmaid."

And Boaz said, "Blessed be thou of the Lord, my daughter, and fear not, for all the city of my people doth know thou art a virtuous woman. And now it is true that I am thy near kinsman; howbeit, there is a kinsman nearer than I. Tarry this night, and it shall be in the morning that if he will perform unto thee the part of a kinsman, well; let him do the kinsman's part. But if he will not do the part of a kinsman to thee, then will I do the part of the kinsman to thee, as the Lord liveth. Bring now the vail that thou hast upon thee and hold it."

And when she held it, he measured six measures of barley and laid it on her, and she returned into the city.

When now she came to her mother, Naomi asked, "Who art thou?" And Ruth told her all that the man had said and done, and said, "These six measures of barley gave he me, for he said to me, 'Go not empty unto thy mother-in-law.'"

Then said Naomi, "Sit still, my daughter, until thou know how the matter will fall; for the man will not be in rest until he have finished the thing this day."

Then went Boaz up to the gate and sat him down there; and, behold, the kinsman of whom Boaz spoke came by. Unto whom Boaz said, "Ho, such a one! Turn aside; sit down here." And he turned aside and sat down.

And Boaz took also ten men of the elders of the city and said, "Sit ye down here." And they sat down.

Then said Boaz unto the kinsman, "Naomi, that is come again out of the land of Moab, selleth a parcel of land, which was our brother's. And I thought to ask thee to buy it before the inhabitants and before the elders of my people. If thou wilt redeem it, redeem it; but if thou wilt not redeem it, then tell me, that I may know. For there is none to redeem it beside thee, and I am after thee. And what day thou buyest it of the hand of Naomi, thou must buy it also of Ruth the Moabitess, the wife of the dead."

And the kinsman said, "I cannot redeem it for myself, lest I mar mine own inheritance. I redeem thou my right to thyself; for I cannot redeem it."

Now this was the manner in former time in Israel, concerning redeeming and concerning changing, for to confirm all things. A man plucked off his shoe and gave it to his neighbor; and this was a testimony in Israel. Therefore the kinsman said unto Boaz, "Buy it for thee." So he drew off his shoe.

And Boaz said unto the elders and all the people, "Ye are witnesses this day that I have bought all that was Naomi's husband's and all that was her son's of the hand of Naomi. Moreover, Ruth the Moabitess, the wife of my kinsman that is dead, have I purchased to be my wife, that the name of the dead be not cut off from among his brethren, and from the gate of his place. Ye are witnesses this day."

And all the people that were there in the gate, and the elders, said, "We are witnesses. The Lord make the woman that is come into thine house like Rachel and like Leah, which two did build the house of Israel, and do thou worthily and be famous in Bethlehem."

So Boaz took Ruth, and she was his wife, and she bare him a son. And the women said unto Naomi, "Blessed be the Lord that hath not left thee this day without a kinsman, that his name may be famous in Israel. And he shall be unto thee a restorer of thy life and a nourisher of thine old age; for thy daughter-in-law which loveth thee, which is better to thee than seven sons, hath borne him."

And Naomi took the child and laid it in her bosom and became nurse unto it. And the women, her neighbors, gave it a name, saying, "There is a son born to Naomi, and his name is Obed."

This same Obed is the father of Jesse, who is the father of David.

Written Summation

And Ruth said unto Naomi, "Let me now go to the field and glean ears of corn after him in whose sight I shall find grace."

And Naomi answered, "Go, my daughter."

Model Practice 1

Model Practice 2

Model Practice 3

The Story of the Fight with the Giant
c. 1037 – c. 967 BC
from The Wonder Book of Bible Stories
by Logan Marshall

All through the reign of Saul, there was constant war with the Philistines, who lived upon the lowlands west of Israel. At one time, when David was still with his sheep, a few years after he had been anointed by Samuel, the camps of the Philistines and the Israelites were set against each other on opposite sides of the valley of Elah. In the army of Israel were the three oldest brothers of David.

Every day a giant came out of the camp of the Philistines and dared some one to come from the Israelites' camp and fight with him. The giant's name was Goliath. He was nine feet high; and he wore armor from head to foot and carried a spear twice as long and as heavy as any other man could hold; and his shield bearer walked before him. He came every day and called out across the little valley:

"I am a Philistine, and you are servants of Saul. Now choose one of your men and let him come out and fight with me. If I kill him, then you shall submit to us; and if he kills me, then we will give up to you. Come, now, send out your man!"

But no man in the army, not even King Saul, dared to go out and fight with the giant. Forty days the camps stood against each other, and the Philistine giant continued his call.

One day, old Jesse, the father of David, sent David from Bethlehem to visit his three brothers in the army. David came, and spoke to his brothers, and while he was talking with them, Goliath the giant came out as before in front of the camp calling for some one to fight with him.

They said one to another:

"If any man will go out and kill this Philistine, the king will give him a great reward and a high rank; and the king's daughter shall be his wife."

And David said:

"Who is this man that speaks in this proud manner against the armies of the living God? Why does not some one go out and kill him?"

David's brother Eliab said to him:

"What are you doing here, leaving your few sheep in the field? I know that you have come down just to see the battle."

But David did not care for his brother's words. He thought he saw a way to kill this boasting giant; and he said:

"If no one else will go, I will go out and fight with this enemy of the Lord's people."

They brought David before King Saul. Some years had passed since Saul had met David, and he had grown from a boy to a man, so that Saul did not know him as the shepherd who had played on the harp before him in other days.

Saul said to David:

"You cannot fight with this great giant. You are very young; and he is a man of war, trained from his youth."

And David answered King Saul:

"I am only a shepherd, but I have fought with lions and bears when they have tried to steal my sheep. And I am not afraid to fight with this Philistine."

Then Saul put his own armor on David—a helmet on his head and a coat of mail on his body and a sword at his waist. But Saul was almost a giant, and his armor was far too large for David. David said:

"I am not used to fighting with such weapons as these. Let me fight in my own way."

So David took off Saul's armor. While everybody in the army had been looking on the giant with fear, David had been thinking out the best way for fighting him; and God had given to David a plan. It was to throw the giant off his guard, by appearing weak and helpless; and while so far away that the giant could not reach him with sword or spear, to strike him down with a weapon which the giant would not expect and would not be prepared for.

David took his shepherd's staff in his hand, as though that were to be his weapon. But out of sight, in a bag under his mantle, he had five smooth stones carefully chosen and a sling—the weapon that he knew how to use. Then he went out to meet the Philistine.

The giant looked down on the youth and despised him and laughed.

"Am I a dog?" he said, "that this boy comes to me with a staff? I will give his body to the birds of the air and the beasts of the field."

And the Philistine cursed David by the gods of his people. And David answered him:

"You come against me with a sword and a spear and a dart; but I come to you in the name of the Lord of hosts, the God of the armies of Israel. This day will the Lord give you into my hand. I will strike you down and take off your head, and the host of the Philistines shall be dead bodies, to be eaten by the birds and the beasts; so that all may know that there is a God in Israel and that He can save in other ways besides with sword and spear."

And David ran toward the Philistine, as if to fight him with his shepherd's staff. But when he was just near enough for a good aim, he took out his sling and hurled a stone aimed at the giant's forehead. David's aim was good; the stone struck the Philistine in his forehead. It stunned him, and he fell to the ground.

While the two armies stood wondering and scarcely knowing what had caused the giant to fall so suddenly, David ran forward, drew out the giant's own sword, and cut off his head. Then the Philistines knew that their great warrior in whom they trusted was dead. They turned to flee to their own land; and the Israelites followed after them and killed them by the hundred and the thousand, even to the gates of their own city of Gath.

So in that day David won a great victory and stood before all the land as the one who had saved his people from their enemies.

Written Summation

You come against me with a sword and a spear and a dart; but I come to you in the name of the Lord of hosts, the God of the armies of Israel. This day will the Lord give you into my hand. I will strike you down and take off your head, and the host of the Philistines shall be dead bodies, to be eaten by the birds and the beasts.

Model Practice 1

Model Practice 2

Model Practice 3

The Story of the Cave of Adullam

c.1037 BC - 967 BC
from The Wonder Book of Bible Stories
by Logan Marshall

Now Saul had a son, Jonathan, near David's own age. He and David became fast friends and loved one another as brothers. Saul the king became very jealous of David because the people praised him after his fight with Goliath. He even threatened to take David's life. He tried to catch him in his own house, but David's wife let him down from a window by a rope and he escaped. He met his friend Jonathan, who told him that he should flee. They renewed their promises of friendship, which they kept ever afterward.

From his meeting with Jonathan, David went forth to be a wanderer, having no home as long as Saul lived. He found a great cave, called the cave of Adullam, and hid in it. Soon people heard where he was, and from all parts of the land, especially from his own tribe of Judah, men who were not satisfied with the rule of King Saul gathered around David.

Saul soon heard that David, with a band of men, was hiding among the mountains of Judah and that among those who aided him were certain priests.

This enraged King Saul, and he ordered his guards to kill all the priests. The guards would not obey him, for they felt that it was a wicked thing to lay hands upon the priests of the Lord.

But he found one man whose name was Doeg, an Edomite, who was willing to obey the king. And Doeg, the Edomite, killed eighty-five men who wore the priestly garments.

All through the land went the news of Saul's dreadful deed, and everywhere the people began to turn from Saul and to look toward David as the only hope of the nation.

When Saul died, he was followed by David, the shepherd boy, now grown to manhood and greatly loved by the people. He had many battles to fight with the Philistines and was nearly always victorious. He was a warrior king, but he was more than a warrior. He played on his harp and composed many beautiful hymns and songs, which are collected in the book of Psalms. He was a good king and tried to obey God's command. He had a long reign and his people were happy and prosperous. He had many sons and daughters and beautiful palaces for them to live in.

Written Summation

From his meeting with Jonathan, David went forth to be a wanderer, having no home as long as Saul lived. He found a great cave, called the cave of Adullam, and hid in it. Soon people heard where he was, and men from his own tribe and from all parts of the land who were not satisfied with the rule of King Saul gathered around David.

Model Practice 1 (adapted from the original)

Model Practice 2

Model Practice 3

The Blind Poet

ca. 800 BC - 701 BC
from The Story of the Greeks
by H. A. Guerber

Three or four centuries after the siege of Troy, there lived a poor old blind poet who wandered about from place to place, playing upon his lyre, and reciting wonderful verses which told about the adventures of the Greek heroes, and their great deeds during the Trojan War.

We are told that this old man, whose name was Homer, had not always been poor and blind, but that, having embarked by mistake upon a vessel manned by pirates, he not only had been robbed of all his wealth and blinded, but had been left upon a lonely shore.

By some happy chance, poor blind Homer found his way to the inhabited parts of the country, where he soon won many friends. Instead of spending all his time in weeping over his troubles, Homer tried to think of some way in which he could earn his living and at the same time give pleasure to others. He soon found such a way in telling the stories of the past to all who cared to listen to them.

As the people in those days had no books, no schools, and no theaters, these stories seemed very wonderful. Little by little Homer turned them into verses so grand and beautiful that we admire them still; and these he recited, accompanying himself on a lyre, which he handled with much skill. As he wandered thus from place to place, old and young crowded around him to listen to his tales; and some young men were so struck by them that they followed him everywhere, until they too could repeat them. This was quite easy to do, because Homer had put them into the most beautiful and harmonious language the world has ever known. As soon as these young men had learned a few of the tales, they too began to travel from place to place, telling them to all they met; and thus Homer's verses became well known throughout all Greece.

The Greeks who could recite Homer's poems went next to the islands and Asia Minor, stopping at every place where Greek was spoken, to tell about the wrath of Achilles, the death of Patroclus, Hector, or old Priam, the burning of Troy, the wanderings of Ulysses, and the return of the Greeks. Other youths learned the poems; and so, although they were not written down for many a year, they were constantly recited and sung, and thus kept alive in the memory of the people.

As for Homer, their author, we know but little about him. We are told that he lived to be very old, and that although he was poor as long as he lived and forced to earn his living by reciting his songs, he was greatly honored after his death.

His two great heroic poems—the Iliad, telling all about the Trojan War, and the Odyssey, relating how Ulysses sailed about for ten years on his way home from Troy—were finally written down, and kept so carefully that they can still be read today. Such was the admiration felt for these poems that some years after Homer's death an attempt was made to find out more about him and about the place where he was born.

Fifty cities claimed the honor of giving him birth; but, although it was never positively found out where he was born, most people thought the Island of Chios was his birthplace. The Greek towns, wishing to show how much they admired the works of Homer, used to send yearly gifts to this place, the native land of the grandest poet the world has ever known.

Written Summation

Homer's two great heroic poems were the <u>Iliad</u>, telling all about the Trojan War, and the <u>Odyssey</u>, relating how Ulysses sailed about for ten years on his way home from Troy. Such was the admiration felt for these poems that years after Homer's death an attempt was made to find out more about him and about the place where he was born.

Model Practice 1 (adapted from the original)

Model Practice 2

Model Practice 3

Death of Romulus

c. 771 BC – 717 BC lifespan of Romulus
from The Story of the Romans
by H. A. Guerber

We are told that Romulus reigned over the Romans for thirty-seven years. Although he was at first a very good ruler, he soon grew proud and cruel. As he was king, he wanted to have his own way in everything; and as he soon ceased to care whether what he wished would be good for the Romans, they began to dislike him.

A man who thinks only of himself can have no real friends, and Romulus soon stood alone. But although the people hated him, they feared him too much to defy him openly and show him their displeasure.

One day, when Romulus and all the people had gone to the plain beyond the citadel, a sudden storm arose. The darkness became so great that the people fled in terror, leaving the senators and king to look out for themselves.

When the storm was over, the Romans all came back again. To their surprise, however, Romulus did not appear. He was sent for, but no one could find him. The people were amazed, and were all talking about his sudden disappearance, and wondering what could have become of him, when one of the senators stood up and called for silence.

As soon as he could make himself heard, this man told the assembled Romans that he had seen Romulus being carried up to heaven. The king, he said, had called out that he was going to live with the gods and wished his people to worship him under the name of Quirinus.

The Romans in those days were so ignorant and superstitious that they believed all this man told them. They therefore built a temple on the hill whence the senator said that Romulus had risen to heaven. This hill was called Mount Quirinal, and here for many years the Romans worshiped Romulus, the founder of their city and their first king, whom they now called Quirinus.

In later times the Romans did not believe that Romulus was carried up to heaven; and many of them thought that the senators were so tired of the king's tyranny that they murdered him during the storm, cut his body to pieces, and carried it off, hidden under their long mantles.

Written Summation

In *The Story of the Romans*, we are told that Romulus reigned over the Romans for thirty-seven years. Although he was at first a very good ruler, he soon grew proud and cruel. As he was king, he wanted to have his own way in everything; and as he ceased to care whether what he wished would be good for the Romans, they began to dislike him.

Model Practice 1 (adapted from the original)

Model Practice 2

Model Practice 3

Laws of Lycurgus
700 BC–630 BC
from The Story of the Greeks
by H. A. Guerber

The Spartan girls, who were brought up by the women, were, like the boys, taught to wrestle, run, and swim, and to take part in gymnastics of all kinds until they too became very strong and supple and could stand almost any fatigue.

They were also taught to read, write, count, sing, play, and dance; to spin, weave, and dye; and to do all kinds of woman's work. In short, they were expected to be strong, intelligent, and capable, so that when they married they might help their husbands and bring up their children sensibly. At some public festivals the girls strove with one another in various games, which were witnessed only by their fathers and mothers and the other married people of the city. The winners in these contests were given beautiful prizes, which were much coveted.

Lycurgus hoped to make the Spartans a strong and good people. To hinder the kings from doing anything wrong, he had the people choose five men, called ephors, to watch over and to advise them.

Then, knowing that great wealth is not desirable, Lycurgus said that the Spartans should use only iron money. All the Spartan coins were therefore bars of iron, so heavy that a yoke of oxen and a strong cart were needed to carry a sum equal to one hundred dollars from one spot to another. Money was so bulky that it could neither be hidden nor stolen, and no one cared to make a fortune, since it required a large space to stow away even a small sum.

When Charilaus, the infant king, had grown up, Lycurgus prepared to go away. Before he left the town, he called all the citizens together, reminded them of all he had done to make them a great people, and ended by asking every man present to swear to obey the laws until he came back.

The Spartans were very grateful for all he had done for them, so they gladly took this oath, and Lycurgus left the place. Some time after, he came back to Greece; but, hearing that the Spartans were thriving under the rules he had laid down, he made up his mind never to visit Sparta again.

It was thus that the Spartans found themselves bound by solemn oath to obey Lycurgus' laws forever. And as long as they remembered this promise, they were a thriving and happy people.

Written Summation

Then, knowing that great wealth is not desirable, Lycurgus said that the Spartans should use only iron money. All the Spartan coins were therefore bars of iron. This made the money so heavy that a yoke of oxen and a strong cart were needed to carry a sum equal to one hundred dollars from one spot to another.

Model Practice 1

Model Practice 2

Model Practice 3

The Laws of Solon
from The Story of the Greeks
by H. A. Guerber
638 BC–558 BC

Shortly after the death of Cylon and the murder of his followers, a great many troubles came upon the city of Athens. The people were frightened, and soon the friends of Cylon began to whisper that the gods were surely punishing the Athenians, and especially Megacles for breaking his promise.

This report spread throughout the city. The terrified people assembled, and voted to exile Megacles and all his family, the Alcmæonidæ. Such was the fury of the Athenians against the archon whose crime had brought misfortunes upon them, that they even dug up the bones of his ancestors and had them carried away beyond the boundary of Attica.

The city had been defiled by the crime which Megacles had committed, and the people felt that they would never be prosperous again until Athens had been purified; but the great question was to find a man holy enough to perform the ceremony.

After much talking, they decided to send for Epimenides, and to ask him to purify the city. This man, when a mere lad, once went into a cave near his native town and there laid himself down to sleep. Instead of taking an ordinary nap, however, he slept fifty-eight years, without awakening or undergoing any change. When he came out of the cave, where he fancied he had spent only a few hours, he was surprised to find everything new and strange to him.

His relatives had all died, no one knew him, and it was only after some time had passed that he found out that he had slept fifty-eight years at a stretch. This man was a poet of note, and, as he had enjoyed so long a sleep, the people thought that he was a favorite of the gods.

When the Athenians asked him to purify the town, he came to do so; but when the ceremonies were ended, he refused to accept any of the rich gifts, which the people offered him as reward. Instead, he humbly begged them to give him a twig of the sacred olive tree which they said Athene herself had planted on the Acropolis.

Their troubles having now ceased, the Athenians began to think of making another and less severe code of laws. This time they chose as lawmaker a wise man called Solon, a descendant of the noble Codrus; and he soon consented to tell them what to do.

Solon was a studious and thoughtful man, and had acquired much of his wisdom by traveling and by learning all he could from the people he visited. He knew so much that he was called a sage, and he loved to meet and talk with wise people.

Solon changed many of Draco's severe laws, arranged that the farmers and poor people should no longer be treated badly by the rich and even took care of the slaves. He also gave the Athenians a court of law called Areopagus. Here there were jurymen to judge all criminals; and here, for the first time, an accused person was allowed to speak in his own defense.

When a man was accused of any wrongdoing, he was brought before this jury, who sat under the open sky at night. No light was provided, and the whole trial was carried on in the dark, so that the jury should not be influenced by the good or bad looks of the prisoner, but should judge merely from what was proved about him.

If the accused person was found guilty, he was also sentenced and executed in the dark, so that the bright sun god, riding across the sky in his golden chariot, should not be offended by the sad sight of a man dying for his misdeeds.

Every citizen of Athens, whether rich or poor, was allowed to vote; and as a salary was now paid to the men who helped govern the city, even a man of small means, if elected to the Tribunal, could afford to give his time to public duties.

By Solon's order the people were encouraged to talk matters over in public in the market place; and, as the Athenians were fond of making speeches, many of them became very eloquent.

Solon saw that his reforms were likely to work all the better if they were fairly tried, and if he were not there to see how the people did. He therefore made the Athenians promise to obey his laws for ten years and again set out on his travels.

Written Summation

This report spread quickly throughout the city. The terrified people assembled and voted to exile Megacles and all his family. Such was the fury of the Athenians against the archon whose crime had brought misfortunes upon them that they even dug up the bones of his ancestors and had them carried away beyond the boundary of Attica.

Model Practice 1 (adapted from the original)

Model Practice 2

Model Practice 3

The Story of the Fiery Furnace

c 630-562 BC
from The Wonder Book of Bible Stories
by Logan Marshall

There was in the land of Judah a wicked king named Jehoiakim, son of the good Josiah. While Jehoiakim was ruling over the land of Judah, Nebuchadnezzar, a great conqueror of the nations, came from Babylon with his army of Chaldean soldiers. He took the city of Jerusalem and made Jehoiakim promise to submit to him as his master. And when he went back to his own land he took with him all the gold and silver that he could find in the Temple; and he carried away as captives very many of the princes and nobles, the best people in the land of Judah.

When these Jews were brought to the land of Chaldea or Babylon, King Nebuchadnezzar gave orders to the prince, who had charge of his palace, to choose among these Jewish captives some young men who were of noble rank, and beautiful in their looks, and also quick and bright in their minds; young men who would be able to learn readily. These young men were to be placed under the care of wise men, who should teach them all that they knew and fit them to stand before the king of Babylon, so that they might be his helpers to carry out his orders; and the king wished them to be wise, so that they might give him advice in ruling his people.

Among the young men thus chosen were four Jewish men who had been brought from Judah. By order of the king the names of these men were changed. One of them, named Daniel, was to be called Belteshazzer; the other three young men were called Shadrach, Meshach and Abednego. They were taught in all the knowledge of the Chaldeans; and after three years of training they were taken into the king's palace.

King Nebuchadnezzar was pleased with them, more than with any others who stood before him. He found them wise and faithful in the work given to them and able to rule over men under them. And these four men came to the highest places in the kingdom of the Chaldeans.

At one time King Nebuchadnezzar caused a great image to be made and to be covered with gold. This image he set up, as an idol to be worshipped, on the plain of Dura, near the city of Babylon. When it was finished, it stood upon its base or foundation almost a hundred feet high; so that upon the plain it could be seen far away. Then the king sent out a command for all the princes, and rulers, and nobles in the land, to come to a great gathering, when the image was to be set apart for worship.

The great men of the kingdom came from far and near and stood around the image. Among them, by command of the king, were Daniel's three friends, the young Jewish men—Shadrach, Meshach, and Abednego. For some reason, Daniel himself was not there. He may have been busy with the work of the kingdom in some other place.

At one moment in the service before the image, all the trumpets sounded, the drums were beaten, and music was made upon musical instruments of all kinds, as a signal for all the people to kneel down and worship the great golden image. But while the people were kneeling, there were three men who stood up and would not bow down. These were the three young Jewish men called Shadrach, Meshach, and Abednego. They knelt down before the Lord God only.

Many of the nobles had been jealous of these young men, because they had been lifted to high places in the rule of the kingdom; and these men who hated Daniel and his friends were glad to find that these three men had not obeyed the command of King Nebuchadnezzar. The king had said that if any one did not worship the golden image he should be thrown into a furnace of fire. These men who hated the Jews came to the king and said:

"O king, may you live for ever! You gave orders that when the music sounded every one should bow down and worship the golden image; and that if any man did not worship, he should be thrown into a furnace of fire. There are some Jews, whom you have made rulers in the land, who have not done as you commanded. Their names are Shadrach, Meshach and Abednego. They do not serve your gods, nor worship the golden image that you have set up."

Then Nebuchadnezzar was filled with rage and fury at knowing that any one should dare to disobey his words. He sent for these three men and said to them:

"O Shadrach, Meshach, and Abednego, was it by purpose that you did not fall down and worship the image of gold? The music shall sound once more, and if you then will worship the image, it will be well. But if you will not, then you shall be thrown into the furnace of fire to die."

These three young men were not afraid of the king. They said:

"O King Nebuchadnezzar, we are ready to answer you at once. The God whom we serve is able to save us from the fiery furnace, and we know that he will save us. But if it is God's will that we should die, even then you may understand, O king, that we will not serve your gods, nor worship the golden image."

This answer made the king more furious than before. He said to his servants:

"Make a fire in the furnace hotter than ever it has been before, as hot as fire can be made; and throw these three men into it."

Then the soldiers of the king's army seized the three young Jews, as they stood in their loose robes, with their turbans on their heads. They tied them with ropes and dragged them to the mouth of the furnace and threw them into the fire. The flames rushed from the opened door with such fury that they burned even to death the soldiers who were holding these men; and the men themselves fell down bound into the middle of the fiery furnace.

But an angel befriended them and they were unhurt.

King Nebuchadnezzar stood in front of the furnace and looked into the open door. As he looked, he was filled with wonder at what he saw; and he said to the nobles around him:

"Did we not throw three men bound into the fire? How is this that I see four men loose, walking in the furnace; and the fourth man looks as though he were a son of the gods?"

And the nobles who stood by could scarcely speak, so great was their surprise.

"It is true, O king," at last they said to Nebuchadnezzar, "that we cast these men into the flames, expecting them to be burned up; and we cannot understand how it happens that they have not been destroyed."

The king came near to the door of the furnace, as the fire became lower; and he called out to the three men within it:

"Shadrach, Meshach, and Abednego, ye who serve the Most High God, come out of the fire and come to me."

They came out and stood before the king, in the sight of all the princes, and nobles, and rulers; and every one could see that they were alive.

Their garments had not been scorched, nor their hair singed, nor was there even the smell of fire upon them.

Then King Nebuchadnezzar said before all his rulers:

"Blessed be the God of Shadrach, Meshach, and Abednego, who has sent his angel, and has saved the lives of these men who trusted in him. I make a law that no man in all my kingdoms shall say a word against their God, for there is no other god who can save in this manner those who worship him. And if any man speaks a word against their God, the Most High God, that man shall be cut in pieces, and his house shall be torn down."

After King Nebuchadnezzar died, his kingdom became weak, and the city of Babylon was taken by the Medes and Persians, under Cyrus, a great warrior.

Written Summation

But while the people were kneeling, there were three men who stood up and would not bow down. These were the three young Jewish men called Shadrach, Meshach, and Abednego. They knelt down before the Lord God only.

Model Practice 1

Model Practice 2

Model Practice 3

Aesop

620-560 BC
from Journeys Through Bookland, Vol. 2
by Charles H. Sylvester

Many centuries ago, more than six hundred years before Christ was born, there lived in Greece a man by the name of Aesop. We do not know very much about him, and no one can tell exactly what he wrote, or even that he ever wrote anything.

We know he was a slave and much wiser than his masters, but whether he was a fine, shapely man or a hunchback and a cripple we cannot be sure, for different people have written very differently about him.

No matter what he was or how he lived, many, many stories are still told about him, and the greater part of the fables we all like to read are said to have been written or told by him, and everybody still calls them Aesop's fables.

Some of the stories told about him are curious indeed. Here are a few of them.

In those days men were sold as slaves in the market, as cattle are sold now. One day Aesop and two other men were put up at auction. Xanthus, a wealthy man, wanted a slave, and he said to the men: "What can you do?"

The two men bragged large about the things they could do, for both wanted a rich master like Xanthus.

"But what can you do?" said Xanthus, turning to Aesop.

"The others can do so much and so well," said Aesop, "that there's nothing left for me to do."

"Will you be honest and faithful if I buy you?"

"I shall be that whether you buy me or not."

"Will you promise not to run away?"

"Did you ever hear," answered Aesop, "of a bird in a cage that promised to stay in it?"

Xanthus was so much pleased with the answers that he bought Aesop.

Some time afterward, Xanthus, wishing to give a dinner to some of his friends, ordered Aesop to furnish the finest feast that money could buy.

The first course Aesop supplied was of tongues cooked in many ways, and the second of tongues and the third and the fourth. Then Xanthus called sharply to Aesop:

"Did I not tell you, sirrah, to provide the choicest dainties that money could procure?"

"And what excels the tongue?" replied Aesop. "It is the great channel of learning and philosophy. By this noble organ everything wise and good is accomplished."

The company applauded Aesop's wit and good humor was restored.

"Well," said Xanthus to the guests, "pray do me the favor of dining with me again tomorrow. And if this is your best," continued he turning to Aesop, "pray, tomorrow let us have some of the worst meat you can find."

The next day, when dinnertime came, the guests were assembled. Great was their astonishment and great the anger of Xanthus at finding that again nothing but tongue was put upon the table.

"How, sir," said Xanthus, "should tongues be the best of meat one day, and the worst another?"

"What," replied Aesop, "can be worse than the tongue? What wickedness is there under the sun that it has not a part in? Treasons, violence, injustice, and fraud are debated and resolved upon by the tongue. It is the ruin of empires, of cities, and of private friendships."

* * * * *

At another time Xanthus very foolishly bet with a scholar that he could drink the sea dry. Alarmed, he consulted Aesop.

"To perform your wager," said Aesop, "you know is impossible, but I will show you how to evade it."

They accordingly met the scholar and went with him and a great number of people to the seashore, where Aesop had provided a table with several large glasses upon it, and men who stood around with ladles with which to fill the glasses.

Xanthus, instructed by Aesop, gravely took his seat at the table. The beholders looked on with astonishment, thinking that he must surely have lost his senses.

"My agreement," said he, turning to the scholar, "is to drink up the sea. I said nothing of the rivers and streams that are everywhere flowing into it. Stop up these, and I will proceed to fulfill my engagement."

* * * * *

It is said that at one time when Xanthus started out on a long journey, he ordered his servants to get all his things together and put them up into bundles so that they could carry them.

When everything had been neatly tied up, Aesop went to his master and begged for the lightest bundle. Wishing to please his favorite slave, the master told Aesop to choose for himself the one he preferred to carry. Looking them all over, he picked up the basket of bread and started off with it on the journey. The other servants laughed at his foolishness, for that basket was the heaviest of all.

When dinnertime came, Aesop was very tired, for he had had a difficult time to carry his load for the last few hours. When they had rested, however, they took bread from the basket, each taking an equal share. Half the bread was eaten at this one meal, and when suppertime came the rest of it disappeared.

For the whole remainder of the journey, which ran far into the night and was over rough roads, up and down hills, Aesop had nothing to carry, while the loads of the other servants grew heavier and heavier with every step.

The people of the neighborhood in which Aesop was a slave one day observed him attentively looking over some poultry in a pen that was near the roadside; and those idlers, who spent more time in prying into other people's affairs than in adjusting their own, asked why he bestowed his attention on those animals.

"I am surprised," replied Aesop, "to see how mankind imitate this foolish animal."

"In what?" asked the neighbors.

"Why, in crowing so well and scratching so poorly," rejoined Aesop.

Written Summation

The next day, when dinnertime came, the guests were assembled. Great was their astonishment and great the anger of Xanthus at finding that again nothing but tongue was put upon the table.

"Tongue again! How, sir," asked Xanthus, "should tongues be the best of meat one day, and the worst another?"

Model Practice 1 (adapted from the original)

Model Practice 2

Model Practice 3

Death of Pericles

495 – 429 BC lifespan of Pericles
from The Story of the Greeks
by H. A. Guerber

Although the Athenian fleet had caused much damage and had come home victorious, the Spartan army was still in Attica. The Spartans had been awed and frightened by the eclipse, but they did not give up their purpose and continued the war.

The Athenians remained within the city walls, not daring to venture out lest they should meet with a defeat, and they soon began to suffer greatly. As there were not enough water and food for the crowded multitude, a terrible disease called the plague soon attacked the people. This sickness was contagious, and it spread rapidly. On all sides one could see the dead and dying. The sufferers were tormented by a burning thirst; and as there was soon no one left to care for the sick, they painfully dragged themselves to the sides of the fountains where many of them died.

Not only were the sick uncared for, but it was also nearly impossible to dispose of the dead; and the bodies lay in the streets day after day, waiting for burial.

When the Athenians were in the greatest distress, Pericles heard that there was a Greek doctor named Hippocrates who had a cure for the plague; and he wrote to him, imploring his help.

Hippocrates received Pericles' letter at the same time that a message arrived from Artaxerxes, King of Persia. The king asked him to come and save the Persians, who were suffering from the same disease and offered the doctor great wealth.

The noble doctor did not hesitate a moment, but sent away the Persian messenger, saying that it was his duty first to save his own countrymen. Then he immediately set out for the plague-stricken city of Athens, where he worked bravely night and day.

His care and skill restored many sufferers; and although thousands died of the plague, the remaining Athenians knew that they owed him their lives. When the danger was over, they all voted that Hippocrates should have a golden crown and said he should be called an Athenian citizen—an honor which they seldom granted to any outsider.

The plague had not only carried away many of the poorer citizens, but had also stricken down the nobles and the rich. Pericles' family suffered from it too. All his children took it and died, with the exception of one.

The great man, in spite of his private cares and sorrows, was always in and out among the people, helping and encouraging them, and he finally caught the plague himself. His friends soon saw that, in spite of all their efforts, he would die. They crowded around his bed in tears, praising him in low tones, and saying how much he had done for the Athenians and for the improvement of their city.

"Why," said one of them warmly, "he found the city bricks and leaves it marble!"

Pericles, whose eyes had been closed, and who seemed unconscious, now suddenly roused himself and said, "Why do you mention those things? They were mostly owing to my large fortune. The thing of which I am proudest is that I never caused any fellow-citizen to put on mourning!"

Pericles then sank back, and soon died; but his friends always remembered that he had ruled Athens for more than thirty years without ever punishing any one unjustly, and that he had always proved helpful and merciful to all.

Written Summation

Although the Athenian fleet had caused much damage and had come home victorious, the Spartan army was still in Attica. The Spartans had been awed and frightened by the eclipse, but they did not give up their purpose and continued the war.

Model Practice 1

Model Practice 2

Model Practice 3

The Philosopher Socrates

from The Story of the Greeks
by H. A. Guerber
c. 469 BC–399 BC

When Pericles died, the Peloponnesian War had already been carried on for more than three years, but was not nearly at an end. As the Athenians felt the need of a leader, they soon chose Nicias to take the place left vacant by Pericles.

This Nicias was an honest man; but he was unfortunately rather dull and very slow about deciding anything. Whenever he was called upon to see to matters of state, he hesitated so long, and was so uncertain, that the Greeks often had cause to regret the loss of Pericles.

There was another man of note in Athens at this time, the philosopher Socrates, a truly wise and good man. He was no politician, however; and instead of troubling himself about the state, he spent all his spare moments in studying or in teaching the young men of Athens.

Like his friend Anaxagoras, Socrates was a very deep thinker. He, too, always tried to find out the exact truth about everything. He was especially anxious to know how the earth had been created, who the Being was who gave us life, and whether the soul died with the body or continued to live after the body had fallen into dust.

Socrates was a poor man, a stonecutter by trade; but he spent every moment he could spare from his work in thinking, studying, and questioning others. Little by little, in spite of the contrary opinion of his fellow citizens, he began to understand that the stories of the Greek gods and goddesses could not be true.

He thought that there must surely be a God far greater than they—a God who was good and powerful and just, who governed the world he had created, and who rewarded the virtuous and punished the wicked.

Socrates believed that everybody should be as good and gentle as possible and freely forgive all injuries. This belief was very different from that of all ancient nations, who, on the contrary, thought that they should try to avenge every insult and return evil for evil.

The philosopher Socrates not only taught this gentleness, but practiced it carefully at home and abroad. He had plenty of opportunity to make use of it; for he had such a cross wife that her name, Xanthippe, is still used to describe a scolding and bad-tempered woman.

Whenever Xanthippe was angry, she used to scold poor Socrates roundly. He always listened without flying into a passion, or even answering her; and when her temper was too unbearable, he quietly left the house and went about his business elsewhere.

This gentleness and meekness only angered Xanthippe the more; and one day, when he was escaping as usual, she caught up a jug full of water and poured it over his head. Socrates good-naturedly shook off the water, smiled, and merely remarked to his companions, "After the thunder, comes the rain."

Written Summation

The philosopher Socrates not only taught this gentleness, but also practiced it carefully at home and abroad. He had plenty of opportunity to make use of it, for he had such a cross wife that her name, Xanthippe, is still used to describe a scolding and bad-tempered woman.

Model Practice 1 (adapted from the original)

Model Practice 2

Model Practice 3

Accusation of Socrates

from The Story of the Greeks
by H. A. Guerber
c. 469 BC–399 BC

Socrates, as you know, was one of the best and gentlest of men, yet he had many enemies. These were principally the people who were jealous of him and of his renown for great wisdom; for his reputation was so well established that the oracle at Delphi, when consulted, replied that the most learned man in Greece was Socrates.

Although Socrates was so wise and good and gentle, he was not at all conceited and showed his wisdom by never pretending to know what he did not know, and by his readiness to learn anything new, provided one could prove it to be true.

Among the noted Athenians of this time was Aristophanes, a writer of comedies or funny plays. He was so witty that his comedies are still admired almost as much as when they were played in the Theater of Dionysus for the amusement of the people.

Like most funny men, Aristophanes liked to turn everything into ridicule. He had often seen Socrates and Alcibiades walking through the streets of Athens and was greatly amused at the contrast they presented.

Now, Aristophanes, with all his cleverness, was not always just; and while his ridicule sometimes did good, at other times it did a great deal of harm. He soon learned to dislike Alcibiades; but he saw how dearly the people loved the young man and fancied that his faults must be owing to the bad advice of his teacher. Such was not the case, for Socrates had tried to bring out all the good in his pupil. Alcibiades' pride, insolence, and treachery were rather the result of the constant flattery to which he had been exposed on the part of those who claimed to be his friends.

Aristophanes disliked Alcibiades so much that he soon wrote a comedy called "The Clouds" in which he made fun of him. Of course, he did not call the people in the play by their real names; but the hero was a good-for-nothing young man, who, advised by his teacher, bought fast horses, ran his father into debt, cheated everybody, and treated even the gods with disrespect.

As the actors who took part in this comedy dressed and acted as nearly as possible like Alcibiades and Socrates, you can imagine that the play, which was very comical and clever, made the Athenians roar with laughter.

Everybody talked about it, repeated the best jokes, and went again and again to see and laugh over it. We are told that Socrates went there himself one day; and when asked why he had come, he quietly said, "I came to find out whether, among all the faults of which I am accused, there may not be some that I can correct."

You see, the philosopher knew that it was never too late to mend and fully intended to be as perfect as possible. He knew, of course, that he could not straighten his crooked nose or make his face good-looking, but he hoped to find some way of improving his character.

"The Clouds" amused the Athenians for about twenty years; and when Alcibiades turned traitor, and caused the ruin of his country, the people still went to see it. In their anger against Alcibiades, they began to think that perhaps Aristophanes was right, and that the youth they had once loved so dearly would never have turned out so badly had he not been influenced for evil.

As the teacher in the play was blamed for all the wrongdoing of his pupil, so Socrates was now accused by the Athenians of ruining Alcibiades. Little by little the philosopher's enemies became so bold that they finally made up their minds to get rid of him. As he was quite innocent and as there was no other excuse for dragging him before the Tribunal, they finally charged him with giving bad advice to young men and speaking ill of the gods.

Written Summation

Socrates was one of the best and gentlest of men, yet he had many enemies. These were principally the people who were jealous of him and of his renown for great wisdom; for his reputation was so well established that the oracle at Delphi, when consulted, replied that the most learned man in Greece was Socrates.

Model Practice 1 (adapted form the original)

Model Practice 2

Model Practice 3

Pythagoras
c. 428 BC - 348 BC
from <u>Little Journeys To The Homes Of Great Teachers</u>
by Elbert Hubbard

Consult and deliberate before you act, that thou mayest not commit foolish actions. For 't is the part of a miserable man to speak and to act without reflection. But do that which will not afflict thee afterwards, nor oblige thee to repentance.
—*Pythagoras*

When Pythagoras was only four or five years old, his mother taught him to take his morning bath in the cold stream and dry his baby skin by running in the wind. As he ran she ran with him and together they sang a hymn to the rising sun that for them represented the god Apollo.

This mother taught him to be indifferent to cold, heat, hunger, to exult in endurance, and to take a joy in the glow of the body.

So the boy grew strong and handsome and proud; and perhaps it was in those early years, from the mother herself, that he gathered the idea, afterward developed, that Apollo had appeared to his mother, and so great was the beauty of the god that the woman was actually overcome, it being the first god at which she had ever had a good look.

The ambition of a great mother centers on her son. Pythagoras was filled with the thought that he was different, peculiar, set apart to teach the human race.

Having compassed all there was to learn in his native place, and, as he thought, being ill appreciated, he started for Egypt, the land of learning. The fallacy that knowledge was a secret to be gained by word of mouth and to be gotten from books existed then as now. The mother of Pythagoras wanted her son to comprehend the innermost secrets of the Egyptian mysteries. He would then know all. To this end she sold her jewels, in order that her son might have the advantages of an Egyptian education.

Women were not allowed to know the divine secrets—only just a few little ones. This woman wanted to know, and she said her son would learn and tell her.

The family had become fairly rich by this time, and influential. Letters were gotten from the great ones of Samos to the Secretary of State in Egypt. And so Pythagoras, aged twenty, "the youth with the beautiful hair," went on his journey to Egypt and knocked boldly at the doors of the temples at Memphis, where knowledge was supposed to be in stock. Religion then monopolized all schools and continued to do so for quite some time after Pythagoras was dead.

He was turned away with the explanation that no foreigner could enter the sacred portals—that the initiates must be those born in the shadows of the temples and nurtured in the faith from infancy by holy virgins.

Pythagoras still insisted, and it was probably then that he found a sponsor who made for him the claim that he was a son of Apollo. And the holy men peeped out of their peepholes in holy admiration for any one who could concoct as big a lie as they themselves had ever invented.

The boy surely looked the part. Perhaps, at last, here was one who was what they pretended to be! Frauds believe in frauds, and rogues are more easily captured by roguery than are honest men.

His admittance to the university became a matter of international diplomacy. At last, being too hard-pressed, the wise ones who ran the mystery monopoly gave in, and Pythagoras was informed that at midnight of a certain night, he should present himself, naked, at the door of a certain temple and he would be admitted.

On the stroke of the hour, at the appointed time, Pythagoras, the youth with the beautiful hair, was there, clothed only in his beautiful hair. He knocked on the great, bronze doors, but the only answer was a faint, hollow echo.

Then he got a stone and pounded, but still no answer.

The wind sprang up fresh and cold. The young man was chilled to the bone, but still he pounded and then called aloud, demanding admittance. His answer now was the growling and barking of dogs within. Still he pounded! After an interval a hoarse voice called out through a little slide, ordering him to be gone or the dogs would be turned loose upon him.

He demanded admittance.

"Fool, do you not know that the law says these doors shall admit no one except at sunrise?"

"I only know that I was told to be here at midnight and I would be admitted."

"All that may be true, but you were not told when you would be admitted—wait, it is the will of the gods." So Pythagoras waited, numbed and nearly dead.

The dogs, which he had heard, had, in some way, gotten out and came tearing around the corner of the great stone building. He fought them with desperate strength. The effort seemed to warm his blood, and whereas before he was about to retreat to his lodgings he now remained.

The day broke in the east, and gangs of slaves went by to work. They jeered at him and pelted him with pebbles.

Suddenly across the desert sands he saw the faint pink rim of the rising sun. On the instant the big bronze doors against which he was leaning swung suddenly in. He fell with them, and coarse, rough hands seized his hair and pulled him into the hall.

The doors swung to and closed with a clang. Pythagoras was in dense darkness, lying on the stone floor.

A voice, seemingly coming from afar, demanded, "Do you still wish to go on?"

And his answer was, "I desire to go on."

A black-robed figure, wearing a mask, then appeared with a flickering light, and Pythagoras was led into a stone cell.

His head was shaved, and he was given a coarse robe and then left alone. Toward the end of the day he was given a piece of black bread and a bowl of water. This he was told was to fortify him for the ordeal to come.

What that ordeal was we can only guess, save that it consisted partially in running over hot sands where he sank to his waist. At a point where he seemed about to perish a voice called loudly, "Do you yet desire to go on?"

And his answer was, "I desire to go on."

Returning to the inmost temple he was told to enter a certain door and wait therein. He was then blindfolded and when he opened the door to enter, he walked off into space and fell into a pool of ice-cold water.

While floundering there the voice again called, "Do you yet desire to go on?"

And his answer was, "I desire to go on."

At another time he was tied upon the back of a donkey and the donkey was led along a rocky precipice, where lights danced and flickered a thousand feet below.

"Do you yet want to go on?" called the voice.

And Pythagoras answered, "I desire to go on."

The priests here pushed the donkey off the precipice, which proved to be only about two feet high, the gulf below being an illusion arranged with the aid of lights that shone through apertures in the wall.

These pleasing little diversions Pythagoras afterward introduced into the college which he founded, so to teach the merry freshmen that nothing, at the last, was as bad as it seemed, and that most dangers are simply illusions.

The Egyptians grew to have such regard for Pythagoras that he was given every opportunity to know the inmost secrets of the mysteries. He said he encompassed them all, save those alone which were incomprehensible.

This was probably true.

The years spent in Egypt were not wasted—he learned astronomy, mathematics, and psychology, a thing then not named, but pretty well understood—the management of men.

It was twenty years before Pythagoras returned to Samos. His mother was dead, so she passed away in ignorance of the secrets of the gods—which perhaps was just as well.

Samos now treated Pythagoras with great honor.

Crowds flocked to his lectures, presents were given him, royalty paid him profound obeisance.

But Samos soon tired of Pythagoras. He was too austere, too severe. And when he began to rebuke the officials for their sloth and indifference, he was invited to go elsewhere and teach his science of life. And so he journeyed into Southern Italy, and at Crotona built his Temple to the Muses and founded the Pythagorean School. He was the wisest as well as the most learned man of his time.

Written Summation

The wind sprang up fresh and cold. The young man was chilled to the bone, but still he pounded and then called aloud, demanding admittance. His answer now was the growling and barking of dogs within.

Model Practice 1 (adapted from the original)

Model Practice 2

Model Practice 3

Birth of Alexander

July 20, 356 BC – June 10, 323 BC lifespan of Alexander the Great
from The Story of the Greeks
by H. A. Guerber

When Philip died, he was succeeded by his son Alexander, a young man of twenty, who had already earned a good name by leading part of the army at the battle of Chæronea. His efforts, as you know, had defeated the Sacred Battalion of the Thebans and helped much to secure the victory.

Through his mother, Olympias, Alexander was a descendant of Achilles, the well-known hero of the Trojan War. He was born at Pella, a city of Macedon, three hundred and fifty-six years before Christ. His father was so pleased to have a son, that he said that all the boys born in his kingdom on the same day should be brought up with Alexander in the palace and become his bodyguard.

Thus you see the young prince had plenty of playmates; and, as there was nothing he liked better than fighting, he soon began to play soldiers and to train his little regiment.

From the very first, the Macedonians had declared that Alexander was born to greatness, and several noted events that took place on the day of his birth served to confirm this belief.

In the first place, Parmenio, Philip's general, won a grand victory on that day; then Philip's horses, which had been sent to Olympia, got the prize at the chariot races; and, lastly, the famous temple at Ephesus, dedicated to Diana, was burned to the ground.

The first two events were joyful in the extreme; but the burning of this temple, which was among the wonders of the world, was a great calamity. Every one was anxious to know how it had happened; and all were very angry when they found out that it was not an accident, but had been done on purpose.

The man who had set fire to it was crazy. His name was Erostratus; and when he was asked why he had done such a wicked thing, he said that it was only to make his name immortal. The people were so indignant that they not only condemned him to die, but forbade all mention of his name, hoping that it would be forgotten.

In spite of this care, Erostratus' name has come down to us. It is immortal indeed, but who except a crazy man would wish to win such fame and could bear to think that all who ever heard of him would condemn his action and consider him as wicked as he was insane?

Alexander was first given over to the care of a nurse. He loved her dearly as long as he lived, and her son Clytus was always one of his best friends and most faithful comrades.

As soon as he was old enough, Alexander began to learn the Iliad and Odyssey by heart; and he loved to hear about the principal heroes, and especially about his own ancestor, Achilles.

He admired these poems so much that he carried a copy of them with him wherever he went and always slept with it under his pillow. Both the Iliad and the Odyssey were kept in a box of the finest gold, because Alexander thought nothing was too good for them.

When only thirteen years of age, Alexander once saw some horse dealers bringing a beautiful steed before the king. The animal had a white spot on his nose shaped somewhat like the head of an ox, and on this account was named Bucephalus, which means "ox-head."

Philip admired the horse greatly and bade the grooms try him to see if his gait was good. One after another mounted, only to be thrown a few minutes later by the fiery, restless steed, which was becoming very much excited.

The horse seemed so skittish that Philip finally told the men to lead him away, adding that a man would be foolish to purchase such a useless animal. Alexander then stepped forward and begged permission to try him.

His father first made fun of him for asking to mount a horse which none of the grooms could manage; but, as Alexander persisted in his wish, he was finally allowed to make the attempt.

The young prince then quietly walked up to the excited horse, took the bridle, held it firmly, and began to speak gently and pat the steed's arched neck. After a moment, Alexander led Bucephalus forward a few steps and then turned him around, for he had noticed that the horse was frightened by his shadow.

Then, when the shadow lay where he could not see it, and where it could no longer frighten him, the young man dropped his cloak quietly and vaulted upon the horse's back. Once more Bucephalus reared, pranced, kicked, and ran; but Alexander sat firmly on his back, spoke to him gently, and, making no effort to hold him in, let him speed across the plain.

In a few moments the horse's wildness was over, and Alexander could ride back to his proud father, sitting upon a steed which obeyed his slightest touch.

Philip was so delighted with the coolness, courage, and good horsemanship that Alexander had shown on this occasion that he made him a present of the steed. Bucephalus became Alexander's favorite mount, and while he would allow no one else to ride him, he obeyed his master perfectly.

Although most young men began the study of philosophy only at sixteen, Alexander was placed under the tuition of Aristotle soon after his first ride on Bucephalus. This philosopher was a pupil of Plato. He was so learned and well known, that Philip, in writing to him to tell him of Alexander's birth, expressed his pleasure that the gods had allowed his son to live in the same age with so great a teacher.

Alexander loved Aristotle dearly and willingly learned all that was required of him. He often said that he was very grateful, for this philosopher had taught him all the good he knew. Alexander's remarkable coolness, judgment, and perseverance were largely owing to his teacher, and, had he always followed Aristotle's advice, he would have been truly great.

But although Alexander did not always practice the virtues which Aristotle had tried to teach him, he never forgot his old tutor. He gave him large sums of money, so that the philosopher could continue his studies and find out new things. And during his journeys, he always sent him complete collections of the animals and plants of the regions he visited.

Written Summation

Philip was so delighted with the coolness, courage, and good horsemanship that Alexander had shown on this occasion that he made him a present of the steed. Bucephalus became Alexander's favorite mount, and while he would allow no one else to ride him, he obeyed his master perfectly.

Model Practice 1

Model Practice 2

Model Practice 3

Alexander and Diogenes

356 BC– 323 BC lifespan of Alexander the Great
from The Story of the Greeks
by H. A. Guerber

Everybody bowed down before Alexander, and all looked at him with awe and respect, as he made his triumphant progress through Greece—all except the sage Diogenes.

This man belonged to a class of philosophers who were called "cynics," which means "doglike," because, as some say, they did not care for the usual comforts of life.

It is said that Diogenes, the principal philosopher of this kind, chose as his home a great earthenware tub near the Temple of Ceres. He wore a rough woolen cloak, summer and winter, as his only garment and ate all his food raw. His only utensil was a wooden bowl, out of which he drank.

One day, however, he saw a child drinking out of its hollow palm. Diogenes immediately threw away the bowl, saying he could do without luxury as well as the child; and he drank henceforth from his hand.

As you see, Diogenes was a very strange man. He prided himself upon always telling the truth and upon treating all men alike. Some of his disciples once met him wandering about the streets with a lantern, anxiously peering into every nook and corner, and staring fixedly at every person he met. When asked what he was looking for so carefully, yet apparently with so little hope, he bluntly answered, "An honest man."

Alexander had heard of this queer philosopher and was anxious to see him. He therefore went to the Temple of Ceres, escorted by all his courtiers, on purpose to visit him. Diogenes was lying on the ground in front of his tub, warming himself in the rays of the sun.

Alexander, drawing near, stood between the philosopher and the sun and tried to begin a conversation; but Diogenes gave surly answers and seemed to pay little heed to his visitor.

At last the young king proudly remarked, "I am Alexander the king!"

"And I," replied the philosopher in exactly the same tone, "am Diogenes the cynic!"

As he could win nothing but short or rude answers, Alexander was about to go away, but he first asked the sage if there was anything he could do for him. "Yes!" snapped Diogenes. "Stand out of my sunshine!"

The courtiers were shocked at this insolent behavior and began to talk of the philosopher in a scornful tone as they were moving away. Alexander, overhearing them, soon stopped them by saying, "If I were not Alexander, I should like to be Diogenes."

By this remark he wished them to understand, that, if he could not be master of all earthly things, he would rather despise them.

Strange to relate, Alexander the king and Diogenes the cynic died on the same night and from the same cause. Diogenes died in his tub after a too plentiful supper from the raw leg of an ox; while Alexander breathed his last in a Babylonian palace after having eaten and drunk to excess at a rich banquet.

As soon as the Greek states had all been brought to a proper state of obedience, Alexander prepared to conquer Persia, although he had a force of only 34,500 men. These men were very well trained, however, and promised to be more powerful on the battlefield than the million warriors of Xerxes.

In his joy at departing, Alexander made rich presents to everybody, until one of his advisers modestly reminded him that his treasure was not boundless and asked him what he would have left when he had given away all he owned.

"My hopes!" answered Alexander proudly, for he expected to conquer not only Persia and Asia Minor, but all the known world.

While his army slowly made its way along the coast and across the Hellespont, Alexander, attended by only a few followers, sailed straight for Troy, the ancient Asiatic city.

He landed on the desert plain where the proud city had once stood, visited all the scenes of the mighty conflict and offered sacrifices on the tomb of Achilles, while his friend Hephæstion did the same on that of Patroclus.

When this pious pilgrimage to the tomb of his ancestor was over, Alexander hastened to join the army, for he longed to do like the ancient Greeks and win a glorious victory.

His wishes were soon granted, for before long he met the Persian army near the Granicus River, where a terrible battle was fought. Alexander himself joined in the fighting and would certainly have been killed had not his friend Clytus, the son of his old nurse, rushed to his rescue and saved his life.

In spite of the size of the Persian army, which was much larger than his own, Alexander won a complete victory at the Granicus. Then, marching southward, he took the cities of Sardis and Ephesus without striking another blow. These towns were very rich and offered of their own free will to pay him the same tribute that they had given to the Persians.

Alexander, however, would not take it, but bade them use the money to rebuild the Temple of Diana, which had been burned to the ground on the night he was born. As the sacred image of the goddess had been saved, the Ephesians gladly built a second magnificent shrine, which was visited many years later by Paul, the disciple of Christ.

From Sardis and Ephesus, Alexander marched on into the province of Caria. Here the queen of the country warmly welcomed him, adopted him as her son, and even proposed to give him her best cooks, so that they might prepare his food for him on the march.

Alexander thanked her heartily for this kind offer, but declined it, saying that his tutor Aristotle had given him the very best recipe for making him relish his meals.

The queen, whose appetite was fanciful, eagerly asked what it was; and Alexander smilingly answered, "A march before daybreak as the sauce for my dinner, and a light dinner as the sauce for my supper."

This was, as you may see, a very good recipe; and if Alexander had always remembered to be temperate, as Aristotle had advised, he would not have died of over eating and drinking at the age of thirty-three.

Written Summation

As he could win nothing but short or rude answers, Alexander was about to go away, but he first asked the sage a question. He wanted to know if there was anything he could do for him. "Yes!" snapped Diogenes. "Stand out of my sunshine!"

Model Practice 1 (adapted from the original)

Model Practice 2

Model Practice 3

A Roman's Honor

from The Ontario Readers, by Ontario Ministry of Education
adapted from The Book of Golden Deeds by Charlotte M. Yonge
249 BC

The Romans had suffered a terrible defeat in B.C. 251, and Regulus, a famous soldier and senator, had been captured and dragged into Carthage where the victors feasted and rejoiced through half the night and testified their thanks to their god by offering in his fires the bravest of their captives.

Regulus himself was not, however, one of these victims. He was kept a close prisoner for two years, pining and sickening in his loneliness; while, in the meantime, the war continued, and at last a victory so decisive was gained by the Romans that the people of Carthage were discouraged and resolved to ask terms of peace. They thought that no one would be so readily listened to at Rome as Regulus, and they therefore sent him there with their envoys, having first made him swear that he would come back to his prison, if there should neither be peace nor an exchange of prisoners. They little knew how much more a truehearted Roman cared for his city than for himself—for his word than for his life.

Worn and dejected, the captive warrior came to the outside of the gates of his own city and there paused, refusing to enter. "I am no longer a Roman citizen," he said. "I am but the barbarian's slave, and the Senate may not give audience to strangers within the walls."

His wife, Marcia, ran out to greet him, with his two sons, but he did not look up and received their caresses as one beneath their notice, as a mere slave, and he continued, in spite of all entreaty, to remain outside the city and would not even go to the little farm he had loved so well.

The Roman Senate, as he would not come in to them, came out to hold their meeting in the Campagna.

The ambassadors spoke first; then Regulus, standing up, said, as one repeating a task: "Conscript fathers, being a slave to the Carthaginians, I come on the part of my masters to treat with you concerning peace and an exchange of prisoners." He then turned to go away with the ambassadors, as a stranger might not be present at the deliberations of the Senate. His old friends pressed him to stay and give his opinion as a senator, who had twice been consul; but he refused to degrade that dignity by claiming it, slave as he was. But, at the command of his Carthaginian masters, he remained, though not taking his seat.

Then he spoke. He told the senators to persevere in the war. He said he had seen the distress of Carthage, and that a peace would be only to her advantage, not to that of Rome, and therefore he strongly advised that the war should continue. Then, as to the exchange of prisoners, the Carthaginian generals, who were in the hands of the Romans, were in full health and strength, whilst he himself was too much broken down to be fit for service again; and, indeed, he believed that his enemies had given him a slow poison, and that he could not live long. Thus he insisted that no exchange of prisoners should be made.

It was wonderful, even to Romans, to hear a man thus pleading against himself; and their chief priest came forward and declared that, as his oath had been wrested from him by force, he was not bound by it to return to his captivity. But Regulus was too noble to listen to this for a moment. "Have you resolved to dishonor me?" he said. "I am not ignorant that death and the most extreme tortures are preparing for me; but what are these to the shame of an infamous action, or the wounds of a guilty mind? Slave as I am to Carthage, I have still the spirit of a Roman. I have sworn to return. It is my duty to go. Let the gods take care of the rest."

The Senate decided to follow the advice of Regulus, though they bitterly regretted his sacrifice. His wife wept and entreated in vain that they would detain him—they could merely repeat their permission to him to remain; but nothing could prevail with him to break his word, and he turned back to the chains and death he expected, as calmly as if he had been returning to his home. This was in the year B.C. 249.

Written Summation

"Have you resolved to dishonor me?" he said. "I am not ignorant that death and the most extreme tortures are preparing for me; but what are these to the shame of an infamous action, or the wounds of a guilty mind? Slave as I am to Carthage, I have still the spirit of a Roman. I have sworn to return. It is my duty to go. Let the gods take care of the rest."

Model Practice 1

Model Practice 2

Model Practice 3

The Story of the Empty Tomb
c. 4 BC to 33 AD
from The Wonder Book of Bible Stories
by Logan Marshall

After Jesus was taken before the high priest where he was ridiculed and the people spat upon him, he was taken before the Roman Governor, Pontius Pilate, who ruled over Judea. He heard their complaints, but did not find any cause for putting him to death. But at last he yielded to their demands, although he declared Jesus was innocent of all wrong.

And so Pontius Pilate, the Roman governor, gave command that Jesus should die by the cross. The Roman soldiers then took Jesus and beat him most cruelly and then led him out of the city to the place of death. This was a place called "Golgotha" in the Jewish language, "Calvary" in that of the Romans; both words meaning "The Skull Place."

With the soldiers went out of the city a great crowd of people—some of them enemies of Jesus, glad to see him suffer, others of them friends of Jesus and the women who had helped him, now weeping as they saw him all covered with his blood and going out to die. But Jesus turned to them and said:

"Daughters of Jerusalem, do not weep for me, but weep for yourselves and for your children. For the days are coming when they shall count those happy who have no little ones to be slain, when they shall wish that the mountain might fall on them and the hills might cover them and hide them from their enemies!"

They had tried to make Jesus bear his own cross, but soon found that he was too weak from his sufferings and could not carry it. They seized a man who was coming out of the country into the city, a man named Simon, and they made him carry the cross to its place at Calvary.

It was the custom among the Jews to give to men about to die by the cross some medicine to deaden their feelings, so that they would not suffer so greatly. They offered this to Jesus, but when he had tasted it and found what it was, he would not take it. He knew that he would die, but he wished to have his mind clear and to understand what was done and what was said, even though his sufferings might be greater.

At the place Calvary, they laid the cross down, and stretched Jesus upon it, and drove nails through his hands and feet to fasten him to the cross; and then they stood it upright with Jesus upon it. While the soldiers were doing this dreadful work, Jesus prayed for them to God, saying: "Father, forgive them; for they know not what they are doing."

The soldiers also took the clothes that Jesus had worn, giving to each one a garment. But when they came to his undergarment, they found that it was woven and had no seams; so they said, "Let us not tear it, but cast lots for it, to see who shall have it." So at the foot of the cross the soldiers threw lots for the garment of Christ.

Two men who had been robbers and had been sentenced to die by the cross were led out to die at the same time with Jesus. One was placed on a cross at his right side, and the other at his left; and to make Jesus appear as the worst his cross stood in the middle. Over the head of Jesus on his cross, they placed, by Pilate's order, a sign on which was written:

"This is Jesus of Nazareth,

The King of the Jews."

This was written in three languages: in Hebrew, which was the language of the Jews, in Latin, the language of the Romans, and in Greek. Many of the people read this writing; but the chief priests were not pleased with it. They urged Pilate to have it changed from "The King of the Jews" to "He said, 'I am King of the Jews.'" But Pilate would not change it. He said:

"What I have written, I have written."

And the people who passed by on the road, as they looked at Jesus on the cross, mocked at him. Some called out to him:

"You that would destroy the Temple and build it in three days, save yourself. If you are the Son of God, come down from the cross!"

And the priests and scribes said:

"He saved others, but he cannot save himself. Come down from the cross, and we will believe in you!"

And one of the robbers, who was on his own cross beside that of Jesus, joined in the cry, and said: "If you are the Christ, save yourself and save us!"

But the other robber said to him: "Have you no fear of God, to speak thus, while you are suffering the same fate with this man? And we deserve to die, but this man has done nothing wrong."

Then this man said to Jesus: "Lord, remember me when thou comest into thy kingdom!"

And Jesus answered him, as they were both hanging on their crosses: "Today you shall be with me in heaven."

Before the cross of Jesus his mother was standing, filled with sorrow for her son, and beside her was one of his disciples, John, the disciple whom he loved best. Other women besides his mother were there—his mother's sister, Mary the wife of Cleophas and a woman named Mary Magdalene, out of whom a year before Jesus had sent an evil spirit. Jesus wished to give his mother, now that he was leaving her, into the care of John, and he said to her, as he looked from her to John: "Woman, see your son."

And then to John he said: "Son, see your mother."

And on that day John took the mother of Jesus home to his own house and cared for her as his own mother.

At about noon, a sudden darkness came over the land and lasted for three hours. And in the middle of the afternoon, when Jesus had been on the cross for six hours of terrible pain, he cried out aloud words which meant:

"My God, my God, why hast thou forsaken me!" words which are the beginning of the twenty-second psalm, a psalm which long before had spoken of many of Christ's sufferings.

After this he spoke again, saying, "I thirst!"

And someone dipped a sponge in a cup of vinegar, and put it upon a reed, and gave him a drink of it. Then Jesus spoke his last words upon the cross:

"It is finished! Father, into thy hands I give my spirit!"

And then Jesus died. And at that moment, the veil in the Temple between the Holy Place and the Holy of Holies was torn apart by unseen hands from the top to the bottom. And when the Roman officer, who had charge of the soldiers around the cross, saw what had taken place, and how Jesus died, he said: "Surely this was a righteous man; he was the Son of God."

After Jesus was dead, one of the soldiers, to be sure that he was no longer living, ran his spear into the side of his dead body; and out of the wound came pouring both water and blood.

There were even among the rulers of the Jews a few who were friends of Jesus, though they did not dare to follow Jesus openly. One of these was Nicodemus, the ruler who came to see Jesus at night. Another was a rich man who came from the town of Arimathea and was named Joseph. Joseph of Arimathea went boldly in to Pilate and asked that the body of Jesus might be given to him. Pilate wondered that he had died so soon, for often men lived on the cross two or three days. But when he found that Jesus was really dead, he gave his body to Joseph.

Then Joseph and his friends took down the body of Jesus from the cross and wrapped it in fine linen. And Nicodemus brought some precious spices, myrrh and aloes, which they wrapped up with the body. Then they placed the body in Joseph's own new tomb, which was a cave dug out of the rock, in a garden near the place of the cross. And before the opening of the cave they rolled a great stone.

And Mary Magdalene, and the other Mary, and some other women saw the tomb and watched while they laid the body of Jesus in it. On the next morning, some of the rulers of the Jews came to Pilate and said:

"Sir, we remember that that man Jesus of Nazareth, who deceived the people, said while he was yet alive, 'After three days I will rise again.' Give orders that the tomb shall be watched and made sure for three days, or else his disciples may steal his body, and then say, 'He is risen from the dead'; and thus even after his death, he may do more harm than he did while he was alive."

Pilate said to them:

"Set a watch and make it as sure as you can."

Then they placed a seal upon the stone, so that no one might break it; and they set a watch of soldiers at the door.

And in the tomb the body of Jesus lay from the evening of Friday, the day when he died on the cross, to the dawn of Sunday, the first day of the week, when he arose from the dead and appeared unto his disciples.

But the brightest day in all the world was this Sunday morning. For on that day the stone was rolled away from the tomb and Jesus came forth from the dead to gladden his disciples. This he had told them he would do. On this Sunday morning, Mary Magdalene and another Mary, called Salome, came to the tomb and found the stone rolled away and an angel standing by the open tomb. He told them that Jesus was not there, but had risen.

Afterward Jesus was with his disciples for forty days, after which he was taken up into heaven.

Written Summation

But the other robber said to him, "Have you no fear of God, to speak thus, while you are suffering the same fate with this man? And we deserve to die, but this man has done nothing wrong."

Then this man said to Jesus, "Lord, remember me when thou comest into thy kingdom!"

Model Practice 1

Model Practice 2

Model Practice 3

The Wild Caligula
from The Story of the Romans
by H. A. Guerber
August 31, 12 – January 24, 41

As Caligula was the son of virtuous parents, everybody expected that he would prove to be a good man. But he had lost both father and mother when he was very young and had been brought up among wicked people. It is no wonder, therefore, that he followed the example he had so long had under his eyes and turned out to be even worse than Tiberius.

Caligula, like his great-uncle, was a hypocrite, so at first he pretended to be very good; but, before many months had passed, the Romans discovered that he was as cruel and vicious as he could be.

Among his many other failings, Caligula was very vain. Not content with adopting all the pomp of an Eastern king, he soon wished to be worshiped as one of the gods; and he struck off the heads of their statues, so as to have them replaced by copies of his own.

Sometimes, too, he stood in the temple, dressed as Mars or even as Venus, and forced the people to worship him. He often pretended to hold conversations with the gods and even to threaten and scold them whenever things did not suit him.

Sometimes he went out to woo the full moon, as if he had been its lover, and he treated his horse far better than any of his subjects. This animal, whose name was Incitatus, lived in a white marble stable and ate out of an ivory manger; and sentinels were placed all around to see that no sound, however slight, should disturb him when asleep.

Caligula often invited Incitatus to his own banquets and there the horse was made to eat oats off a golden plate and drink wine out of the emperor's own cup. Caligula was on the point of sending the name of Incitatus to the senate and of having him elected as consul of Rome when this favorite horse died and thus put a stop to his master's extravagance.

Many historians think that Caligula was not responsible for all the harm that he did; for he was once very ill, and it was only after that illness that he began to do all these crazy things. Some of his courtiers had exclaimed that they would gladly die if the emperor could only be well; so as soon as he was able to be up again, he forced them to kill themselves.

As time went on, Caligula's madness and cruelty increased, and he did many more absurd things. For instance, he once started out with a large army, saying that he was going to make war against the Germans. But, when he came to the Rhine, he gave orders that a few German slaves should hide on the other side of the river. Then, rushing into their midst, he made believe to take them captive; and when he came back to Rome he insisted upon having a triumph.

Before going back home, however, he started out to conquer Britain. But when he came to the sea, he directed his soldiers to pick up a lot of shells on the shore. These he brought back to Rome as booty, and he pompously called them the spoils of the ocean.

An astrologer once told him that he was as likely to become emperor as to walk over the sea; and he wished to prove his ability to do both. As he was emperor already, he ordered that a bridge of boats should be built across an arm of the sea; and then he walked over it simply to show how wrong the astrologer had been.

An ordinary boat to travel about in would not have suited Caligula, so he had a galley built of cedar wood. The oars were gilded, the sails were made of silk, and on the deck was a pleasure garden with real plants and trees bearing fruit of all kinds.

The cruelty of this emperor was quite as great as his folly. We are told that he killed his own grandmother, caused many Romans to die in slow torture, and once exclaimed, "I wish that the Roman people had but one head so that I might cut it off at a blow!"

Caligula's tyranny lasted about three years. Unable to endure it any longer, some of the Romans formed a conspiracy, and Caligula was murdered by one of his guards whom he had taunted. The first blow having been struck by this man, the other conspirators closed around Caligula, and it was found later that he had been pierced by no less than thirty mortal wounds.

Such was the end of this monster of whom Seneca, a Roman writer, has said: "Nature seemed to have brought him forth to show what mischief could be effected by the greatest vices supported by the greatest authority."

Written Summation

An ordinary boat to travel about in would not have suited Caligula, so he had a galley built of cedar wood. The oars were gilded, the sails were made of silk, and on the deck was a pleasure garden with real plants and trees bearing fruit of all kinds.

Model Practice 1

Model Practice 2

Model Practice 3

Nero's First Crimes

December 15, 37 – June 9, 68
from The story of the Romans
by H. A. Guerber

Claudius was dead, but the fact was at first made known only to a few faithful servants. Then Agrippina arranged that Britannicus, the real heir of the empire, should be kept out of sight until her own son Nero had been set upon the vacant throne.

The senate and people made no objection to her choice, and everybody hoped that Nero would rule very wisely, because he was a grandson of Germanicus and was advised by Seneca and Burrhus, who were both very able and upright men.

Because they were honest, these men first of all told Nero that he had better send his mother away from court, where her influence could do no good. Nero followed this advice, and during the first months of his reign he was generous, clement, and humane. We are told that when he was first asked to sign the death warrant of a criminal, he did so regretfully and exclaimed: "Oh! I wish I did not know how to write!"

Nero was only about seventeen years of age when he began his reign. He was handsome, well educated, and pleasant-mannered, but unfortunately he, too, was a hypocrite. Although he pretended to admire all that was good, he was in reality very wicked.

His mother, Agrippina, had set him on the throne only that she herself might reign; and she was very angry at being sent away from court. However, she did not give up all hopes of ruling, but made several attempts to win her son's confidence once more, and to get back her place at court. Seeing that coaxing had no effect, she soon tried bolder means. One day she entered the hall where Nero was talking with some ambassadors and tried to take a place by his side.

Nero saw her come in and guessed what she intended to do. He rushed forward with exaggerated politeness, took her gently by the hand, and solemnly led her—not to a seat of honor by his side, but to a quiet corner where she could see all, but where she would hardly be seen.

Agrippina was so angry at being thus set aside that she began to plan to dethrone Nero and give the crown to Britannicus instead. This plot, however, was revealed to the young emperor. As soon as he heard it, he sent for Locusta and made her prepare a deadly poison, which he tested upon animals to make sure of its effect.

When quite satisfied that the poison would kill any one who took it, Nero invited his stepbrother to his own table and cleverly poisoned him. Although Britannicus died there, before his eyes, the emperor showed no emotion whatever; but later on he saw that the people mourned the young victim, and then he pretended to weep too.

His wife, Octavia, the gentle sister of Britannicus, was sent away soon after, and in her place Nero chose Poppæa, a woman who was as wicked as Messalina or Agrippina. This woman gave him nothing but bad advice, which he was now only too glad to follow.

Having killed his brother, Nero next began to plan how he might kill his mother. He did not wish to poison Agrippina, so he had a galley built in such a way that it could suddenly be made to fall apart.

As soon as this ship was ready, he asked his mother to come and visit him. Then, after treating her with pretended affection, he sent her home on the treacherous galley.

As soon as it was far enough from the shore, the bolts were loosened, and the ship parted, hurling Agrippina and her attendants into the sea.

One of the queen's women swam ashore and cried out that she was Agrippina in order to secure prompt aid from some men who stood there. Instead of helping her, the men thrust her back into the water and held her under until she was drowned; for they had been sent there by Nero to make sure that no one escaped.

The real Agrippina, seeing this, pretended to be only a waiting maid and came ashore safely. The young emperor was at table when the news of his mother's escape was brought to him. He flew into a passion on hearing that his plans had failed and at once sent a slave to finish the work that had been begun.

In obedience to this cruel order, the slave forced his way into Agrippina's room. When she saw him coming with drawn sword, she bared her breast and cried: "Strike here where Nero's head once rested!" The slave obeyed, and Nero was soon told that his mother was dead.

Written Summation

Nero was only about seventeen years of age when he began his reign. He was handsome, well educated, and pleasant-mannered, but unfortunately he, too, was a hypocrite. Although he pretended to admire all that was good, he was in reality very wicked.

Model Practice 1

Model Practice 2

Model Practice 3

The Christians Persecuted
37-68 AD
from The Story of the Romans
By H. A. Guerber

At first, Nero was rather frightened at his own crimes. The Romans, however, did not resent the murder of Agrippina, but gave public thanks because the emperor's life had been spared; and when Nero heard of this he was quite reassured. Shortly afterwards, the gentle Octavia died too, and then Nero launched forth into a career of extravagance as wild as that of Caligula.

Always fond of gladiatorial combats and games of all kinds, Nero himself took part in the public chariot races. Then, too, although he had a very poor voice, he liked to go on the stage and perform and sing before his courtiers, who told him that he was a great actor and a very fine singer.

Encouraged by these flatterers, Nero grew more conceited and more wild. To win his favor, many great people followed his example; and noble ladies soon appeared on the stage, where they sought the applause of the worst class in Rome.

The poor people were admitted free of charge at these games, provided that they loudly applauded Nero and his favorites. As they could not attend to their work, owing to the many festivities, the emperor ordered that they should be fed at the expense of the state; and he made lavish gifts of grain.

A comet having appeared at this time, some of the superstitious Romans ventured to suggest that it was a sign of a new reign. These words were repeated to Nero and displeased him greatly; so he ordered that all the people who spoke of it should be put to death, and that their property should be confiscated for his use.

Some of these unfortunate Romans took their own lives in order to escape the tortures which awaited them. There were others whom the emperor did not dare to arrest openly, lest the people should rise up against him; and these received secret orders to open their veins in a bath of hot water, and thus bleed to death.

For the sake of the excitement, Nero used to put on a disguise and go out on the highways to rob and murder travelers. On one occasion he attacked a senator, who, failing to recognize him, struck him a hard blow. The very next day the senator found out who the robber was, and, hoping to disarm Nero's rage, went up to the palace and humbly begged his pardon for striking him.

Nero listened to the apologies in haughty silence, and then exclaimed: "What, wretch, you have struck Nero and are still alive?" And, although he did not kill the senator then and there, he nevertheless gave the man strict orders to kill himself; and the poor senator did not dare to disobey.

Nero had received a very good education, and so he was familiar with the great poem of Homer which tells about the war of Troy. He wished to enjoy the sight of a fire, such as Homer describes when the Greeks became masters of that city. He therefore, it is said, gave orders that Rome should be set afire, and sat up on his palace tower, watching the destruction and singing the verses about the fall of Troy, while he accompanied himself on his lyre.

A great part of the city was thus destroyed, many lives were lost, and countless people were made poor; but the sufferings of others did not trouble the monster Nero, who delighted in seeing misery of every kind.

Ever since the crucifixion of our Lord, during the reign of Tiberius, the apostles had been busy preaching the gospel. Peter and Paul had even visited Rome, and talked to so many people that there were by this time a large number of Roman Christians.

The Christians, who had been taught to love one another and to be good, could not of course approve of the wicked Nero's conduct. They boldly reproved him for his vices, and Nero soon took his revenge by accusing them of having set fire to Rome and by having them seized and tortured in many ways.

Some of the Christians were beheaded, some were exposed to the wild beasts of the circus, and some were wrapped up in materials, which would easily catch fire, set upon poles, and used as living torches for the emperor's games. Others were plunged in kettles of boiling oil or water or hunted like wild beasts.

All of them, however, died with great courage, boldly confessing their faith in Christ; and because they suffered death for their religion, they have ever since been known as Martyrs. During this first Roman persecution, St. Paul was beheaded and St. Peter was crucified. St. Peter was placed on the cross head downward, at his own request, because he did not consider himself worthy to die as his beloved Master had died.

Written Summation

During this first Roman persecution, St. Paul was beheaded and St. Peter was crucified. St. Peter was placed on the cross head downward, at his own request, because he did not consider himself worthy to die as his beloved master had died.

Model Practice 1

Model Practice 2

Model Practice 3

The Siege of Jerusalem
from The Story of the Romans
By H. A. Guerber
November 17, 9 – June 23, 79

The new emperor, Vitellius, was not cruel like Tiberius, Caligula, and Nero, nor imbecile like Claudius, nor a victim of his favorites like Galba; but he had a fault that was as disastrous as any. This was gluttony. He is said to have been so greedy that even now, over eighteen hundred years after he died, his name is still used as a byword.

All his thoughts were about eating and drinking. He lived in great luxury at home; but he often invited himself out to dinner, breakfast, or supper at the house of one of his courtiers, where he expected to be treated to the most exquisite viands.

Such was his love of eating, it is said, that when he had finished one good meal, he would take an emetic, so that he might begin at once on the next; and thus he was able to enjoy four dinners a day instead of one. This disgusting gluttony became so well know that many Romans made up their minds not to obey any longer a man whose habits were those of the meanest animals.

They therefore determined to select as emperor the general Vespasian, who had won many victories during the reigns of Claudius, Nero, Galba, and Otho, and who was now besieging Jerusalem. In obedience to the soldiers' wishes, Vespasian left his son Titus to finish the siege and sent an army toward Rome, which met and defeated the forces of Vitellius.

The greedy emperor cared little for the imperial title and now offered to give it up, on condition that he should be allowed a sum of money large enough to enable him to end his life in luxury. When this was refused him, he made a feeble effort to defend himself in Rome.

Vespasian's army, however, soon forced its way into the city. Vitellius tried first to flee and then to hide; but he was soon found and killed by the soldiers, who dragged his body through the streets and then flung it into the Tiber.

The senate now confirmed the army's choice, and Vespasian became emperor of Rome. Although he had been wild in his youth, Vespasian now gave the best example to his people, for he spent all his time in thinking of their welfare and in trying to improve Rome. He also began to build the Coliseum, the immense circus whose ruins can still be seen and where there were seats for more than one hundred thousand spectators.

While Vespasian was thus occupied at home, his son Titus had taken command of the army which was besieging the city of Jerusalem. As the prophets had foretold, these were terrible times for the Jews. There were famines and earthquakes, and strange signs were seen in the sky.

In spite of all these signs, Titus battered down the heavy walls, scaled the ramparts, and finally took the city where famine and pestilence now reigned. The Roman soldiers robbed the houses and then set fire to them. The flames, thus started, soon reached the beautiful temple built by Herod, and in spite of all that Titus could do to save it, this great building was burned to the ground.

Amid the lamentations of the Jews, the walls of the city were razed and the site plowed; and soon, as Christ had foretold, not one stone remained upon another. Nearly one million Jews are said to have perished during this awful siege, and the Romans led away one hundred thousand captives.

On his return to Rome, Titus was honored by a triumph. The books of the law and the famous golden candlestick, which had been in the temple at Jerusalem, were carried as trophies in the procession. The Romans also commemorated their victory by erecting the Arch of Titus, which is still standing. The carving on this arch represents the Roman soldiers carrying the booty.

Vespasian reigned ten years and was beloved by all his subjects. He was taken ill at his country house and died there. Even when the end was near, and he was too weak to stand, he bade his attendants help him to his feet, saying, "An emperor should die standing."

Written Summation

All his thoughts were about eating and drinking. He lived in great luxury at home; but he often invited himself out to dinner, breakfast, or supper at the house of one of his courtiers, where he expected to be treated to the most exquisite viands.

Model Practice 1 (adapted from the original)

Model Practice 2

Model Practice 3

A Prophecy Fulfilled

from The Story of the Romans
by H. A. Guerber
c. 272 – 337

Several other emperors succeeded Tacitus at short intervals and all died violent deaths after very brief reigns. Finally the army called Diocletian, an Illyrian soldier, to the throne.

It seems that a northern priestess had once foretold that Diocletian would gain the Roman throne when he had "killed the boar." All the people at this time were more or less superstitious, so Diocletian spent much time hunting. But, although he killed many boars, he was not for a long time named Emperor.

Now the two emperors who came before Diocletian were murdered by a burly soldier named Aper, a Latin word meaning "boar." Some of the legions then elected Diocletian to this office; and he, wishing to punish the murderer for his double crime, struck Aper down with his own hand.

His soldiers were familiar with the prophecy of the priestess, and they now cried that he would surely gain the throne, because he had killed the Boar. True enough, Diocletian's only rival was soon slain, and he was declared emperor by all the Romans.

Diocletian, however, found that the Roman Empire was too large and hard to govern for a single ruler. He therefore made his friend Maximian associate emperor. Then he said that Galerius and Constantius should be called Cæsars, and gave them also a portion of the empire to govern. These four Roman rulers had their capitals at Nicomedia, Milan, Sirmium, and Treves; and now a new epoch begins, with Rome no longer the central point of the government.

Diocletian remained the head and acknowledged leader and adviser of the other rulers. But his reign was troubled by invasions of the barbarians, a war in Persia, and a persecution of the Christians—the worst and bloodiest that had yet been known.

A lover of solitude and simplicity, Diocletian soon tired of the imperial life. Therefore, when he felt that his strength no longer permitted him to serve the people, he withdrew to a quiet retreat in his native city of Salona, where he spent his last eight years in growing vegetables for his amusement.

As Maximian had retired at the same time as Diocletian, the Roman Empire was now divided between Galerius and Constantius, who were known as emperors of the East and of the West, respectively. Constantius, having obtained the West for his share, went to Britain to suppress a revolt. He died at York, and his son Constantine became emperor in his stead.

Constantine's claim to the empire was disputed by several rivals; but the strongest among them was Maxentius, who ruled Italy and had a large army. On his way to meet him, Constantine became a Christian, thanks to a miracle, which the ancient writers relate about as follows.

At noontide, on the day before his battle with Maxentius, Constantine and his army were startled by a brilliant cross which suddenly appeared in the sky. Around the cross were the Greek words meaning, "By this sign conquer."

Constantine was so moved by this vision that he made a vow to become a Christian if he won the victory. He also ordered a new standard, called a Labarum, which bore the cross and the inscription he had seen in the skies. This was always carried before him in battle.

The two armies met near Rome. Maxentius was defeated, and Constantine entered the city in triumph. In memory of his victory a fine arch was built, which is standing still, and is always called the Arch of Constantine.

Written Summation

Diocletian, however, found that the Roman Empire was too large and hard to govern for a single ruler. He therefore made his friend Maximian associate emperor. Then he said that Galerius and Constantius should be called Caesars, and gave them also a portion of the empire to govern.

Model Practice 1

Model Practice 2

Model Practice 3

CHAPTER II

Text Excerpts from
Primary Source Documents

Lines for written summations have not been included in this section. These selections are somewhat complicated, detailed, and advanced for written summations by students at this stage. These selections are best used for oral narrations as an introduction to ideas from the time period studied.

They also serve as a great introduction to primary source material, introducing children to the idea that they are capable of evaluating history for themselves. Copywork and dictation from primary source documents are excellent selections of living literature (aka living books).

The Babylonian Story of the Deluge as Told by Assyrian Tablets from Nineveh (excerpt)
c. 2600 BC Rule of Gilgamesh
by E. A. Wallis Budge

The form of the Legend of the Deluge given below is that which is found on the Eleventh of the Series of Twelve Tablets in the Library of Nebo at Nineveh, which described the life and exploits of Gilgamish, an early king of the city of Erech. As we have seen above, the Legend of the Deluge has in reality no connection with the Epic of Gilgamish, but was introduced into it by the editors of the Epic at a comparatively late period, perhaps even during the reign of Ashurbani-pal (B.C. 668-626). A summary of the contents of the other Tablets of the Gilgamish Series is given in the following section of this short monograph. It is therefore only necessary to state here that Gilgamish, who was horrified and almost beside himself when his bosom friend and companion Enkidu (Eabâni) died, meditated deeply how he could escape death himself. He knew that his ancestor Uta-Napishtim had become immortal, therefore he determined to set out for the place where Uta-Napishtim lived so that he might obtain from him the secret of immortality. Guided by a dream in which he saw the direction of the place where Uta-Napishtim lived, Gilgamish set out for the Mountain of the Sunset, and, after great toil and many difficulties, came to the shore of a vast sea. Here he met Ur-Shanabi, the boatman of Uta-Napishtim, who was persuaded to carry him in his boat over the "waters of death," and at length he landed on the shore of the country of Uta-Napishtim. The immortal came down to the shore and asked the newcomer the object of his visit, and Gilgamish told him of the death of his great friend Enkidu, and of his desire to escape from death and to find immortality. Uta-Napishtim having made to Gilgamish some remarks which seem to indicate that in his opinion death was inevitable,

1. Gilgamish said unto Uta-Napishtim, to Uta-Napishtim the remote:
2. "I am looking at thee, Uta-Napishtim.
3. Thy person is not altered; even as am I so art thou.
4. Verily, nothing about thee is changed; even as am I so art thou.
5. [Moved is my] heart to do battle,
6. But thou art at leisure and dost lie upon thy back.
7. How then wast thou able to enter the company of the gods and see life?"

Thereupon Uta-Napishtim related to Gilgamish the Story of the Deluge, and the Eleventh Tablet continues thus: --

8. Uta-Napishtim said unto him, to Gilgamish:
9. "I will reveal unto thee, O Gilgamish, a hidden mystery,
10. And a secret matter of the gods I will declare unto thee.
11. Shurippak, a city which thou thyself knowest,
12. On [the bank] of the river Puratti (Euphrates) is situated,
13. That city was old and the gods [dwelling] within it --
14. Their hearts induced the great gods to make a wind-storm (a-bu-bi), [12]
15. Their father Anu,
16. Their counsellor, the warrior Enlil,
17. Their messenger En-urta [and]
18. Their prince Ennugi.
19. Nin-igi-azag, Ea, was with them [in council] and
20. reported their word to the house of reeds.

[First Speech of Ea to Uta-Napishtim who is sleeping in a reed hut.]

21. O House of reeds, O House of reeds! O Wall, O Wall!
22. O House of reeds, hear! O Wall, understand!
23. O man of Shurippak, son of Ubara-Tutu.
24. Throw down the house, build a ship,
25. Forsake wealth, seek after life,
26. Abandon possessions, save thy life,
27. Carry grain of every kind into the ship.
28. The ship which thou shalt build,
29. The dimensions thereof shall be measured,
30. The breadth and the length thereof shall be the same.
31. ... the ocean, provide it with a roof."

[Uta-Napishtim's answer to Ea.]

32. "I understood and I said unto Ea, my lord:
33. [I comprehend] my lord, that which thou hast ordered,
34. I will regard it with great reverence, and will perform it.
35. But what shall I say to the town, to the multitude, and to the elders?"

[Second Speech of Ea.]

36. "Ea opened his mouth and spake
37. And said unto his servant, myself,
38. ... Thus shalt thou say unto them:
39. Ill-will hath the god Enlil formed against me,
40. Therefore I can no longer dwell in your city,
41. And never more will I turn my countenance upon the soil of Enlil.
42. I will descend into the ocean to dwell with my lord Ea.
43. But upon you he will rain riches:
44. A catch of birds, a catch of fish
45. ... an [abundant] harvest,
46. ... the prince (?) of the darkness
47. ... shall make a violent cyclone [to fall upon you]."

[The Building of the Ship.]

48. As soon as [the dawn] broke...
[Lines 49-54 broken away.]

55. The weak [man] ... brought bitumen,
56. The strong [man] ... brought what was needed.
57. On the fifth day I decided upon its plan.
58. According to the plan its walls were 10 Gar (i.e. 120 cubits) high,
59. And the circuit of the roof thereof was equally 10 Gar.
60. I measured out the hull thereof and marked it out (?)
61. I covered (?) it six times.
62. Its exterior I divided into seven,
63. Its interior I divided into nine,
64. Water bolts I drove into the middle of it.
65. I provided a steering pole, and fixed what was needful for it,
66. Six sar of bitumen I poured over the inside wall,
67. Three sar of pitch I poured into the inside.
68. The men who bear loads brought three sar of oil,
69. Besides a sar of oil which the offering consumed,
70. And two sar of oil which the boatman hid.
71. I slaughtered oxen for the [work]people,

72. I slew sheep every day.
73. Beer, sesame wine, oil and wine
74. I made the people drink as if they were water from the river.
75. I celebrated a feast-day as if it had been New Year's Day.
76. I opened [a box of ointment], I laid my hands in unguent.
77. Before the sunset the ship was finished.
78. [Since] ... was difficult.
79. The shipbuilders brought the ... of the ship, above and below,
80. ... two-thirds of it.

[The Loading of the Ship.]

81. With everything that I possessed, I loaded it (i.e. the ship).
82. With everything that I possessed of silver, I loaded it.
83. With everything that I possessed of gold, I loaded it.
84. With all that I possessed of living grain, I loaded it.
85. I made to go up into the ship all my family and kinsfolk,
86. The cattle of the field, the beasts of the field, all handicraftsmen I made them go up into it.
87. The god Shamash had appointed me a time (saying)
88. The Power of Darkness will at eventide make a rain-flood to fall;
89. Then enter into the ship and shut thy door.
90. The appointed time drew nigh;
91. The Power of Darkness made a rain-flood to fall at eventide.
92. I watched the coming of the [approaching] storm,
93. "When I saw it terror possessed me,
94. I went into the ship and shut my door.
95. To the pilot of the ship, Puzur-Bêl (or Puzur-Amurri) the sailor
96. I committed the great house (i.e. ship), together with the contents thereof.

[The Abubu (Cyclone) and its effects Described.]

97. As soon as the gleam of dawn shone in the sky
98. A black cloud from the foundation of heaven came up.
99. Inside it the god Adad (Rammânu) thundered,
100. The gods Nabû and Sharru (i.e. Marduk) went before,
101. Marching as messengers over high land and plain,
102. Irragal (Nergal) tore out the post of the ship,
103. En-urta (Ninib) went on, he made the storm to descend.
104. The Anunnaki [13] brandished their torches,
105. With their glare they lighted up the land.
106. The whirlwind (or, cyclone) of Adad swept up to heaven.
107. Every gleam of light was turned into darkness.
108. ...... the land ...... as if ...... had laid it waste.
109. A whole day long [the flood descended] ...
110. Swiftly it mounted up ..... [the water] reached to the mountains
111. [The water] attacked the people like a battle.
112. Brother saw not brother.
113. Men could not be known (or, recognized) in heaven.
114. The gods were terrified at the cyclone.
115. They betook themselves to flight and went up into the heaven of Anu.
116. The gods crouched like a dog and cowered by the wall.
117. The goddess Ishtar cried out like a woman in travail.
118. The Lady of the Gods lamented with a loud voice [saying]:

[Ishtar's Lament.]

119. "Verily the former dispensation is turned into mud,

120. Because I commanded evil among the company of the gods.
121. When I commanded evil among the company of the gods,
122. I commanded battle for the destruction of my people.
123. Did I of myself bring forth my people
124. That they might fill the sea like little fishes?"

[Uta-Napishtim's Story continued.]

125. The gods of the Anunnaki wailed with her.
126. The gods bowed themselves, and sat down, and wept.
127. Their lips were shut tight (in distress) ...
128. For six days and nights
129. The storm raged, and the cyclone overwhelmed the land.

[The Abating of the Storm.]

130. When the seventh day approached the cyclone and the raging flood ceased:
131. --now it had fought like an army.
132. The sea became quiet and went down, and the cyclone and the rain-storm ceased.
133. I looked over the sea and a calm had come,
134. And all mankind were turned into mud,
135. The land had been laid flat like a terrace.
136. I opened the air-hole and the light fell upon my face,
137. I bowed myself, I sat down, I cried,
138. My tears poured down over my cheeks.
139. I looked over the quarters of the world --open sea!
140. After twelve days an island appeared.
141. The ship took its course to the land of Nisir.
142. The mountain of Nisir held the ship, it let it not move.
143. The first day, the second day, the mountain of Nisir held the ship and let it not move.
144. The third day, the fourth day, the mountain of Nisir held the ship and let it not move.
145. The fifth day, the sixth day, the mountain of Nisir held the ship and let it not move.
146. When the seventh day had come
147. I brought out a dove and let her go free.
148. The dove flew away and [then] came back;
149. Because she had no place to alight on, she came back.
150. I brought out a swallow and let her go free.
151. The swallow flew away and [then] came back;
152. Because she had no place to alight on she came back.
153. I brought out a raven and let her go free.
154. The raven flew away; she saw the sinking waters.
155. She ate, she pecked in the ground, she croaked, she came not back.

[Uta-Napishtim Leaves the Ship.]

With everything that I possessed, I loaded it.
With everything that I possessed of silver, I loaded it.
With everything that I possessed of gold, I loaded it.
With all that I possessed of living grain, I loaded it.

Model Practice 1

Model Practice 2

Model Practice 3

The Oldest Code of Laws in the World, by Hammurabi, King of Babylon
c. 1760 BC
by C. H. W. JOHNS, M.A.

(Note: The oldest code of laws is now considered to be the Code of Ur-Nammu. It was translated in 1952, and is dated back to c. 2100 BC)

"The discovery and decipherment of this Code is the greatest event in Biblical Archæology for many a day. A translation of the Code, done by Mr. Johns of Queens' College, Cambridge, the highest living authority on this department of study, has just been published by Messrs. T. & T. Clark in a cheap and attractive booklet. Winckler says it is the most important Babylonian record which has thus far been brought to light."—The Expository Times.

INTRODUCTION (excerpt)

The Code of Hammurabi is one of the most important monuments in the history of the human race, containing as it does the laws which were enacted by a king of Babylonia in the third millennium B.C., whose rule extended over the whole of Mesopotamia from the mouths of the rivers Tigris and Euphrates to the Mediterranean coast, we must regard it with interest. But when we reflect that the ancient Hebrew tradition ascribed the migration of Abraham from Ur of the Chaldees to this very period, and clearly means to represent their tribe father as triumphing over this very same Hammurabi (Amraphel, Gen. xiv. 1), we can hardly doubt that these very laws were part of that tradition. At any rate, they must have served to mould and fix the ideas of right throughout that great empire, and so form the state of society in Canaan when, five hundred years later, the Hebrews began to dominate that region.

The monument itself consists of a block of black diorite, nearly eight feet high, found in pieces, but readily rejoined. It contains on the obverse a very interesting representation of the King Hammurabi, receiving his laws from the seated sun-god Šamaš, 'the judge of heaven and earth.' Then follow, on the obverse, sixteen columns of writing with 1114 lines. There were five more columns on this side, but they have been erased and the stone repolished, doubtless by the Elamite conqueror, who meant to inscribe his name and titles there. As we have lost those five columns we may regret that he did not actually do this, but there is now no trace of any hint as to who carried off the stone. On the reverse side are twenty-eight columns with more than 2500 lines of inscription.

C. H. W. JOHNS.

Cambridge,
January 31, 1903

The Text of the Code (excerpt)

§ 1. If a man weave a spell and put a ban upon a man, and has not justified himself, he that wove the spell upon him shall be put to death.

§ 2. If a man has put a spell upon a man, and has not justified himself, he upon whom the spell is laid shall go to the holy river, he shall plunge into the holy river, and if the holy river overcome him, he who wove the spell upon him shall take to himself his house. If the holy river makes that man to be innocent, and has saved him, he who laid the spell upon him shall be put to death. He who plunged into the holy river shall take to himself the house of him who wove the spell upon him.

§ 3. If a man, in a case pending judgement, has uttered threats against the witnesses, or has not justified the word that he has spoken, if that case be a capital suit, that man shall be put to death.

§ 5. If a judge has judged a judgement, decided a decision, granted a sealed sentence, and afterwards has altered his judgement, that judge, for the alteration of the judgement that he judged, one shall put him to account, and he shall pay twelve fold the penalty which was in the said judgement, and in the assembly one shall expel him from his judgement seat, and he shall not return, and with the judges at a judgement he shall not take his seat.

§ 6. If a man has stolen the goods of temple or palace, that man shall be killed, and he who has received the stolen thing from his hand shall be put to death.

§ 7. If a man has bought silver, gold, manservant or maidservant, ox or sheep or ass, or anything whatever its name, from the hand of a man's son, or of a man's slave, without witness and bonds, or has received the same on deposit, that man has acted the thief, he shall be put to death.

§ 8. If a man has stolen ox or sheep or donkey or pig or ship, whether from the temple or the palace, he shall pay thirty fold. If he be a poor man, he shall render tenfold. If the thief has nought to pay, he shall be put to death.

§ 15. If a man has caused either a palace slave or palace maid, or a slave of a poor man or a poor man's maid, to go out of the gate, he shall be put to death.

§ 16. If a man has harbored in his house a manservant or a maidservant, fugitive from the palace, or a poor man, and has not produced them at the demand of the commandant, the owner of that house shall be put to death.

§ 17. If a man has captured either a manservant or a maidservant, a fugitive, in the open country and has driven him back to his master, the owner of the slave shall pay him two shekels of silver.

§ 141. If the wife of a man who is living in the house of her husband has set her face to go out and has acted the fool, has wasted her house, has belittled her husband, one shall put her to account, and if her husband has said, 'I put her away,' he shall put her away and she shall go her way, he shall not give her anything for her divorce. If her husband has not said 'I put her away,' her husband shall marry another woman, that woman as a maidservant shall dwell in the house of her husband.

§ 162. If a man has married a wife and she has borne him children, and that woman has gone to her fate, her father shall have no claim on her marriage portion, her marriage portion is her children's forsooth.

§ 178. If a lady, votary, or a vowed woman whose father has granted her a marriage portion, has written her a deed, in the deed he has written her has not, however, written her 'after her wherever is good to her to give,' has not permitted her all her choice, after the father has gone to his fate, her brothers shall take her field and her garden, and according to the value of her share shall give her corn, oil, and wool, and shall content her heart. If her brothers have not given her corn, oil, and wool according to the value of her share, and have not contented her heart, she shall give her field or her garden to a cultivator, whoever pleases her, and her cultivator shall sustain her. The field, garden, or whatever her father has given her she shall enjoy as long as she lives, she shall not give it for money, she shall not answer to another, her sonship is her brothers' forsooth.

§ 180. If a father to his daughter a votary, bride, or vowed woman has not granted a marriage portion, after the father has gone to his fate, she shall share in the goods of the father's house a share like one son, as long as she lives she shall enjoy, after her it is her brothers' forsooth.

§ 186. If a man has taken a young child to sonship, and when he took him his father and mother rebelled, that nursling shall return to his father's house.

§ 188. If an artisan has taken a son to bring up and has caused him to learn his handicraft, no one has any claim.

§ 189. If he has not caused him to learn his handicraft, that nursling shall return to his father's house.

§ 215. If a doctor has treated a gentleman for a severe wound with a bronze lancet and has cured the man, or has opened an abscess of the eye for a gentleman with the bronze lancet and has cured the eye of the gentleman, he shall take ten shekels of silver.

§ 216. If he (the patient) be the son of a poor man, he shall take five shekels of silver.

§ 217. If he be a gentleman's servant, the master of the servant shall give two shekels of silver to the doctor.

§ 218. If the doctor has treated a gentleman for a severe wound with a lancet of bronze and has caused the gentleman to die, or has opened an abscess of the eye for a gentleman with the bronze lancet and has caused the loss of the gentleman's eye, one shall cut off his hands.

§ 219. If a doctor has treated the severe wound of a slave of a poor man with a bronze lancet and has caused his death, he shall render slave for slave.

§ 220. If he has opened his abscess with a bronze lancet and has made him lose his eye, he shall pay money, half his price.

§ 221. If a doctor has cured the shattered limb of a gentleman, or has cured the diseased bowel, the patient shall give five shekels of silver to the doctor.

§ 224. If a cow doctor or a sheep doctor has treated a cow or a sheep for a severe wound and cured it, the owner of the cow or sheep shall give one-sixth of a shekel of silver to the doctor as his fee.

§ 225. If he has treated a cow or a sheep for a severe wound and has caused it to die, he shall give a quarter of its price to the owner of the ox or sheep.

If a man has harbored in his house a manservant or a maidservant, fugitive from the palace, or a poor man, and has not produced them at the demand of the commandant, the owner of that house shall be put to death.

Model Practice 1

Model Practice 2

Model Practice 3

The Babylonian Legends of the Creation
by British Museum

Discovery of the Tablets

The baked clay tablets and portions of tablets which describe the views and beliefs of the Babylonians and Assyrians about the Creation were discovered by Mr. (later Sir) A.H. Layard, Mormuzd Rassam and George Smith, Assistant in the Department of Oriental Antiquities in the British Museum. They were found among the ruins of the Palace and Library of Ashur-bani-pal (B.C. 668-626) at Ḳuyûnjiḳ (Nineveh), between the years 1848 and 1876.

Description of Contents

In the beginning nothing whatever existed except APSÛ, which may be described as a boundless, confused and disordered mass of watery matter; how it came into being is unknown. Out of this mass there were evolved two orders of beings, namely, demons and gods. The demons had hideous forms, even as Berosus said, which were part animal, part bird, part reptile and part human. The gods had wholly human forms, and they represented the three layers of the comprehensible world, that is to say, heaven or the sky, the atmosphere, and the underworld. The atmosphere and the underworld together formed the earth as opposed to the sky or heaven. The texts say that the first two gods to be created were LAKHMU and LAKHAMU. Their attributes cannot at present be described, but they seem to represent two forms of primitive matter. They appear to have had no existence in popular religion, and it has been thought that they may be described as theological conceptions containing the notions of matter and some of its attributes.

After countless eons had passed the gods ANSHAR and KISHAR came into being; the former represents the "hosts of heaven," and the latter the "hosts of earth."

After another long and indefinite period the independent gods of the Babylonian pantheon came into being, *e.g.*, ANU, EA, who is here called NUDIMMUD, and others.

As soon as the gods appeared in the universe "order" came into being. When APSÛ, the personification of confusion and disorder of every kind, saw this "order," he took counsel with his female associate TIÂMAT with the object of finding some means of destroying the "way" (*al-ka-at*) or "order" of the gods. Fortunately the Babylonians and Assyrians have supplied us with representations of Tiâmat, and these show us what form ancient tradition assigned to her. She is depicted as a ferocious monster with wings and scales and terrible claws, and her body is sometimes that of a huge serpent, and sometimes that of an animal. In the popular imagination she represented all that was physically terrifying, and foul, and abominable; she was nevertheless the mother of everything, and was the possessor of the DUP SHIMATI or "TABLET OF DESTINIES". No description of this Tablet or its contents is available, but from its name we may assume that it was a sort of Babylonian Book of Fate. Theologically, Tiâmat represented to the Babylonians the same state in the development of the universe as did *tôhû wâ-bhôhû* (Genesis I. 2), *i.e.*, formlessness and voidness, of primeval matter, to the Hebrews She is depicted both on bas-reliefs and on cylinder seals in a form which associates her with LABARTU, a female devil that prowled about the desert at night suckling wild animals but killing men. And it is tolerably certain that she was the type, and symbol, and head of the whole community of fiends, demons and devils.

In the consultation which took place between APSÛ and TIÂMAT, their messenger MU-UM-MU took part; of the history and attributes of this last-named god nothing is known. The result of the consultation was that a long struggle began between the demons and the gods, and it is clear that the object of the powers of darkness was to destroy the light. The whole story of this struggle is the subject of the Seven Tablets of Creation. The gods are deifications of the sun, moon, planets and other stars, and APSÛ, or CHAOS, and his companions the demons, are personifications of darkness, night and evil. The story of the fight between them is nothing more nor less than a picturesque allegory of natural phenomena.

FIRST TABLET (lines 1-61)
story may date to the 18th century BC

[Footnote 1: This translation is made from transcripts of the British Museum fragments (_Cuneiform Texts_, Part XIII), and transcripts of the Berlin fragments (Ebeling, _Keilschrifttexte aus Assur_, Nos. 117, 118).]

1. When the heavens above were yet unnamed,[1]

[Footnote 1: The name of an object was the object itself, and it was believed that nothing could exist apart from its name.]

2. And the name of the earth beneath had not been recorded,

3. Apsu, the oldest of beings, their progenitor,

4. "Mummu" Tiâmat, who bare each and all of them

5. Their waters were merged into a single mass.

6. A field had not been measured, a marsh had not been searched out,

7. When of the gods none was shining,

8. A name had not been recorded, a fate had not been fixed,

9. The gods came into being in the midst of them.
10. The god Lakhmu and the goddess Lakhamu were made to shine, they were named.
11. [Together] they increased in stature, they grew tall.
12. Anshar and Kishar came into being, and others besides them.
13. Long were the days, the years increased.
14. The god Anu, their son, the equal of his fathers, [was created].
15. The god Anshar made his eldest son Anu in his own image.
16. And the god Anu begat Nudimmud (Ea) the image of himself.
17. The god Nudimmud was the first among his fathers,
18. Endowed with understanding, he who thinketh deeply, the orator
19. Exceedingly mighty in strength above his father Anshar who begat him.
20. Unrivalled amongst the gods his brothers ...
21. The confraternity of the gods was established.
22. Tiâmat was troubled and she ... their guardian.
23. Her belly was stirred up to its uttermost depths.
24. ....
25. Apsu (the watery abyss) could not diminish their brawl
26. And Tiâmat gathered herself together ...
27. She struck a blow, and their works ...
28. Their way was not good,...
29. At that time Apsu, the progenitor of the great gods,
30. Shouted out and summoned Mummu, the steward of his house, saying
31. "[O] Mummu, my steward, who makest my liver to rejoice,
32. "Come, to Tiâmat we will go."
33. They went, they lay down [on a couch] facing Tiâmat.
34. They took counsel together about the gods [their children].
35. Apsu took up his word and said,
36. To Tiâmat, the holy (?) one, he made mention of a matter, [saying],
37. "... their way ...
38. "By day I find no peace; by night I have no rest.
39. "Verily I will make an end of their way; I will sweep them away.
40. "There shall be a sound of lamentation; lo, then we shall rest."
41. Tiâmat on hearing this
42. Was stirred up to wrath and shrieked to her husband,[1]

[Footnote 1: Tiâmat's wrath was roused by Apsu, who had proposed to slay the gods, her children. She took no part in the first struggle of Apsu and Mummu against the gods, and only engaged in active hostilities to avenge Apsu.]

43. ... unto sickness. She raged all alone,
44. She uttered a curse, and unto [Apsu, spake, saying,],
45. "Whatsoever we have made we will destroy.
46. "Verily their way shall be filled with disaster; lo, then we shall rest."
47. Mummu answered and gave counsel unto Apsu,
48. The counsel of Mummu was ... and dire [in respect of the gods]:
49. "Come, [do thou destroy] their way which is strong.

50. "Then verily by day thou shalt find peace, [and] by night thou shalt have rest."
51. Apsu heard him, his face grew bright,
52. For that they were planning evil against the gods, his children.
53. Mummu embraced his neck ...
54. He took him on his knee, he kissed him ...
55. They (i.e. Mummu and Apsu) planned the cursing in the assembly,
56. They repeated the curses to the gods their eldest sons.
57. The gods made answer ...
58. They began a lamentation...
59. [Endowed] with understanding, the prudent god, the exalted one,
60. Ea, who pondereth everything that is, searched out their [plan].
61. He brought it to nought (?), he made the form of everything to stand still.

[In the British Museum tablets lines 63-108 are either wanting entirely, or are too broken to translate, and the last 130 lines of the Berlin fragment are much mutilated. The fragments of text show that Ea waged war against Apsu and Mummu. Ea recited an incantation which caused Apsu to fall asleep. He then "loosed the joints" of Mummu, who in some way suffered, but he was strong enough to attack Ea when he turned to deal with Apsu. Ea overcame both his adversaries and divided Apsu into chambers and laid fetters upon him. In one of the chambers of Apsu a god was begotten and born.

According to the Ninevite theologians Ea begat by his wife, who is not named, his son Marduk, and according to the theologians of the City of Ashur, Lakhmu begat by his wife Lakhamu a son who is no other than Anshar, or Ashur. A nurse was appointed to rear him, and he grew up a handsome child, to the great delight of his father. He had four ears and four eyes, a statement which suggests that he was two-headed, and resembled the Latin god Janus.]

By day I find no peace; by night I have no rest.
Verily I will make an end of their way; I will sweep them away.
There shall be a sound of lamentation; lo, then we shall rest.

Model Practice 1

Model Practice 2

Model Practice 3

The Shih King or Book of Poetry (excerpt)

c. 1763 BC – c. 1123 BC Shang Dynasty
by James Legge
from the Sacred Books of the East, Vol. 3

THE SACRIFICIAL ODES OF SHANG

These Odes of Shang constitute the last Book in the ordinary editions of the Shih. I put them here in the first place, because they are the oldest pieces in the collection. There are only five of them.

The sovereigns of the dynasty of Shang who occupied the throne from B.C. 1766 to 1123. They traced their lineage to Hsieh, appears in the Shû as Minister of Instruction to Shun. By Yâo or by Shun, Hsieh was invested with the principality of Shang, corresponding to the small department which is so named in Shen-hsî. Fourteenth in descent from him came Thien-Yî, better known as Khang Thang, or Thang the Successful, who dethroned the last descendant of the line of Hsiâ, and became the founder of a new dynasty. We meet with him first at a considerable distance from the ancestral fief (which, however, gave name to the dynasty), having as his capital the southern Po, which seems correctly referred to the present district of Shang-khiû, in the department of Kwei-teh, Ho-nan. Among the twenty-seven sovereigns who followed Thang, there were three especially distinguished: --Thâi Kiâ, his grandson and successor (B.C. 1753 to 1721), who received the title of Thai Zung; Thai Mâu (B.C. 1637 to 1563), canonized as Kung Zung; and Wû-ting (B.C. 1324 to 1266), known as Kâo Zung. The shrines of these three sovereigns and that of Thang retained their places in the ancestral temple ever after they were first set up and if all the sacrificial odes of the dynasty had been preserved, most of them would have been in praise of one or other of the four. But it so happened that at least all the odes of which Thai Zung was the subject were lost; and of the others we have only the small portion that has been mentioned above.

ODE 1. THE NÂ [1a]

APPROPRIATE TO A SACRIFICE TO THANG, THE FOUNDER OF THE SHANG DYNASTY, DWELLING ESPECIALLY ON THE MUSIC AND THE REVERENCE WITH WHICH THE SACRIFICE WAS PERFORMED.

(We cannot tell by which of the kings of Shang the sacrifice here referred to was first performed. He is simply spoken of as 'a descendant of Thang.' The ode seems to have been composed by some one, probably a member of the royal House, who had taken part in the service.)

How admirable! How complete! Here are set our hand-drums and drums. The drums resound harmonious and loud, To delight our meritorious ancestor [2a].

The descendant of Thang invites him with this music, That he may soothe us with the realization of our thoughts[3a]. Deep is the sound of our hand-drums and drums; Shrilly sound the flutes; All harmonious and blending together, According to the notes of the sonorous gem. Oh! majestic is the descendant of Thang; Very admirable is his music.

The large bells and drums fill the ear; The various dances are grandly performed[1b]. We have the admirable visitors[2b], who are pleased and delighted.

From of old, before our time, The former men set us the example—How to be mild and humble from morning to night, And to be reverent in discharging the service.

May he regard our sacrifices of winter and autumn[3b], (Thus) offered by the descendant of Thang!

[1a. The piece is called the Nâ, because a character so named is an important part of the first line. So generally the pieces in the Shih receive their names from a character or phrase occurring in them. This point will not be again touched on.
2a. The 'meritorious ancestor' is Thang. The sacrifices of the Shang dynasty commenced with music; those of the Kâu with libations of fragrant spirits; --in both cases with the same object, to attract the spirit, or spirits, sacrificed to, and secure their presence at the service. Khan Hâo (Ming dynasty) says, 'The departed spirits hover between heaven and earth, and sound goes forth, filling the region of the air. Hence in sacrificing, the people of Yin began with a performance of music.'
3a. The Lî Kî, XXIV, i, parr. 2, 3, tells us, that the sacrificer, as preliminary to the service, had to fast for some days, and to think of the person of his ancestor, --where he had stood and sat, how he had smiled and spoken, what had been his cherished aims, pleasures, and delights; and on the third day he would have a complete image of him in his mind's eye. Then on the day of sacrifice, when he entered the temple, he would seem to see him in his shrine, and to hear him, as he went about in the discharge of the service. This line seems to indicate the realization of all this.]

[1b. Dancing thus entered into the service as an accompaniment of the music. Two terms are employed; one denoting the movements appropriate to a dance Of war, the other those appropriate to a dance of peace.
2b. The visitors would be the representatives of the lines of Hsiâ, Shun, and Yâo.
3b. Two of the seasonal sacrifices are thus specified, by synecdoche, for all the four.]

ODE 4. THE KHANG FÂ

CELEBRATING HSIEH, THE ANCESTOR OF THE HOUSE OF SHANG; HSIANG-THÛ, HIS GRANDSON; THANG, THE FOUNDER OF THE DYNASTY; AND Î-YIN, THANG'S CHIEF MINISTER AND ADVISER.

(It does not appear on occasion of what sacrifice this piece was made. The most probable view is that of Mâo, that it was the 'great Tî sacrifice,' when the principal object of honour would be the ancient Khû, the father of Hsieh, with Hsieh as his correlate, and all the kings of the dynasty, with the earlier lords of Shang, and their famous ministers and advisers, would have their places at the service. I think this is the oldest of the odes of Shang.)

Profoundly wise were (the lords of) Shang, And long had there appeared the omens (of their dignity).

When the waters of the deluge spread vast abroad, Yû arranged and divided the regions of the land, And assigned to the exterior great states their boundaries, With their borders extending all over (the kingdom). (Even) then the chief of Sung was beginning to be great, And God raised up the son (of his daughter), and founded (the line of) Shang[1].

The dark king exercised an effective sway[2]. Charged with a small state, he commanded success: Charged with a large state, he commanded success[3]. He followed his rules of conduct without error; Wherever he inspected (the people), they responded (to his instructions[4]. (Then came) Hsiang-thû all ardent [5], And all within the four seas, beyond (the middle regions), acknowledged his restraints.

[1. This line refers to the birth of Hsieh, as described in the previous ode, and his being made lord of Shang.
2. It would be hard to say why Hsieh is here called 'the dark king.' There may be an allusion to the legend about the connexion of the swallow, --'the dark bird,' --with his birth, He never was 'a king;' but his descendants here represented him as such.
3. All that is meant here is, that the territory of Shang was enlarged under Hsieh.
4. There is a reference here to Hsieh's appointment by Shun to be Minister of Instruction.
5. Hsiang-thû appears in the genealogical lists as grandson of Hsieh. We know nothing of him but what is related here.]

The favour of God did not leave (Shang), And in Thang was found the fit object for its display. Thang was not born too late, And his wisdom and reverence daily advanced: Brilliant was the influence of his character (on Heaven) for long. God he revered, And God appointed him to be the model for the nine regions.

He received the rank-tokens of the states, small and large, Which depended on him like the pendants of a banner:--So did he receive the blessing of Heaven. He was neither violent nor remiss, Neither hard nor soft. Gently he spread his instructions abroad, And all dignities and riches were concentrated in him.

He received the tribute of the states, small and large, And he supported them as a strong steed (does its burden): -So did he receive the favour of Heaven. He displayed everywhere his valour, Unshaken, unmoved, Unterrified, unscared: -All dignities were united in him.

The martial king displayed his banner, And with reverence grasped his axe. It was like (the case of) a blazing fire which no one can repress. The root, with its three shoots, Could make no progress, no growth[1c]. The nine regions were effectually secured by Thang. Having smitten (the princes of) Wei and Kû, He dealt with (him of) Kün-wû and with Kieh of Hsiâ.

Formerly, in the middle of the period (before Thang), There was a time of shaking and peril. But truly did Heaven (then) deal with him as a son, And sent him down a high minister, Namely, Â-hang, Who gave his assistance to the king of Shang.

[1c. By 'the root' we are to understand Thang's chief opponent, Kieh, the last king of Hsiâ. Kieh's three great helpers were 'the three shoots,' --the princes of Wei, Kû, and Kün-wû; but the exact sites of their principalities cannot be made out.]

The large bells and drums fill the ear. The various dances are grandly performed. We have the admirable visitors, who are pleased and delighted.

From of old, before our time, the former men set us the example – how to be mild and humble from morning to night and to be reverent in discharging the service.

Model Practice 1 (grammatically adapted from the original--poetry)

Model Practice 2

Model Practice 3

The Literature of the Ancient Egyptians (excerpt)
by E. A. Wallis Budge
1479 BC to 1425 BC reign of Thotmes III

The Conquests of Thothmes III
summarized by Amen-Rā, King of the Gods (excerpt)

The text is supposed to be a speech of Amen-Rā, the lord of the thrones of the Two Lands, to the king. He says:

"Thou hast come to me, thou hast rejoiced in beholding my beneficence, O my son, my advocate, Menkheperrā, living for ever! I rise upon thee through my love for thee. My heart rejoiceth at thy auspicious comings to my temple. My hands knit together thy limbs with the fluid of life; sweet unto me are thy gracious acts towards my person. I have established thee in my sanctuary. I have made thee to be a source of wonder [to men]. I have given unto thee strength and conquests over all lands. I have set thy Souls and the fear of thee in all lands. The terror of thee hath penetrated to the four pillars of the sky. I have made great the awe of thee in all bodies. I have set the roar of Thy Majesty everywhere [in the lands of] the Nine Bows (i.e. Nubia). The Chiefs of all lands are grouped in a bunch within thy fist. I put out my two hands; I tied them in a bundle for thee. I collected the Antiu of Ta-sti[1] in tens of thousands and thousands, and I made captives by the hundred thousand of the Northern Nations. I have cast down thy foes under thy sandals, thou hast trampled upon the hateful and vile-hearted foes even as I commanded thee. The length and breadth of the earth are thine, and those who dwell in the East and the West are vassals unto thee. Thou hast trodden upon all countries, thy heart is expanded (i.e. glad). No one dareth to approach Thy Majesty with hostility, because I am thy guide to conduct thee to them. Thou didst sail over the Great Circuit of water (the Euphrates) of Nehren (Aram Naharayim, or Mesopotamia) with strength and power. I have commanded for thee that they should hear thy roarings and run away into holes in the ground. I stopped up their nostrils [shutting out] the breath of life. I have set the victories of Thy Majesty in their minds. The fiery serpent Khut which is on thy forehead burnt them up. It made thee to grasp as an easy prey the Ketu peoples, it burnt up the dwellers in their marshes with its fire. The Princes of the Āamu (Asiatics) have been slaughtered, not one of them remains, and the sons of the mighty men have fallen. I have made thy mighty deeds to go throughout all lands, the serpent on my crown hath illumined thy territory, nothing that is an abomination unto thee existeth in all the wide heaven, and the people come bearing offerings upon their backs, bowing to the ground before Thy Majesty, in accordance with my decree. I made impotent those who dared to attack thee, their hearts melted and their limbs quaked.

[1] The natives of the Eastern Desert of Nubia."I have come, making thee to trample under foot the Chief of Tchah (Syria), I have cast them down under thy feet in all the lands, I have made them to behold Thy Majesty as the 'lord of beams' (i.e. the Sun-god), thou hast shone on their faces as the image of me.

"I have come, making thee to trample under foot the people of Asia, thou hast led away captive the Chiefs of the Āamu of Retenu, I have made them to behold Thy Majesty arrayed in thy decorations, grasping the weapons for battle, [mounted] on thy chariot.

"I have come, making thee to trample under foot the land of the East, thou hast trodden upon those who dwell in the districts of the Land of the God, I have made them to see thee as the brilliant star that shooteth out light and fire and scattereth its dew.

"I have come, making thee to trample under foot the land of the West, Kefti (Phœnicia) and Asi (Cyprus) are in awe of thee. I have made them to see Thy Majesty as a young bull, steady-hearted, with horns ready to strike, invincible.

"I have come, making thee to trample under foot those who are in their marshes, the Lands of Methen (Mitani) quake through their fear of thee. I have made them to see Thy Majesty as the crocodile, the lord of terror in the water, unassailable.

"I have come, making thee to trample under foot those who dwell in the Islands, those who live in the Great Green (Mediterranean) hear thy roarings, I have made them to see Thy Majesty as the slayer when he mounteth on the back of his sacrificial animal.

"I have come, making thee to trample under foot the Thehenu (Libyans), the Islands of the Uthentiu [have submitted to] the power of thy Souls. I have made them to see Thy Majesty as a savage lion, which hath scattered the dead bodies of the people throughout their valleys.

"I have come, making thee to trample under foot the uttermost ends of the earth, the Circuit of the Great Circuit is in thy grasp, I have made them to see Thy Majesty as the hawk, which seizeth what it seeth when it pleaseth.

"I have come, making thee to trample upon those who are on their frontiers(?), thou hast smitten 'those on their sand' (i.e. the desert dwellers), making them living captives. I have made them to see Thy Majesty as a jackal of the south, moving fleetly and stealthily, and traversing the Two Lands.

"I have come, making thee to trample under foot the Antiu of Ta-sti, as far as ... they are in thy grasp. I have made them to see Thy Majesty as the Two Brothers (Set and Horus), I have gathered together their arms about thee with [strength].

"I have placed thy Two Sisters (Isis and Nephthys) near thee as protectresses for thee, the arms of Thy Majesty are [lifted] upwards to drive away evil. I have made thee strong and glorious, O my beloved Son, thou Mighty Bull, crowned in Thebes, begotten by me ..., Thothmes, the ever-living, who hast performed for me all that my Ka wished. Thou hast set up my sanctuary with work that shall endure for ever, thou hast lengthened it and broadened it more than ever was done before. The great pylon ... Thou hast celebrated the festival of the beauties of Amen-Rā, thy monuments are greater than those of any king who hath existed, I commanded thee to do it. I am satisfied with it. I have established thee upon the throne of Horus for hundreds of thousands of years. Thou shalt guide life ..."

"I have come, making thee to trample under foot the uttermost ends of the earth. The Circuit of the Great Circuit is in thy grasp. I have made them to see Thy Majesty as the hawk, which seizeth what it seeth when it pleaseth."

Model Practice 1

Model Practice 2

Model Practice 3

David and Goliath

c.1037 – c. 967 BC
dead sea scrolls c. 2nd Century BC
from The King James Bible,
1 Samuel 17: 20-50

Note: LORD in all caps is representative of a different translation than Lord with only a capital L. It is meant to represent the name of God.

20 And David rose up early in the morning, left the sheep with a keeper, and went as Jesse had commanded him; and he came to the trench, as the host was going forth to the fight and shouted for the battle.

21 For Israel and the Philistines had put the battle in array, army against army.

22 And David left his carriage in the hand of the keeper of the carriage and ran into the army and came and saluted his brethren.

23 And as he talked with them, behold, there came up the champion, the Philistine of Gath, Goliath by name, out of the armies of the Philistines, and spake according to the same words: and David heard them.

24 And all the men of Israel, when they saw the man, fled from him and were sore afraid.

25 And the men of Israel said, "Have ye seen this man that is come up? Surely to defy Israel is he come up: and it shall be that the man who killeth him the king will enrich him with great riches and will give him his daughter and make his father's house free in Israel."

26 And David spake to the men that stood by him, saying, "What shall be done to the man that killeth this Philistine and taketh away the reproach from Israel? For who is this uncircumcised Philistine that he should defy the armies of the living God?"

27 And the people answered him after this manner, saying, "So shall it be done to the man that killeth him."

28 And Eliab his eldest brother heard when he spake unto the men; and Eliab's anger was kindled against David, and he said, "Why camest thou down hither? And with whom hast thou left those few sheep in the wilderness? I know thy pride, and the naughtiness of thine heart; for thou art come down that thou mightest see the battle."

29 And David said, "What have I now done? Is there not a cause?"

30 And he turned from him toward another, and spake after the same manner: and the people answered him again after the former manner.

31 And when the words were heard which David spake, they rehearsed them before Saul: and he sent for him.

32 And David said to Saul, "Let no man's heart fail because of him; thy servant will go and fight with this Philistine."

33 And Saul said to David, "Thou art not able to go against this Philistine to fight with him; for thou art but a youth, and he a man of war from his youth."

34 "And David said unto Saul, "Thy servant kept his father's sheep, and there came a lion and a bear and took a lamb out of the flock.

35 "And I went out after him and smote him and delivered it out of his mouth: and when he arose against me, I caught him by his beard and smote him and slew him.

36 "Thy servant slew both the lion and the bear; and this uncircumcised Philistine shall be as one of them, seeing he hath defied the armies of the living God."

37 David said moreover, "The LORD that delivered me out of the paw of the lion, and out of the paw of the bear, he will deliver me out of the hand of this Philistine." And Saul said unto David, "Go, and the LORD be with thee."

38 And Saul armed David with his armour, and he put a helmet of brass upon his head; also he armed him with a coat of mail.

39 And David girded his sword upon his armour, and he assayed to go; for he had not proved it. And David said unto Saul, I cannot go with these; for I have not proved them. And David put them off him.

40 And he took his staff in his hand and chose him five smooth stones out of the brook and put them in a shepherd's bag which he had, even in a scrip; and his sling was in his hand: and he drew near to the Philistine.

41 And the Philistine came on and drew near unto David; and the man that bare the shield went before him.

42 And when the Philistine looked about, and saw David, he disdained him: for he was but a youth, ruddy and of a fair countenance.

43 And the Philistine said unto David, "Am I a dog, that thou comest to me with staves?" And the Philistine cursed David by his gods.

44 And the Philistine said to David, "Come to me, and I will give thy flesh unto the fowls of the air, and to the beasts of the field."

45 Then said David to the Philistine, "Thou comest to me with a sword and with a spear and with a shield, but I come to thee in the name of the LORD of hosts, the God of the armies of Israel, whom thou hast defied.

46 "This day will the LORD deliver thee into mine hand; and I will mite thee and take thine head from thee; and I will give the carcasses of the host of the Philistines this day unto the owls of the air and to the wild beasts of the earth that all the earth may know that there is a God in Israel.

47 "And all this assembly shall know that the LORD saveth not with word and spear; for the battle is the LORD's, and he will give you into our hands."

48 And it came to pass, when the Philistine arose and came and drew nigh to meet David that David hastened and ran toward the army to meet the Philistine.

49 And David put his hand in his bag and took thence a stone and slang it and smote the Philistine in his forehead, that the stone sunk into his forehead and he fell upon his face to the earth.

50 So David prevailed over the Philistine with a sling and with a stone, and smote the Philistine, and slew him; but there was no sword in the hand of David.

And David said to Saul, "Let no man's heart fail because of him; thy servant will go and fight with this Philistine."

And Saul said to David, "Thou art not able to go against this Philistine to fight with him; for thou art but a youth, and he a man of war from his youth."

Model Practice 1

Model Practice 2

Model Practice 3

Works And Days (excerpt)
by Hesiod 700 BC
translated by Hugh G. Evelyn-White

(ll. 352-369) Do not get base gain: base gain is as bad as ruin. Be friends with the friendly and visit him who visits you. Give to one who gives, but do not give to one who does not give. A man gives to the freehanded, but no one gives to the close-fisted. Give is a good girl, but Take is bad and she brings death. For the man who gives willingly, even though he gives a great thing, rejoices in his gift and is glad in heart; but whoever gives way to shamelessness and takes something himself, even though it be a small thing, it freezes his heart. He who adds to what he has will keep off bright-eyed hunger; for if you add only a little to a little and do this often, soon that little will become great. What a man has by him at home does not trouble him: it is better to have your stuff at home, for whatever is abroad may mean loss. It is a good thing to draw on what you have; but it grieves your heart to need something and not to have it, and I bid you mark this. Take your fill when the cask is first opened and when it is nearly spent, but midways be sparing: it is poor saving when you come to the less.

(ll. 370-372) Let the wage promised to a friend be fixed; even with your brother smile -- and get a witness; for trust and mistrust, alike ruin men.

Do not get base gain: base gain is as bad as ruin. Be friends with the friendly and visit him who visits you. Give to one who gives, but do not give to one who does not give. A man gives to the freehanded, but no one gives to the close-fisted.

Model Practice 1

Model Practice 2

Model Practice 3

Apocryphal Life of Esop, the Fabulist (interesting excerpt, but not a primary source)
620-560 BC (life of Aesop)
from Flowers from a Persian Garden and Other Papers
by W. A. Clouston

Little is authentically known regarding the career of the renowned fabulist, who is supposed to have been born about B.C. 620, and, as in the case of Homer, various places are assigned as that of his nativity—Samos, Sardis, Mesembria in Thrace, and Cotiæium in Phrygia. He is said to have been brought as a slave to Athens when very young, and after serving several masters was enfranchised by Iadmon, the Samian. His death is thus related by Plutarch: Having gone to Delphos, by the order of Crœsus, with a large quantity of gold and silver, to offer a costly sacrifice to Apollo and to distribute a considerable sum among the inhabitants, a quarrel arose between him and the Delphians, which induced him to return the money, and inform the king that the people were unworthy of the liberal benefaction he had intended for them. The Delphians, incensed, charged him with sacrilege, and, having procured his condemnation, precipitated him from a rock and caused his death. The popular notion that Esop was a monster of ugliness and deformity is derived from a "Life" of the fabulist, prefixed to a Greek collection of fables purporting to be his, said to have been written by Maximus Planudes, a monk of the 14th century, which, however apocryphal, is both curious and entertaining, from whatever sources the anecdotes may have been drawn.

According to Planudes, Esop was born at Amorium, in the Greater Phrygia, a slave, ugly exceedingly: he was sharp-chinned, snub-nosed, bull-necked, blubber-lipped, and extremely swarthy (whence his name, Ais-ôpos, or Aith-ôpos: burnt-face, blackamoor); pot-bellied, crook-legged, and crook-backed; perhaps uglier even than the Thersites of Homer; worst of all, tongue-tied, obscure and inarticulate in his speech; in short, everything but his mind seemed to mark him out for a slave. His first master sent him out to dig one day. A husbandman having presented the master with some fine fresh figs, they were given to a slave to be set before him after his bath. Esop had occasion to go into the house; meanwhile the other slaves ate the figs, and when the master missed them they accused Esop, who begged a moment's respite: he then drank some warm water and caused himself to vomit, and as he had not broken his fast his innocence was thus manifest. The same test discovered the thieves, who by their punishment illustrated the proverb:

Whoso against another worketh guile
Thereby himself doth injure unaware.

Next day the master goes to town. Esop works in the field, and entertains with his own food some travellers who had lost their way, and sets them on the right road again. They are really priests of Artemis, and having received their blessing he falls asleep, and dreams that Tychê (i.e. Fortune) looses his tongue, and gives him eloquence. Waking, he finds he can say bous, onos, dikella, (ox, ass, mattock). This is the reward of piety, for "well-doing is full of good hopes." Zenas, the overseer, is rebuked by Esop for beating a slave. This is the first time he has been heard to speak distinctly. Zenas goes to his master and accuses Esop of having blasphemed him and the gods, and is given Esop to sell or give away as he pleases. He sells him to a trader for three obols (4½d.), Esop pleading that, if useless for aught else, he will do for a bugbear to keep his children quiet. When they arrive home the little ones begin to cry. "Was I not right?" quoth Esop, and the other slaves think he has been bought to avert the Evil Eye.

The merchant sets out for Asia with all his household. Esop is offered the lightest load, as being a raw recruit. From among the bags, beds, and baskets, he chooses a basket full of bread—a load for two men. They laugh at his folly, but let him have his will, and he staggers under the burden to the wonder of his master. But at the first halt for ariston, or breakfast, the basket is half-emptied, and by the evening wholly so, and then Esop marches triumphantly ahead, all commending his wit. At Ephesus the merchant sells all his slaves, excepting a musician, a scribe, and Esop. Thence he goes to Samos, where he puts new garments on the two former (he had none left for Esop), and sets them out for sale, Esop between them. Xanthus, the philospher, lived at Samos. He goes to the slave market, and, seeing the three, praises the dealer's cunning in making the two look handsomer than they were by contrast with the ugly one. Asking the scribe and the musician what they know, their answer is, "Everything," upon which Esop laughs. The price of the musician (1000 obols, or six guineas) and of the scribe (three times that sum) prevents the philosopher from buying them, and he turns to Esop to see what he is made of. He gives him the customary salutation, "Khaire!" (Rejoice). "I wasn't grieving," retorts Esop. "I greet thee," says Xanthus. "And I thee," replies Esop. "What are thou?" "Black." "I don't mean that, but in what sort of place wast thou born?" "My mother didn't tell me whether in the second floor or the cellar." "What can you do?" "Nothing." "How?" "Why, these fellows here say they know how to do everything, and they haven't left me a single thing." "By Jove," cries Xanthus, "he has answered right well; for there is no man who knows everything. That was why he laughed, it is clear." In the end, Xanthus buys Esop for sixty obols (about 7s. 6d.) and takes him home, where his wife (who is "very cleanly") receives him only on sufferance.

One day Xanthus, meeting friends at the bath, sends Esop home to boil pease (idiomatically using the word in the singular), for his friends are coming to eat with him. Esop boils one pea and sets it before Xanthus, who tastes it and bids him serve up. The water is then placed on the table, and Esop justifies himself to his distracted master, who then sends him for four pig's feet. While they boil, Xanthus slyly abstracts one, and when Esop discovers this he takes it for a plot against him of the other slaves. He runs into the yard, cuts a foot from the pig feeding there, and tosses it into the pot. Presently the other foot is put back, and Esop is confounded to see five trotters on the boil. He serves them up, however, and when Xanthus asks him what the five mean he replies:

"How many feet have two pigs?" Xanthus saying, "Eight," quoth Esop: "Then here are five, and the porker feeding below goes on three." On being reproached he urges: "But, master, there is no harm in doing a sum in addition and subtraction, is there?" For very shame Xanthus forbears whipping him.

One morning Xanthus gives a breakfast, for which Esop is sent to buy "the best and most useful." He buys tongues, and the guests (philosophers all) have nothing else. "What could be better for man than tongue?" quoth Esop. Another time he is ordered to get "the worst and most worthless"; again he brings tongues, and again is ready with a similar defence. A guest reviles him, and Esop retorts that he is "malicious and a busy-body." On hearing this Xanthus commands him to find some one who is not a busybody. In the road Esop finds a simple soul and brings him home to his master, who persuades his wife to bear with him in anything he should pretend to do to her; if the guest is a busybody (or one who meddles) Esop will get a beating. The plan fails; for the good man continues eating and takes no notice of the wife-cuffing going on, and when his host seems about to burn her, he only asks leave to bring his own wife to be also placed on the pile.

At a symposium Xanthus takes too much wine, and in bravado wagers his house and all that it contains that he will drink up the waters of the sea. Out of this scrape Esop rescues him by suggesting that he should demand that all the rivers be stopped from flowing into the sea, for he did not undertake to drink them too, and the other party is satisfied.

A party of scientific guests are coming to dinner one day, and Esop is set just within the door to keep out "all but the wise." When there is a knock at the door Esop shouts: "What does the dog shake?" and all save one go away in high dudgeon, thinking he means them; but this last answers: "His tail," and is admitted.

At a public festival an eagle carries off the municipal ring, and Esop obtains his freedom by order of the state for his interpretation of this omen—that some king purposes to annex Samos. This, it turns out, is Crœsus, who sends to claim tribute. Hereupon Esop relates his first fable, that of the Wolf, the Dog, and the Sheep, and, going on an embassy to Crœsus, that of the Grasshopper who was caught by the Locust-gatherer. He brings home "peace with honour." After this Esop travels over the world, showing his wisdom and wit. At Babylon he is made much of by the king. He then visits Egypt and confounds the sages in his monarch's behalf. Once more he returns to Greece, and at Delphi is accused of stealing a sacred golden bowl and condemned to be hurled from a rock. He pleads the fables of the Matron of Ephesus, the Frog and the Mouse, the Beetle and the Eagle, the Old Farmer and his Ass-waggon, and others, but all is of no avail, and the villains break his neck.

The merchant sets out for Asia with all his household. Esop is offered the lightest load, as being a raw recruit. From among the bags, beds, and baskets, he chooses a basket full of bread — a load for two men. They laugh at his folly, but let him have his will, and he staggers under the burden to the wonder of his master.

Model Practice 1

Model Practice 2

Model Practice 3

The Tao Teh King, or the Tao and its Characteristics
by Lao-Tse
c. 6th century BC
translated by James Legge

Ch. 1. 1. The Tao that can be trodden is not the enduring and unchanging Tao. The name that can be named is not the enduring and unchanging name.

2. (Conceived of as) having no name, it is the Originator of heaven and earth; (conceived of as) having a name, it is the Mother of all things.

3. Always without desire we must be found,
   If its deep mystery we would sound;
   But if desire always within us be,
   Its outer fringe is all that we shall see.

4. Under these two aspects, it is really the same; but as development takes place, it receives the different names. Together we call them the Mystery. Where the Mystery is the deepest is the gate of all that is subtle and wonderful.

2. 1. All in the world know the beauty of the beautiful, and in doing this they have (the idea of) what ugliness is. They all know the skill of the skillful, and in doing this they have (the idea of) what the want of skill is.

2. So it is that existence and non-existence give birth the one to (the idea of) the other; that difficulty and ease produce the one (the idea of) the other; that length and shortness fashion out the one the figure of the other; that (the ideas of) height and lowness arise from the contrast of the one with the other; that the musical notes and tones become harmonious through the relation of one with another; and that being before and behind give the idea of one following another.

3. Therefore the sage manages affairs without doing anything, and conveys his instructions without the use of speech.

4. All things spring up, and there is not one which declines to show itself; they grow, and there is no claim made for their ownership; they go through their processes, and there is no expectation (of a reward for the results). The work is accomplished, and there is no resting in it (as an achievement).

   The work is done, but how no one can see;
   'Tis this that makes the power not cease to be.

3. 1. Not to value and employ men of superior ability is the way to keep the people from rivalry among themselves; not to prize articles which are difficult to procure is the way to keep them from becoming thieves; not to show them what is likely to excite their desires is the way to keep their minds from disorder.

2. Therefore the sage, in the exercise of his government, empties their minds, fills their bellies, weakens their wills, and strengthens their bones.

3. He constantly (tries to) keep them without knowledge and without desire, and where there are those who have knowledge, to keep them from presuming to act (on it). When there is this abstinence from action, good order is universal.

4. 1. The Tao is (like) the emptiness of a vessel; and in our employment of it we must be on our guard against all fullness. How deep and unfathomable it is, as if it were the Honoured Ancestor of all things!

2. We should blunt our sharp points, and unravel the complications of things; we should attemper our brightness, and bring ourselves into agreement with the obscurity of others. How pure and still the Tao is, as if it would ever so continue!

3. I do not know whose son it is. It might appear to have been before God.

9. 1. It is better to leave a vessel unfilled, than to attempt to carry it when it is full. If you keep feeling a point that has been sharpened, the point cannot long preserve its sharpness.

2. When gold and jade fill the hall, their possessor cannot keep them safe. When wealth and honours lead to arrogancy, this brings its evil on itself. When the work is done, and one's name is becoming distinguished, to withdraw into obscurity is the way of Heaven.

15. 1. The skillful masters (of the Tao) in old times, with a subtle and exquisite penetration, comprehended its mysteries, and were deep (also) so as to elude men's knowledge. As they were thus beyond men's knowledge, I will make an effort to describe of what sort they appeared to be.

2. Shrinking looked they like those who wade through a stream in winter; irresolute like those who are afraid of all around them; grave like a guest (in awe of his host); evanescent like ice that is melting away; unpretentious like wood that has not been fashioned into anything; vacant like a valley, and dull like muddy water.

3. Who can (make) the muddy water (clear)? Let it be still, and it will gradually become clear. Who can secure the condition of rest? Let movement go on, and the condition of rest will gradually arise.

4. They who preserve this method of the Tao do not wish to be full (of themselves). It is through their not being full of themselves that they can afford to seem worn and not appear new and complete.

18. 1. When the Great Tao (Way or Method) ceased to be observed, benevolence and righteousness came into vogue. (Then) appeared wisdom and shrewdness, and there ensued great hypocrisy.

2. When harmony no longer prevailed throughout the six kinships, filial sons found their manifestation; when the states and clans fell into disorder, loyal ministers appeared.

19. 1. If we could renounce our sageness and discard our wisdom, it would be better for the people a hundredfold. If we could renounce our benevolence and discard our righteousness, the people would again become filial and kindly. If we could renounce our artful contrivances and discard our (scheming for) gain, there would be no thieves nor robbers.

2. Those three methods (of government)
   Thought olden ways in elegance did fail
   And made these names their want of worth to veil;
   But simple views, and courses plain and true
   Would selfish ends and many lusts eschew.

20. 1. When we renounce learning, we have no troubles.
   The (ready) 'yes,' and (flattering) 'yea;' --
   Small is the difference they display.
   But mark their issues, good and ill; --
   What space the gulf between shall fill?

What all men fear is indeed to be feared; but how wide and without end is the range of questions (asking to be discussed)!

2. The multitude of men look satisfied and pleased; as if enjoying a full banquet, as if mounted on a tower in spring. I alone seem listless and still, my desires having as yet given no indication of their presence. I am like an infant which has not yet smiled. I look dejected and forlorn, as if I had no home to go to. The multitude of men all have enough and to spare. I alone seem to have lost everything. My mind is that of a stupid man; I am in a state of chaos.

Ordinary men look bright and intelligent, while I alone seem to be benighted. They look full of discrimination, while I alone am dull and confused. I seem to be carried about as on the sea, drifting as if I had nowhere to rest. All men have their spheres of action, while I alone seem dull and incapable, like a rude borderer. (Thus) I alone am different from other men, but I value the nursing-mother (the Tao).

25. 1. There was something undefined and complete, coming into existence before Heaven and Earth. How still it was and formless, standing alone, and undergoing no change, reaching everywhere and in no danger (of being exhausted)! It may be regarded as the Mother of all things.

2. I do not know its name, and I give it the designation of the Tao (the Way or Course). Making an effort (further) to give it a name I call it The Great.

3. Great, it passes on (in constant flow). Passing on, it becomes remote. Having become remote, it returns. Therefore the Tao is great; Heaven is great; Earth is great; and the (sage) king is also great. In the universe there are four that are great, and the (sage) king is one of them.

4. Man takes his law from the Earth; the Earth takes its law from Heaven; Heaven takes its law from the Tao. The law of the Tao is its being what it is.

27. 1. The skillful traveler leaves no traces of his wheels or footsteps; the skillful speaker says nothing that can be found fault with or blamed; the skillful reckoner uses no tallies; the skillful closer needs no bolts or bars, while to open what he has shut will be impossible; the skillful binder uses no strings or knots, while to unloose what he has bound will be impossible. In the same way the sage is always skillful at saving men, and so he does not cast away any man; he is always skillful at saving things, and so he does not cast away anything. This is called 'Hiding the light of his procedure.'

2. Therefore the man of skill is a master (to be looked up to) by him who has not the skill; and he who has not the skill is the helper of (the reputation of) him who has the skill. If the one did not honour his master, and the other did not rejoice in his helper, an (observer), though intelligent, might greatly err about them. This is called 'The utmost degree of mystery.'

32. 1. The Tao, considered as unchanging, has no name.
2. Though in its primordial simplicity it may be small, the whole world dares not deal with (one embodying) it as a minister. If a feudal prince or the king could guard and hold it, all would spontaneously submit themselves to him.
3. Heaven and Earth (under its guidance) unite together and send down the sweet dew, which, without the directions of men, reaches equally everywhere as of its own accord.
4. As soon as it proceeds to action, it has a name. When it once has that name, (men) can know to rest in it. When they know to rest in it, they can be free from all risk of failure and error.
5. The relation of the Tao to all the world is like that of the great rivers and seas to the streams from the valleys.

36. 1. When one is about to take an inspiration, he is sure to make a (previous) expiration; when he is going to weaken another, he will first strengthen him; when he is going to overthrow another, he will first have raised him up; when he is going to despoil another, he will first have made gifts to him: --this is called 'Hiding the light (of his procedure).'
2. The soft overcomes the hard; and the weak the strong.
3. Fishes should not be taken from the deep; instruments for the profit of a state should not be shown to the people.

All in the world know the beauty of the beautiful, and in doing this they have the idea of what ugliness is. They all know the skill of the skillful, and in doing this they have the idea of what the want of skill is.

Model Practice 1

Model Practice 2

Model Practice 3

The Sayings of Confucius (excerpt)
by Confucius
551 BC-479 BC
translated by Leonard A. Lyall

INTRODUCTION
Confucius was born in the year 550 BC. in the land of Lu, in a small village, situated in the western part of the modern province of Shantung. His name was K'ung Ch'iu, and his style (corresponding to our Christian name) was Chung-ni. His countrymen speak of him as K'ung Fu-tzu, the Master, or philosopher K'ung. This expression was altered into Confucius by the Jesuit missionaries who first carried his fame to Europe.
LEONARD A. LYALL

BOOK II (Footnotes are on the following page.)
1. The Master said, He that rules by mind is like the north star, steady in his seat, whilst the stars all bend to him.
2. The Master said, The three hundred poems are summed up in the one line, Think no evil.
3. The Master said, Guide the people by law, aline them by punishment; they may shun crime, but they will want shame. Guide them by mind, aline them by courtesy; they will learn shame and grow good.
4. The Master said, At fifteen, I had the will to learn; at thirty, I could stand; at forty, I had no doubts; at fifty, I understood the heavenly Bidding; at sixty, my ears were opened [9]; at seventy, I could do as my heart lusted without trespassing from the square.
5. Meng Yi asked the duty of a son.
The Master said, Not to transgress.
As Fan Chi'ih[10] was driving him, the Master said, Meng-sun[11] asked me the duty of a son; I answered, Not to transgress.
What did ye mean? said Fan Chi'ih.
To serve our father and mother with courtesy whilst they live; to bury them with courtesy when they die, and to worship them with courtesy.
6. Meng Wu asked the duty of a son.
The Master said, He should not grieve his father and mother by anything but illness.
7. Tzu-yu[12] asked the duty of a son.
The Master said, He that can feed his parents is now called a good son. But both dogs and horses are fed, and unless we honour our parents, what is the difference?
8. Tzu-hsia[13] asked the duty of a son.
The Master said, Our manner is the hard part. For the young to be a stay in toil and leave the wine and food to their elders, is this to fulfill their duty?
9. The Master said, If I talk all day to Hui,[14] like a dullard, he never differs from me. But when he is gone, if I watch him when alone, he can carry out what I taught. No, Hui is no dullard!
10. The Master said, See what he does; watch what moves him; search what pleases him: can the man lie hidden? Can the man lie hidden?
11. The Master said, To keep old knowledge warm and get new makes the teacher.
12. The Master said, A gentleman is not a vessel.
13. Tzu-kung[15] asked, What is a gentleman?

The Master said, He puts words into deeds first, and follows these up with words.

14. The Master said, A gentleman is broad and fair; the small man takes sides and is narrow.

15. The Master said, Learning without thought is naught; thought without learning is dangerous.

16. The Master said, To fight strange doctrines does harm.

17. The Master said, Yu,[16] shall I teach thee what is wisdom? To know what we know, and know what we do not know, is wisdom.

18. Tsu-chang[17] learned with an eye to pay.

The Master said, Hear much, leave all that is doubtful alone, speak warily of everything else, and few will be offended. See much, leave all that is dangerous alone, deal warily with everything else, and thou wilt have little to rue. If thy words seldom give offence, and thy deeds leave little to rue, pay will follow.

19. Duke Ai[18] asked, What should I do to win the people?

Confucius answered, Lift up the straight, put away the crooked; and the people will be won. Lift up the crooked, put away the straight; and the people will not be won.

20. Chi K'ang[19] asked how to make the people lowly, faithful and painstaking.

The Master said, Meet them with dignity, they will be lowly; be a good son and merciful, they will be faithful; lift up the good and teach the unskilled, and they will take pains.

21. One said to Confucius, Why do ye not govern, Sir?

The Master said, What does the Book[20] say of a good son? 'To be a good son and a friend to thy brothers is to show how to govern.' This, too, is to govern. Must one be in office to govern?

22. The Master said, A man without truth, I know not what good he is! A cart without a cross pole, a carriage without a yoke, how can they be moved?

23. Tzu-chang[21] asked whether we can know what is to be ten generations hence.

The Master said, The Yin[22] took over the manners of the Hsia; the harm and the good that they did them can be known. The Chou took over the manners of the Yin; the harm and the good that they did them can be known. And we may know what shall be, even an hundred generations hence, whoever follows Chou.

24. The Master said, To worship the ghosts of men not akin to us is fawning. To see the right and not do it is want of courage.

FOOTNOTES:
[9] *Lit.*, obedient.
[10] A disciple.
[11] Meng Yi.
[12] A disciple.
[13] A disciple.
[14] The disciple Yen Yüan.
[15] A disciple.
[16] The disciple Tzu-lu.
[17] A disciple.
[18] Of Lu.
[19] The head of the Chi clan.
[20] The Book of History.
[21] A disciple.
[22] Up to the time of Confucius, China had been ruled by three lines of kings. First the T'ang, next the Yin or Shang, then the Chou.

13. Tzu-kung asked, "What is a gentleman?" The Master said, "He puts words into deeds first, and follows these up with words."
14. The Master said, "A gentleman is broad and fair; the small man takes sides and is narrow."
15. The Master said, "Learning without thought is naught; thought without learning is dangerous."

Model Practice 1

Model Practice 2

Model Practice 3

An Account of Egypt (excerpt)
by Herodotus
5th century BC (c. 484 BC–c. 425 BC)
translated by G. C. Macaulay

The Egyptians in agreement with their climate, which is unlike any other, and with the river, which shows a nature different from all other rivers, established for themselves manners and customs in a way opposite to other men in almost all matters: for among them the women frequent the market and carry on trade, while the men remain at home and weave; and whereas others weave pushing the woof upwards, the Egyptians push it downwards: the men carry their burdens upon their heads and the women upon their shoulders: the women make water standing up and the men crouching down: they ease themselves in their houses and they eat without in the streets, alleging as reason for this that it is right to do secretly the things that are unseemly though necessary, but those which are not unseemly, in public: no woman is a minister either of male or female divinity, but men of all, both male and female: to support their parents the sons are in no way compelled, if they do not desire to do so, but the daughters are forced to do so, be they never so unwilling. The priests of the gods in other lands wear long hair, but in Egypt they shave their heads. Among other men, the custom is that in mourning, those whom the matter concerns most nearly, have their hair cut short, but the Egyptians, when deaths occur, let their hair grow long, both that on the head and that on the chin, having before been close shaven: other men have their daily living separated from beasts, but the Egyptians have theirs together with beasts: other men live on wheat and on barley, but to any one of the Egyptians who makes his living on these it is a great reproach; they make their bread of maize, which some call spelt: they knead dough with their feet and clay with their hands, with which also they gather up dung.... finally in the writing of characters and reckoning with pebbles, while the Hellenes carry the hand from the left to the right, the Egyptians do this from the right to the left; and doing so they say that they do it themselves rightwise and the Hellenes leftwise: and they use two kinds of characters for writing, of which the one kind is called sacred and the other common.

They are religious excessively beyond all other men, and with regard to this they have customs as follows:—they drink from cups of bronze and rinse them out every day, and not some only do this but all: they wear garments of linen always newly washed, and this they make a special point of practice... The priests shave themselves all over their body every other day, so that no lice or any other foul thing may come to be upon them when they minister to the gods; and the priests wear garments of linen only and sandals of papyrus, and any other garment they may not take nor other sandals; these wash themselves in cold water twice in a day and twice again in the night; and other religious services they perform (one may almost say) of infinite number. They enjoy also good things not a few, for they do not consume or spend anything of their own substance, but there is sacred bread baked for them and they have each great quantity of flesh of oxen and geese coming in to them each day, and also wine of grapes is given to them; but it is not permitted to them to taste of fish: beans moreover the Egyptians do not at all sow in their land, and those which they grow they neither eat raw nor boil for food; nay the priests do not endure even to look upon them, thinking this to be an unclean kind of pulse: and there is not one priest only for each of the gods but many, and of them one is chief-priest, and whenever a priest dies his son is appointed to his place.

Now all who have a temple set up to the Theban Zeus or who are of the district of Thebes, these, I say, all sacrifice goats and abstain from sheep: for not all the Egyptians equally reverence the same gods, except only Isis and Osiris (who they say is Dionysos), these they all reverence alike: but they who have a temple of Mendes or belong to the Mendesian district, these abstain from goats and sacrifice sheep. Now the men of Thebes and those who after their example abstain from sheep, say that this custom was established among them for the cause which follows:—Heracles (they say) had an earnest desire to see Zeus, and Zeus did not desire to be seen of him; and at last when Heracles was urgent in entreaty Zeus contrived this device, that is to say, he flayed a ram and held in front of him the head of the ram which he had cut off, and he put on over him the fleece and then showed himself to him. Hence the Egyptians make the image of Zeus with the face of a ram; and the Ammonians do so also after their example, being settlers both from the Egyptians and from the Ethiopians, and using a language which is a medley of both tongues: and in my opinion it is from this god that the Egyptians call Zeus Amun. The Thebans then do not sacrifice rams but hold them sacred for this reason; on one day however in the year, on the feast of Zeus, they cut up in the same manner and flay one single ram and cover with its skin the image of Zeus, and then they bring up to it another image of Heracles. This done, all who are in the temple beat themselves in lamentation for the ram, and then they bury it in a sacred tomb.

About Heracles I heard the account given that he was of the number of the twelve gods; but of the other Heracles whom the Hellenes know I was not able to hear in any part of Egypt: and moreover to prove that the Egyptians did not take the name of Heracles from the Hellenes, but rather the Hellenes from the Egyptians,—that is to say those of the Hellenes who gave the name Heracles to the son of Amphitryon,—of that, I say, besides many other evidences there is chiefly this, namely that the parents of this Heracles, Amphitryon and Alcmene, were both of Egypt by descent, and also that the Egyptians say that they do not know the names either of Poseidon or of the Dioscuroi, nor have these been accepted by them as gods among the other gods; whereas if they had received from the Hellenes the name of any divinity, they would naturally have preserved the memory of these most of all, assuming that in those times as now some of the Hellenes were wont to make voyages and were seafaring folk, as I suppose and as my judgment compels me to think; so that the Egyptians would have learnt the names of these gods even more than that of Heracles. In fact however Heracles is a very ancient Egyptian god; and (as they say themselves) it is seventeen thousand years to the beginning of the reign of Amasis from the time when the twelve gods, of whom they count that Heracles is one, were begotten of the eight gods. I moreover, desiring to know something certain of these matters so far as might be, made a voyage also to Tyre of Phenicia, hearing that in that place there was a holy temple of Heracles; and I saw that it was richly furnished with many votive offerings besides, and especially there were in it two pillars, the one of pure gold and the other of an emerald stone of such size as to shine by night: and having come to speech with the priests of the god, I asked them how long a time it was since their temple had been set up: and these also I found to be at variance with the Hellenes, for they said that at the same time when Tyre was founded, the temple of the god also had been set up, and that it was a period of two thousand three hundred years since their people began to dwell at Tyre. I saw also at Tyre another temple of Heracles, with the surname Thasian; and I came to Thasos also and there I found a temple of Heracles set up by the Phenicians, who had sailed out to seek for Europa and had colonised Thasos; and these things happened full five generations of men before Heracles the son of Amphitryon was born in Hellas. So then my inquiries show clearly that Heracles is an ancient god, and those of the Hellenes seem to me to act most rightly who have two temples of Heracles set up, and who sacrifice to the one as an immortal god and with the title Olympian, and make offerings of the dead to the other as a hero. Moreover, besides many other stories which the Hellenes tell without due consideration, this tale is especially foolish which they tell about Heracles, namely that when he came to Egypt, the Egyptians put on him wreaths and led him forth in procession to sacrifice him to Zeus; and he for some time kept quiet, but when they were beginning the sacrifice of him at the altar, he betook himself to prowess and slew them all. I for my part am of opinion that the Hellenes when they tell this tale are altogether without knowledge of the nature and customs of the Egyptians; for how should they for whom it is not lawful to sacrifice even beasts, except swine and the males of oxen and calves (such of them as are clean) and geese, how should these sacrifice human beings? Besides this, how is it in nature possible that Heracles, being one person only and moreover a man (as they assert), should slay many myriads? Having said so much of these matters, we pray that we may have grace from both the gods and the heroes for our speech.

The priests of the gods in other lands wear long hair, but in Egypt they shave their heads. Among other men, the custom is that in mourning, those whom the matter concerns most nearly, have their hair cut short, but the Egyptians, when deaths occur, let their hair grow long.

Model Practice 1

Model Practice 2

Model Practice 3

The Apology (excerpt)
by Xenophon
c. 431 BC- c. 350 BC
translation by H. G. Dakyns

"I admit it," Socrates replied, "in the case of education, for they know that I have made the matter a study; and with regard to health a man prefers to obey his doctor rather than his parents; in the public assembly the citizens of Athens, I presume, obey those whose arguments exhibit the soundest wisdom rather than their own relations. And is it not the case that, in your choice of generals, you set your fathers and brothers, and, bless me! your own selves aside, by comparison with those whom you believe to be the wisest authorities on military matters?"

"No doubt, Socrates," replied Meletus, "because it is expedient and customary so to do."

"Well then," rejoined Socrates, "does it not strike even you, Meletus, as wonderful when in all ordinary concerns the best people should obtain, I do not say only an equal share, but an exclusive preference; but in my case, simply because I am selected by certain people as an adept in respect of the greatest treasure men possess—education, I am on that account to be prosecuted by you, sir, on the capital charge?"

Much more than this, it stands to reason, was urged, whether by himself or by the friends who advocated his cause. But my object has not been to mention everything that arose out of the suit. It suffices me to have shown on the one hand that Socrates, beyond everything, desired not to display impiety to heaven, and injustice to men; and on the other, that escape from death was not a thing, in his opinion, to be clamoured for importunately—on the contrary, he believed that the time was already come for him to die. That such was the conclusion to which he had come was made still more evident later when the case had been decided against him. In the first place, when called upon to suggest a counter-penalty, he would neither do so himself nor suffer his friends to do so for him, but went so far as to say that to propose a counter-penalty was like a confession of guilt. And afterwards, when his companions wished to steal him out of prison, he would not follow their lead, but would seem to have treated the idea as a jest, by asking, "whether they happened to know of some place outside Attica where death was forbidden to set foot?"

When the trial drew to an end, we are told, the master said: "Sirs, those who instructed the witnesses that they ought to perjure themselves and bear false witness against me, alike with those who listened to their instruction, must be conscious to themselves of a deep impiety and injustice. But for myself, what reason have I at the present time to hold my head less high than I did before sentence was passed against me, if I have not been convicted of having done any of those things whereof my accusers accused me? It has not been proved against me that I have sacrificed to novel divinities in place of Zeus and Hera and the gods who form their company. I have not taken oath by any other gods, nor named their name.

"And then the young—how could I corrupt them by habituating them to manliness and frugality? since not even my accusers themselves allege against me that I have committed any of those deeds of which death is the penalty, such as robbery of temples, breaking into houses, selling freemen into slavery, or betrayal of the state; so that I must still ask myself in wonderment how it has been proved to you that I have done a deed worthy of death. Nor yet again, because I die innocently is that a reason why I should lower my crest, for that is a blot not upon me but upon those who condemned me.

"For me, I find a certain consolation in the case of Palamedes, whose end was not unlike my own; who still even to-day furnishes a far nobler theme of song than Odysseus who unjustly slew him; and I know that testimony will be borne to me also by time future and time past that I never wronged another at any time or ever made a worse man of him, but ever tried to benefit those who practiced discussion with me, teaching them gratuitously every good thing in my power."

And when he perceived those who followed by his side in tears, "What is this?" he asked. "Why do you weep now? Do you not know that for many a long day, ever since I was born, sentence of death was passed upon me by nature? If so be I perish prematurely while the tide of life's blessings flows free and fast, certainly I and my well-wishers should feel pained; but if it be that I am bringing my life to a close on the eve of troubles, for my part I think you ought all of you to take heart of grace and rejoice in my good fortune."

Now there was a certain Apollodorus, who was an enthusiastic lover of the master, but for the rest a simple-minded man. He exclaimed very innocently, "But the hardest thing of all to bear, Socrates, is to see you put to death unjustly."

Whereupon Socrates, it is said, gently stroked the young man's head: "Would you have been better pleased, my dear one, to see me put to death for some just reason rather than unjustly?" and as he spoke he smiled tenderly.

It is also said that, seeing Anytus pass by, Socrates remarked: "How proudly the great man steps; he thinks, no doubt, he has performed some great and noble deed in putting me to death, and all because, seeing him deemed worthy of the highest honours of the state, I told him it ill became him to bring up his son in a tan-yard. What a scamp the fellow is! he appears not to know that of us two whichever has achieved what is best and noblest for all future time is the real victor in this suit. Well! well!" he added, "Homer has ascribed to some at the point of death a power of forecasting things to be, and I too am minded to utter a prophecy. Once, for a brief space, I associated with the son of Anytus, and he seemed to me not lacking in strength of soul; and what I say is, he will not adhere long to the slavish employment which his father has prepared for him, but, in the absence of any earnest friend and guardian, he is like to be led into some base passion and go to great lengths in depravity."

The prophecy proved true. The young man fell a victim to the pleasures of wine; night and day he never ceased drinking, and at last became a mere good-for-nothing, worthless alike to his city, his friends, and himself. As to Anytus, even though the grave has closed upon him, his evil reputation still survives him, due alike to his son's base bringing-up and his own want of human feeling.

Socrates did, it is true, by his self-laudation draw down upon him the jealousy of the court and caused his judges all the more to record their votes against him. Yet even so, I look upon the lot of destiny which he obtained as providential, chancing as he did upon the easiest amidst the many shapes of death, and escaping as he did the one grievous portion of existence. And what a glorious chance, moreover, he had to display the full strength of his soul, for when once he had decided that death was better for him than life, just as in the old days he had never harshly opposed himself to the good things of life morosely, so even in face of death he showed no touch of weakness, but with gaiety welcomed death's embrace, and discharged life's debt.

He exclaimed very innocently, "But the hardest thing of all to bear, Socrates, is to see you put to death unjustly."

Whereupon Socrates, it is said, gently stroked the young man's head: "Would you have been better pleased, my dear one, to see me put to death for some just reason rather than unjustly?"

Model Practice 1

Model Practice 2

Model Practice 3

The Categories (excerpt)
by Aristotle
translated by E. M. Edghill
384 BC – 322 BC

Section 1

Part 1

Things are said to be named 'equivocally' when, though they have a common name, the definition corresponding with the name differs for each. Thus, a real man and a figure in a picture can both lay claim to the name 'animal'; yet these are equivocally so named, for, though they have a common name, the definition corresponding with the name differs for each. For should any one define in what sense each is an animal, his definition in the one case will be appropriate to that case only.

On the other hand, things are said to be named 'univocally' which have both the name and the definition answering to the name in common. A man and an ox are both 'animal', and these are univocally so named, inasmuch as not only the name, but also the definition, is the same in both cases: for if a man should state in what sense each is an animal, the statement in the one case would be identical with that in the other.

Things are said to be named 'derivatively', which derive their name from some other name, but differ from it in termination. Thus, the grammarian derives his name from the word 'grammar', and the courageous man from the word 'courage'.

Part 2

Forms of speech are either simple or composite. Examples of the latter are such expressions as 'the man runs', 'the man wins'; of the former 'man', 'ox', 'runs', 'wins'.

Of things themselves, some are predicable of a subject and are never present in a subject. Thus 'man' is predicable of the individual man and is never present in a subject.

By being 'present in a subject' I do not mean present as parts are present in a whole, but being incapable of existence apart from the said subject.

Some things, again, are present in a subject, but are never predicable of a subject. For instance, a certain point of grammatical knowledge is present in the mind, but is not predicable of any subject; or again, a certain whiteness may be present in the body (for colour requires a material basis), yet it is never predicable of anything.

Other things, again, are both predicable of a subject and present in a subject. Thus while knowledge is present in the human mind, it is predicable of grammar.

There is, lastly, a class of things which are neither present in a subject nor predicable of a subject, such as the individual man or the individual horse. But, to speak more generally, that which is individual and has the character of a unit is never predicable of a subject. Yet in some cases, there is nothing to prevent such being present in a subject. Thus a certain point of grammatical knowledge is present in a subject.

Part 3

When one thing is predicated of another, all that which is predicable of the predicate will be predicable also of the subject. Thus, 'man' is predicated of the individual man; but 'animal' is predicated of 'man'; it will, therefore, be predicable of the individual man also: for the individual man is both 'man' and 'animal'.

If genera are different and co-ordinate, their differentiae are themselves different in kind. Take as an instance the genus 'animal' and the genus 'knowledge'. 'With feet', 'two-footed', 'winged', 'aquatic', are differentiae of 'animal'; the species of knowledge are not distinguished by the same differentiae. One species of knowledge does not differ from another in being 'two-footed'.

But where one genus is subordinate to another, there is nothing to prevent their having the same differentiae: for the greater class is predicated of the lesser, so that all the differentiae of the predicate will be differentiae also of the subject.

Part 4

Expressions which are in no way composite signify substance, quantity, quality, relation, place, time, position, state, action, or affection. To sketch my meaning roughly, examples of substance are 'man' or 'the horse', of quantity, such terms as 'two cubits long' or 'three cubits long', of quality, such attributes as 'white', 'grammatical'. 'Double', 'half', 'greater', fall under the category of relation; 'in the market place', 'in the Lyceum', under that of place; 'yesterday', 'last year', under that of time. 'Lying', 'sitting', are terms indicating position, 'shod', 'armed', state; 'to lance', 'to cauterize', action; 'to be lanced', 'to be cauterized', affection.

No one of these terms, in and by itself, involves an affirmation; it is by the combination of such terms that positive or negative statements arise. For every assertion must, as is admitted, be either true or false, whereas expressions which are not in any way composite such as 'man', 'white', 'runs', 'wins', cannot be either true or false.

Things are said to be named 'derivatively', which derive their name from some other name, but differ from it in termination. Thus, the grammarian derives his name from the word 'grammar', and the courageous man from the word 'courage'.

Model Practice 1

Model Practice 2

Model Practice 3

On Old Age (excerpt)
by Marcus Tullius Cicero January 3
106 BC – 43 BC
translated by E. S. Shuckburgh

10. But to return to my own case: I am in my eighty-fourth year. I could wish that I had been able to make the same boast as Cyrus; but, after all, I can say this: I am not indeed as vigorous as I was as a private soldier in the Punic war, or as quaestor in the same war, or as consul in Spain, and four years later when as a military tribune I took part in the engagement at Thermopylae under the consul Manius Acilius Glabrio; but yet, as you see, old age has not entirely destroyed my muscles, has not quite brought me to the ground. The Senate-house does not find all my vigour gone, nor the rostra, nor my friends, nor my clients, nor my foreign guests. For I have never given in to that ancient and much-praised proverb:

Old when young
Is old for long.

For myself, I had rather be an old man a somewhat shorter time than an old man _before_ my time. Accordingly, no one up to the present has wished to see me, to whom I have been denied as engaged. But, it may be said, I have less strength than either of you. Neither have you the strength of the centurion T. Pontius: is he the more eminent man on that account? Let there be only a proper husbanding of strength, and let each man proportion his efforts to his powers. Such an one will assuredly not be possessed with any great regret for his loss of strength. At Olympia Milo is said to have stepped into the course carrying a live ox on his shoulders. Which then of the two would you prefer to have given to you-bodily strength like that, or intellectual strength like that of Pythagoras? In fine, enjoy that blessing when you have it; when it is gone, don't wish it back-unless we are to think that young men should wish their childhood back, and those somewhat older their youth! The course of life is fixed, and nature admits of its being run but in one way, and only once; and to each part of our life there is something specially seasonable; so that the feebleness of children, as well as the high spirit of youth, the soberness of maturer years, and the ripe wisdom of old age-all have a certain natural advantage which should be secured in its proper season. I think you are informed, Scipio, what your grandfather's foreign friend Masinissa does to this day, though ninety years old. When he has once begun a journey on foot, he does not mount his horse at all; when on horseback he never gets off his horse. By no rain or cold can he be induced to cover his head. His body is absolutely free from unhealthy humours, and so he still performs all the duties and functions of a king. Active exercise, therefore, and temperance can preserve some part of one's former strength even in old age.

11. Bodily strength is wanting to old age; but neither is bodily strength demanded from old men. Therefore, both by law and custom, men of my time of life are exempt from those duties which cannot be supported without bodily strength. Accordingly, not only are we not forced to do what we cannot do; we are not even obliged to do as much as we can. But, it will be said, many old men are so feeble that they cannot perform any duty in life of any sort or kind. That is not a weakness to be set down as peculiar to

old age: it is one shared by ill health. How feeble was the son of P. Africanus, who adopted you! What weak health he had, or rather no health at all! If that had not been the case, we should have had in him a second brilliant light in the political horizon; for he had added a wider cultivation to his father's greatness of spirit. What wonder, then, that old men are eventually feeble, when even young men cannot escape it? My dear Laelius and Scipio, we must stand up against old age and make up for its drawbacks by taking pains. We must fight it as we should an illness. We must look after our health, use moderate exercise, take just enough food and drink to recruit, but not to overload, our strength. Nor is it the body alone that must be supported, but the intellect and soul much more. For they are like lamps: unless you feed them with oil, they too go out from old age. Again, the body is apt to get gross from exercise; but the intellect becomes nimbler by exercising itself. For what Caecilius means by "old dotards of the comic stage " are the credulous, the forgetful, and the slipshod. These are faults that do not attach to old age as such, but to a sluggish, spiritless, and sleepy old age. Young men are more frequently wanton and dissolute than old men; but yet, as it is not all young men that are so, but the bad set among them, even so senile folly-usually called imbecility-applies to old men of unsound character, not to all. Appius governed four sturdy sons, five daughters, that great establishment, and all those clients, though he was both old and blind. For he kept his mind at full stretch like a bow, and never gave in to old age by growing slack. He maintained not merely an influence, but an absolute command over his family: his slaves feared him, his sons were in awe of him, all loved him. In that family, indeed, ancestral custom and discipline were in full vigour. The fact is that old age is respectable just as long as it asserts itself, maintains its proper rights, and is not enslaved to any one. For as I admire a young man who has something of the old man in him, so do I an old one who has something of a young man. The man who aims at this may possibly become old in body—in mind he never will. I am now engaged in composing the seventh book of my _Origins_. I collect all the records of antiquity. The speeches delivered in all the celebrated cases which I have defended I am at this particular time getting into shape for publication. I am writing treatises on augural, pontifical, and civil law. I am, besides, studying hard at Greek, and after the manner of the Pythagoreans—to keep my memory in working order-I repeat in the evening whatever I have said, heard, or done in the course of each day. These are the exercises of the intellect, these the training grounds of the mind: while I sweat and labour on these I don't much feel the loss of bodily strength. I appear in court for my friends; I frequently attend the Senate and bring motions before it on my own responsibility, prepared after deep and long reflection. And these I support by my intellectual, not my bodily forces. And if I were not strong enough to do these things, yet I should enjoy my sofa-imagining the very operations which I was now unable to perform. But what makes me capable of doing this is my past life.

For a man who is always living in the midst of these studies and labours does not perceive when old age creeps upon him. Thus, by slow and imperceptible degrees life draws to its end. There is no sudden breakage; it just slowly goes out.

Bodily strength is wanting to old age; but neither is bodily strength demanded from old men. Therefore, both by law and custom, men of my time of life are exempt from those duties which cannot be supported without bodily strength. Accordingly, not only are we not forced to do what we cannot do; we are not even obliged to do as much as we can.

Model Practice 1

Model Practice 2

Model Practice 3

The Crucifixion of Christ

c. 4 BC to 33 AD
Matthew 27:1-54
from the King James Bible
written c. 70 AD

01 When the morning was come, all the chief priests and elders of the people took counsel against Jesus to put him to death:

02 And when they had bound him, they led him away and delivered him to Pontius Pilate, the governor.

03 Then Judas, which had betrayed him, when he saw that he was condemned, repented himself and brought again the thirty pieces of silver to the chief priests and elders,

04 Saying, "I have sinned in that I have betrayed the innocent blood." And they said, "What is that to us? See thou to that."

05 And he cast down the pieces of silver in the temple and departed and went and hanged himself.

06 And the chief priests took the silver pieces and said, "It is not lawful for to put them into the treasury, because it is the price of blood."

07 And they took counsel and bought with them the potter's field to bury strangers in.

08 Wherefore that field was called, The Field of Flood, unto this day.

09 Then was fulfilled that which was spoken by Jeremy the prophet, saying, "And they took the thirty pieces of silver, the price of him that was valued, whom they of the children of Israel did value;

10 "And gave them for the potter's field, as the Lord appointed me."

11 And Jesus stood before the governor. And the governor asked him, saying, "Art thou the King of the Jews?" And Jesus said unto him, "Thou sayest."

12 And when he was accused of the chief priests and elders, he answered nothing.

13 Then said Pilate unto him, "Hearest thou not how many things they witness against thee?"

14 And he answered him to never a word; insomuch that the governor marvelled greatly.

15 Now at that feast the governor was wont to release unto the people a prisoner, whom they would.

16 And they had then a notable prisoner, called Barabbas.

17 Therefore when they were gathered together, Pilate said unto them, "Whom will ye that I release unto you? Barabbas, or Jesus which is called Christ?"

18 For he knew that for envy they had delivered him.

19 When he was set down on the judgment seat, his wife sent unto him, saying, "Have thou nothing to do with that just man: for I have suffered many things this day in a dream because of him."

20 But the chief priests and elders persuaded the multitude that they should ask Barabbas, and destroy Jesus.

21 The governor answered and said unto them, "Whether of the twain will ye that I release unto you?" They said, "Barabbas."

22 Pilate saith unto them, "What shall I do then with Jesus which is called Christ?" They all said unto him, "Let him be crucified."

23 And the governor said, "Why, what evil hath he done?" But they cried out the more, saying, "Let him be crucified."

24 When Pilate saw that he could prevail nothing, but that rather a tumult was made, he took water, and washed his hands before the multitude, saying, "I am innocent of the blood of this just person: see ye to it."

25 Then answered all the people, and said, "His blood be on us, and on our children."

26 Then released he Barabbas unto them: and when he had scourged Jesus, he delivered him to be crucified.

27 Then the soldiers of the governor took Jesus into the common hall and gathered unto him the whole band of soldiers.

28 And they stripped him and put on him a scarlet robe.

29 And when they had platted a crown of thorns, they put it upon his head and a reed in his right hand: and they bowed the knee before him and mocked him, saying, "Hail, King of the Jews!"

30 And they spit upon him and took the reed and smote him on the head.

31 And after that they had mocked him they took the robe off from him and put his own raiment on him and led him away to crucify him.

32 And as they came out, they found a man of Cyrene, Simon by name: him they compelled to bear his cross.

33 And when they were come unto a place called Golgotha, that is to say, a place of a skull,

34 They gave him vinegar to drink mingled with gall: and when he had tasted thereof, he would not drink.

35 And they crucified him and parted his garments, casting lots: that it might be fulfilled which was spoken by the prophet, "They parted my garments among them, and upon my vesture did they cast lots."

36 And sitting down they watched him there;

37 And set up over his head his accusation written, THIS IS JESUS THE KING OF THE JEWS.

38 Then were there two thieves crucified with him—one on the right hand, and another on the left.

39 And they that passed by reviled him, wagging their heads,

40 And saying, "Thou that destroyest the temple, and buildest it in three days, save thyself. If thou be the Son of God, come down from the cross."

41 Likewise also the chief priests mocking him, with the scribes and elders, said,

42 "He saved others; himself he cannot save. If he be the King of Israel, let him now come down from the cross, and we will believe him.

43 "He trusted in God; let him deliver him now, if he will have him: for he said, I am the Son of God."

44 The thieves also, which were crucified with him, cast the same in his teeth.

45 Now from the sixth hour there was darkness over all the land unto the ninth hour.

46 And about the ninth hour, Jesus cried with a loud voice, saying, "Eli, Eli, lama sabachthani?" that is to say, My God, my God, why hast thou forsaken me?

47 Some of them that stood there, when they heard that, said, "This man calleth for Elias."

48 And straightway one of them ran and took a spunge and filled it with vinegar and put it on a reed and gave him to drink.

49 The rest said, "Let be, let us see whether Elias will come to save him."

50 Jesus, when he had cried again with a loud voice, yielded up the ghost.

51 And, behold, the veil of the temple was rent in twain from the top to the bottom; and the earth did quake, and the rocks rent;

52 And the graves were opened; and many bodies of the saints which slept arose,

53 And came out of the graves after his resurrection and went into the holy city and appeared unto many.

54 Now when the centurion and they that were with him, watching Jesus, saw the earthquake, and those things that were done, they feared greatly, saying, "Truly this was the Son of God."

And Jesus stood before the governor. And the governor asked him, saying, "Art thou the King of the Jews?" And Jesus said unto him, "Thou sayest."

And when he was accused of the chief priests and elders, he answered nothing.

Model Practice 1

Model Practice 2

Model Practice 3

Marcus Aurelius Antoninus (excerpt)

121 AD - 180 AD
Roman Emperor and Stoic Philosopher
from the Library of the World's Best Literature, Ancient and Modern—Vol. 3
edited by Charles Dudley Warner

THE SUPREME NOBILITY OF DUTY
As A Roman and as a man, strive steadfastly every moment to do thy duty, with dignity, sincerity, and loving-kindness, freely and justly, and freed from all disquieting thought concerning any other thing. And from such thought thou wilt be free if every act be done as though it were thy last, putting away from thee slothfulness, all loathing to do what Reason bids thee, all dissimulation, selfishness, and discontent with thine appointed lot. Behold, then, how few are the things needful for a life which will flow onward like a quiet stream, blessed even as the life of the gods. For he who so lives, fulfills their will. (Book ii., §5.)

I strive to do my duty; to all other considerations I am indifferent, whether they be material things or unreasoning and ignorant people. (Book vi., §22.)

THE GOOD MAN
In the mind of him who is pure and good will be found neither corruption nor defilement nor any malignant taint. Unlike the actor who leaves the stage before his part is played, the life of such a man is complete whenever death may come. He is neither cowardly nor presuming; not enslaved to life nor indifferent to its duties; and in him is found nothing worthy of condemnation nor that which putteth to shame. (Book iii., § 8.)

Test by a trial how excellent is the life of the good man—the man who rejoices at the portion given him in the universal lot and abides therein, content; just in all his ways and kindly minded toward all men. (Book iv., § 25.)

This is moral perfection: to live each day as though it were the last; to be tranquil, sincere, yet not indifferent to one's fate. (Book vii., § 69.)

PRAYER
The gods are all-powerful or they are not. If they are not, why pray to them at all? If they are, why dost thou not pray to them to remove from thee all desire and all fear, rather than to ask from them the things thou longest for, or the removal of those things of which thou art in fear? For if the gods can aid men at all, surely they will grant this request. Wilt thou say that the removal of all fear and of all desire is within thine own power? If so, is it not better, then, to use the strength the gods have given, rather than in a servile and fawning way to long for those things which our will cannot obtain? And who hath said to thee that the gods will not strengthen thy will? I say unto thee, begin to pray that this may come to pass, and thou shalt see what shall befall thee...Another man prays that he may not be forced to do his duty: let thy prayer be that thou mayest

not even desire to be relieved of its performance. Another man prays that he may not lose his beloved son: let thy prayer be that even the fear of losing him may be taken away. Let these be thy prayers, and thou shalt see what good will befall thee. (Book ix., §41.)

FAITH
The Universe is either a chaos or a fortuitous aggregation and dispersion of atoms; or else it is builded in order and harmony and ruled by Wisdom. If then it is the former, why should one wish to tarry in a haphazard disordered mass? Why should I be concerned except to know how soon I may cease to be? Why should I be disquieted concerning what I do, since whatever I may do, the elements of which I am composed will at last, at last be scattered? But if the latter thought be true, then I reverence the Divine One; I trust; I possess my soul in peace. (Book vi., § 10.)

PAIN
If pain cannot be borne, we die. If it continue a long time it becomes endurable; and the mind, retiring into itself, can keep its own tranquillity and the true self be still unharmed. If the body feel the pain, let the body make its moan. (Book vii., §30.)

LOVE AND FORGIVENESS FOR THE EVIL-DOER
If it be in thy power, teach men to do better. If not, remember it is always in thy power to forgive. The gods are so merciful to those who err, that for some purposes they grant their aid to such men by conferring upon them health, riches, and honor. What prevents thee from doing likewise? (Book ix., §11.)

ETERNAL CHANGE THE LAW OF THE UNIVERSE
Think, often, of how swiftly all things pass away and are no more--the works of Nature and the works of man. The substance of the Universe--matter--is like unto a river that flows on forever. All things are not only in a constant state of change, but they are the cause of constant and infinite change in other things. Upon a narrow ledge thou standest! Behind thee, the bottomless abyss of the Past! In front of thee, the Future that will swallow up all things that now are! Over what things, then, in this present life, wilt thou, O foolish man, be disquieted or exalted--making thyself wretched; seeing that they can vex thee only for a time--a brief, brief time! (Book v., §23.)

In the mind of him who is pure and good will be found neither corruption nor defilement nor any malignant taint. Unlike the actor who leaves the stage before his part is played, the life of such a man is complete whenever death may come.

Model Practice 1

Model Practice 2

Model Practice 3

The Nicene Creed

modified 381 AD at the second Ecumenical Council
notes from the Exposition of the Apostles' Creed
by the Rev. James Dodds, D.D.

I believe in one God, the Father Almighty, Maker of heaven and earth, and of all things visible and invisible.

And in one Lord Jesus Christ, the only-begotten Son of God, begotten of the Father before all worlds, God of God, Light of Light, very God of very God, begotten, not made, being of one substance with the Father; by whom all things were made; who for us men, and for our salvation, came down from heaven, and was incarnate by the Holy Ghost of the Virgin Mary, and was made man, and was crucified also for us under Pontius Pilate; He suffered and was buried, and the third day He rose again according to the Scriptures and ascended into heaven and sitteth on the right hand of the Father. And He shall come again with glory to judge the quick and the dead, whose kingdom shall have no end.

And I believe in the Holy Ghost, the Lord and Giver of life, who proceedeth from the Father and the Son; who with the Father and the Son together is worshiped and glorified; who spake by the Prophets. And I believe in one holy Catholic and Apostolic Church. I acknowledge one Baptism for the remission of sins; and I look for the resurrection of the dead, and the life of the world to come. Amen.

The word "creed"—derived from the Latin "*credo*, I believe"—is, in its ecclesiastical sense, used to denote a summary or concise statement of doctrines formulated and accepted by a church. Although usually connected with religious belief, it has a wider meaning, and designates the principles which an individual or an associated body so holds that they become the springs and guides of conduct. Some sects of Christians reject formal creeds and profess to find the Scriptures sufficient for all purposes that creeds are meant to serve.

In estimating the value of creeds in the early ages of the Christian Church, it is important to bear in mind that the converts were almost wholly dependent on oral instruction for their knowledge of Divine truth. Copies of the Old and New Testaments existed in manuscript only. These were few in number, and the cost of production placed them beyond the reach of the great majority. A single copy served for a community or a district in which the Hebrew or the Greek tongue was understood, but in localities where other languages were in use the living voice was needed to make revelation known. It is only since the invention of printing and the application of the steam-engine to the economical and rapid production of books, and since modern linguists have multiplied the translations of the Bible, that it has become in their own tongues accessible to believers in all lands, available for private perusal and family reading. It was therefore a necessity that Christians should possess "a form of sound words," comprehensive enough to embody the leading doctrines of Christianity, yet brief enough to be easily committed to memory.

He suffered and was buried, and the third day He rose again according to the Scriptures and ascended into heaven and sitteth on the right hand of the Father. And He shall come again with glory to judge the quick and the dead, whose kingdom shall have no end.

Model Practice 1

Model Practice 2

Model Practice 3

CHAPTER III

Poetry from Ancient History

Note: Poetry models should be written in the same manner that the author wrote them, meaning indentions and punctuation.

Each line of poetry should begin on a new line. If the student cannot fit the line of the model on one line, he should continue the sentence on the next line with an indention at the beginning.

For examples, see the cursive model to "Night" on page III-28 and the model to "The Destruction of Sennacherib" on page III-13.

The poetry selections do not lend themselves as easily to written summations; written summation pages are not included.

Age

by Anacreon
c. 570 BC – 480 BC
from the Library Of The World's Best Literature, Ancient And Modern, Vol. 2
by Charles Dudley Warner
Cowley's Translation.

    Oft am I by the women told,
    Poor Anacreon, thou grow'st old!
    Look how thy hairs are falling all;
    Poor Anacreon, how they fall!
    Whether I grow old or no,
    By th' effects I do not know;
    This I know, without being told,
    'Tis time to live, if I grow old;
    'Tis time short pleasures now to take,
    Of little life the best to make,
    And manage wisely the last stake.

Of the life of this lyric poet we have little exact knowledge. We know that he was an Ionian Greek, and therefore by racial type a luxury-loving, music-loving Greek, born in the city of Teos on the coast of Asia Minor. The year was probably B.C. 562.

Anacreon was a lyrist of the first order. Plato's poet says of him in the 'Symposium,' "When I hear the verses of Sappho or Anacreon, I set down my cup for very shame of my own performance."

His metres, like his matter, are simple and easy. So imitators, perhaps as brilliant as the master, have sprung up and produced a mass of songs; and at this time it remains in doubt whether any complete poem of Anacreon remains untouched. For this reason the collection is commonly termed 'Anacreontics'.

Whether I grow old or no,
By th' effects I do not know;
This I know, without being told,
'Tis time to live, if I grow old;

Model Practice 1

Model Practice 2

Model Practice 3

The Boaster
620 BC - 560 BC
by Aesop, W. J. Linton, and Walter Crane
from the Baby's Own Aesop 1887

In the house, in the market, the streets,
Everywhere he was boasting his feats;
Till one said, with a sneer,
"Let us see it done here!
What's so oft done with ease, one repeats."

                Deeds not words.

The Crow and the Pitcher
620 BC - 560 BC
by Aesop, W. J. Linton, and Walter Crane
from the Baby's Own Aesop 1887

How the cunning old Crow got his drink
When 'twas low in the pitcher, just think!
Don't say that he spilled it!
With pebbles he filled it,
Till the water rose up to the brink.

                Use your wits

In the house, in the market, the streets,
Everywhere he was boasting his feats;
Till one said, with a sneer,
"Let us see it done here!
What's so oft done with ease, one repeats."

Model Practice 1

Model Practice 2

Model Practice 3

The Cloud Chorus (excerpt)
From the 'The Clouds'
By Aristophanes
c. 456 BC – c. 386 BC
from the Library of the World's Best Literature, Ancient and Modern, Vol. 2
translation by Andrew Lang's
edited by Charles Dudley Warner

Socrates Speaks:
  Hither, come hither, ye Clouds renowned, and unveil yourselves here;
   Come, though ye dwell on the sacred crests of Olympian snow,
   Or whether ye dance with the Nereid Choir in the gardens clear,
   Or whether your golden urns are dipped in Nile's overflow,
     Or whether you dwell by Mæotis mere
     Or the snows of Mimas, arise! appear!
   And hearken to us, and accept our gifts ere ye rise and go.

The Clouds Sing:
  Immortal Clouds from the echoing shore
   Of the father of streams from the sounding sea,
  Dewy and fleet, let us rise and soar;
   Dewy and gleaming and fleet are we!
  Let us look on the tree-clad mountain-crest,
   On the sacred earth where the fruits rejoice,
  On the waters that murmur east and west,
   On the tumbling sea with his moaning voice.
  For unwearied glitters the Eye of the Air,
   And the bright rays gleam;
  Then cast we our shadows of mist, and fare
  In our deathless shapes to glance everywhere
  From the height of the heaven, on the land and air,
   And the Ocean Stream.
  Let us on, ye Maidens that bring the Rain,
   Let us gaze on Pallas's citadel,
  In the country of Cecrops fair and dear,
   The mystic land of the holy cell,
   Where the Rites unspoken securely dwell,
  And the gifts of the gods that know not stain,
   And a people of mortals that know not fear.
  For the temples tall and the statues fair,
   And the feasts of the gods are holiest there;
  The feasts of Immortals, the chaplets of flowers,
   And the Bromian mirth at the coming of spring,
  And the musical voices that fill the hours,
   And the dancing feet of the maids that sing!

['The Clouds,' B.C. 423: an attack on Socrates, unfairly taken as an embodiment of the deleterious and unsettling "new learning," both in the form of Sophistical rhetoric and "meteorological" speculation. Worthy Strepsiades, eager to find a new way to pay the debts in which the extravagance of his horseracing son Pheidippides has involved him, seeks to enter the youth as a student in the Thinking-shop or Reflectory of Socrates, that he may learn to make the worse appear the better reason, and so baffle his creditors before a jury. The young man, after much demur and the ludicrous failure of his father, who at first matriculates in his stead, consents. He listens to the pleas of the just and unjust argument in behalf of the old and new education, and becomes himself such a proficient that he demonstrates, in flawless reasoning, that Euripides is a better poet than Aeschylus, and that a boy is justified in beating his father for affirming the contrary. Strepsiades thereupon, cured of his folly, undertakes a subtle investigation into the timbers of the roof of the Reflectory, with a view to smoking out the corrupters of youth. Many of the songs sung by or to the clouds, the patron deities of Socrates's misty lore, are extremely beautiful. Socrates is made to allude to these attacks of comedy by Plato in the 'Apology,' and, on his last day in prison, in the 'Phædo.' In the 'Symposium' or 'Banquet' of Plato, Aristophanes bursts in upon a company of friends with whom Socrates is feasting, and drinks with them till morning; while Socrates forces him and the tragic poet Agathon, both of them very sleepy, to admit that the true dramatic artist will excel in both tragedy and comedy.   by Paul Shorey]

Immortal Clouds from the echoing shore
    Of the father of streams from the sounding sea,
Dewy and fleet, let us rise and soar;
    Dewy and gleaming and fleet are we!

Model Practice 1

Model Practice 2

Model Practice 3

The Destruction of Sennacherib
reign 705-681 BC
by Lord Byron
from Children's Literature
edited by Charles Madison Curry and Erle Elsworth Clippinger
based on 2 Kings 18-19

    The Assyrian came down like a wolf on the fold,
    And his cohorts were gleaming in purple and gold;
    And the sheen of their spears was like stars on the sea,
    When the blue wave rolls nightly on deep Galilee.

    Like the leaves of the forest when summer is green,
    That host with their banners at sunset were seen:
    Like the leaves of the forest when autumn hath blown,
    The host on the morrow lay wither'd and strown.

    For the Angel of Death spread his wings on the blast,
    And breathed in the face of the foe as he passed;
    And the eyes of the sleepers waxed deadly and chill,
    And their hearts but once heaved, and for ever grew still!

    And there lay the steed with his nostril all wide,
    But through it there rolled not the breath of his pride:
    And the foam of his gasping lay white on the turf,
    And cold as the spray of the rock-beating surf.

    And there lay the rider distorted and pale,
    With the dew on his brow and the rust on his mail;
    And the tents were all silent, the banners alone,
    The lances unlifted, the trumpet unblown.

    And the widows of Ashur are loud in their wail,
    And the idols are broke in the temple of Baal;
    And the might of the Gentile, unsmote by the sword,
    Hath melted like snow in the glance of the Lord.

Like the leaves of the forest when summer is green,
That host with their banners at sunset were seen:
Like the leaves of the forest when autumn hath blown,
The host on the morrow lay wither'd and strown.

Model Practice 1

Model Practice 2

Model Practice 3

Horatius (excerpt)

c. 6th Century BC
from Lays of Ancient Rome
by Thomas Babbington Macaulay

A Lay Made About the Year Of The City CCCLX

XXIX

"Haul down the bridge, Sir Consul,
   With all the speed ye may;
I, with two more to help me,
   Will hold the foe in play.
In yon strait path a thousand
   May well be stopped by three.
Now who will stand on either hand,
   And keep the bridge with me?"

XXX

Then out spake Spurius Lartius;
   A Ramnian proud was he:
"Lo, I will stand at thy right hand,
   And keep the bridge with thee."
And out spake strong Herminius;
   Of Titian blood was he:
"I will abide on thy left side,
   And keep the bridge with thee."

XXXI

"Horatius," quoth the Consul,
   "As thou sayest, so let it be."
And straight against that great array
   Forth went the dauntless Three.
For Romans in Rome's quarrel
   Spared neither land nor gold,
Nor son nor wife, nor limb nor life,
   In the brave days of old.

LV

But with a crash like thunder
   Fell every loosened beam,
And, like a dam, the mighty wreck
   Lay right athwart the stream:
And a long shout of triumph
   Rose from the walls of Rome,
As to the highest turret-tops
   Was splashed the yellow foam.

LVI

And, like a horse unbroken
    When first he feels the rein,
The furious river struggled hard,
    And tossed his tawny mane,
And burst the curb and bounded,
    Rejoicing to be free,
And whirling down, in fierce career,
Battlement, and plank, and pier,
    Rushed headlong to the sea.

LVII

Alone stood brave Horatius,
    But constant still in mind;
Thrice thirty thousand foes before,
    And the broad flood behind.
"Down with him!" cried false Sextus,
    With a smile on his pale face.
"Now yield thee," cried Lars Porsena,
    "Now yield thee to our grace."

LVIX

"Oh, Tiber! Father Tiber!
    To whom the Romans pray,
A Roman's life, a Roman's arms,
    Take thou in charge this day!"
So he spake, and speaking sheathed
    The good sword by his side,
And with his harness on his back,
    Plunged headlong in the tide.

LX

No sound of joy or sorrow
    Was heard from either bank;
But friends and foes in dumb surprise,
With parted lips and straining eyes,
    Stood gazing where he sank;
And when above the surges,
    They saw his crest appear,
All Rome sent forth a rapturous cry,
And even the ranks of Tuscany
    Could scarce forbear to cheer.

But friends and foes in dumb surprise,
With parted lips and straining eyes,
    Stood gazing where he sank;
And when above the surges,
    They saw his crest appear,
All Rome sent forth a rapturous cry,
And even the ranks of Tuscany
    Could scarce forbear to cheer.

Model Practice 1

Model Practice 2

Model Practice 3

Hymn to the Nile

c. 2100 BC
from Ancient Egypt
by George Rawlinson and Arthur Gilman

The Egyptians were not unaware of the source of their blessings. From a remote date, they speculated on their mysterious river. They deified it under the name of Hapi, "the Hidden," they declared that "his abode was not known;" that he was an inscrutable god, that none could tell his origin: they acknowledged him as the giver of all good things, and especially of the fruits of the earth. They said—

"Hail to thee, O Nile!
Thou showest thyself in this land,
Coming in peace, giving life to Egypt;
O Ammon, thou leadest night unto day,
A leading that rejoices the heart!
Overflowing the gardens created by Ra;
Giving life to all animals;
Watering the land without ceasing:
The way of heaven descending:
Lover of food, bestower of corn,
Giving life to every home, O Phthah!...

O inundation of Nile, offerings are made to thee;
Oxen are slain to thee;
Great festivals are kept for thee;
Fowls are sacrificed to thee;
Beasts of the field are caught for thee;
Pure flames are offered to thee;
Offerings are made to every god,
As they are made unto Nile.
Incense ascends unto heaven,
Oxen, bulls, fowls are burnt!
Nile makes for himself chasms in the Thebaid;
Unknown is his name in heaven,
He doth not manifest his forms!
Vain are all representations!

Mortals extol him, and the cycle of gods!
Awe is felt by the terrible ones;
His son is made Lord of all,
To enlighten all Egypt.
Shine forth, shine forth, O Nile! shine forth!
Giving life to men by his omen:
Giving life to his oxen by the pastures!
Shine forth in glory, O Nile!"

O inundation of Nile, offerings are made to thee;
Oxen are slain to thee;
Great festivals are kept for thee;
Fowls are sacrificed to thee;
Beasts of the field are caught for thee;
Pure flames are offered to thee;

Model Practice 1

Model Practice 2

Model Practice 3

Moderation

65 BC-8 BC
translation of Horace, Bk. II. Ode X_. W. COWPER.
from the World's Best Poetry, Vol. 10
edited by Bliss Carman

    He that holds fast the golden mean,
      And lives contentedly between
        The little and the great,
     Feels not the wants that pinch the poor,
    Nor plagues that haunt the rich man's door.

He that holds fast the golden mean,
And lives contentedly between
The little and the great,
Feels not the wants that pinch the poor,
Nor plagues that haunt the rich man's door.

Model Practice 1

Model Practice 2

Model Practice 3

The Mouse and the Lion
by Aesop, W. J. Linton, and Walter Crane
from the Baby's Own Aesop 1887

    A poor thing the Mouse was, and yet,
    When the Lion got caught in a net,
    All his strength was no use
    'Twas the poor little Mouse
    Who nibbled him out of the net.

        Small causes may produce great results.

A poor thing the Mouse was, and yet,
When the Lion got caught in a net,
All his strength was no use
'Twas the poor little Mouse
Who nibbled him out of the net.

Model Practice 1

Model Practice 2

Model Practice 3

Night

by Alcman
c. 7th Century BC
translation by Colonel Mure
edited by Charles Dudley Warner

    Over the drowsy earth still night prevails;
        Calm sleep the mountain tops and shady vales,
            The rugged cliffs and hollow glens;
The cattle on the hill. Deep in the sea,
        The countless finny race and monster brood
            Tranquil repose. Even the busy bee
                Forgets her daily toil. The silent wood
        No more with noisy hum of insect rings;
And all the feathered tribes, by gentle sleep subdued,
        Roost in the glade, and hang their drooping wings.

According to legend, this illustrious Grecian lyric poet was born in Lydia, and taken to Sparta as a slave when very young, but emancipated by his master on the discovery of his poetic genius. He flourished probably between 670 and 630, during the peace following the Second Messenian War. It was that remarkable period in which the Spartans were gathering poets and musicians from the outer world of liberal accomplishment to educate their children; for the Dorians thought it beneath the dignity of a Dorian citizen to practice these things themselves.

His descriptive passages are believed to have been his best. The best known and most admired of his fragments is his beautiful description of night, which has been often imitated and paraphrased.

Over the drowsy earth still night prevails;
　　Calm sleep the mountain tops and shady vales,
The rugged cliffs and hollow glens;
The cattle on the hill. Deep in the sea,
　　The countless finny race and monster brood
Tranquil repose. Even the busy bee
　　Forgets her daily toil. The silent wood
No more with noisy hum of insect rings;

Model Practice 1

Model Practice 2

Model Practice 3

The People Who Are Really Happy
from the Children's Bible
translated and arranged by Henry A. Sherman
Matthew 5:3-10
written c. 70 AD

Jesus said to his disciples:

"Blessed are the poor in spirit,
For theirs is the Kingdom of Heaven.
Blessed are the meek,
For they shall inherit the earth.
Blessed are they who mourn,
For they shall be comforted.
Blessed are they who hunger and thirst for righteousness,
For they shall be satisfied.
Blessed are the merciful,
For they shall receive mercy.
Blessed are the pure in heart,
For they shall see God.
Blessed are the peacemakers,
For they shall be called the sons of God.
Blessed are they who are persecuted because of their righteousness,
For theirs is the Kingdom of Heaven.
Blessed are you when you are reviled, persecuted, and falsely maligned because of loyalty to me;
Rejoice and be glad, for great is your reward in heaven, for so the prophets were persecuted who came before you."

Blessed are the poor in spirit,
For theirs is the Kingdom of Heaven.
Blessed are the meek,
For they shall inherit the earth.
Blessed are they who mourn,
For they shall be comforted.

Model Practice 1

Model Practice 2

Model Practice 3

Psalms 23 and 121

by King David
c.1037 – 967 BC
from the King James Bible

Psalms 23

01 The LORD is my shepherd; I shall not want.
02 He maketh me to lie down in green pastures: he leadeth me beside the still waters.
03 He restoreth my soul: he leadeth me in the paths of righteousness for his name's sake.
04 Yea, though I walk through the valley of the shadow of death, I will fear no evil: for thou art with me; thy rod and thy staff, they comfort me.
05 Thou preparest a table before me in the presence of mine enemies: thou anointest my head with oil; my cup runneth over.
06 Surely goodness and mercy shall follow me all the days of my life: and I will dwell in the house of the LORD for ever.

Psalms 121

01 I will lift up mine eyes unto the hills, from whence cometh my help.
02 My help cometh from the LORD, which made heaven and earth.
03 He will not suffer thy foot to be moved: he that keepeth thee will not slumber.
04 Behold, he that keepeth Israel shall neither slumber nor sleep.
05 The LORD is thy keeper: the LORD is thy shade upon thy right hand.
06 The sun shall not smite thee by day, nor the moon by night.
07 The LORD shall preserve thee from all evil: he shall preserve thy soul.
08 The LORD shall preserve thy going out and thy coming in from this time forth and even for evermore.

The LORD is my shepherd; I shall not want.
He maketh me to lie down in green pastures: he leadeth me beside the still waters.
He restoreth my soul: he leadeth me in the paths of righteousness for his name's sake.

Model Practice 1

Model Practice 2

Model Practice 3

The Two Paths
from Proverbs IV
by Solomon
c. 1000 BC - 931 BC
from an <u>Ontario Reader</u>

Hear, O my son, and receive my sayings;
And the years of thy life shall be many.
I have taught thee in the way of wisdom;
I have led thee in paths of uprightness.
When thou goest, thy steps shall not be straitened;
And if thou runnest, thou shalt not stumble.
        Take fast hold of instruction;
        Let her not go:
        Keep her;
        For she is thy life.
Enter not into the Path of the Wicked,
And walk not in the way of evil men.
        Avoid it,
        Pass not by it;
        Turn from it,
        And pass on.
For they sleep not, except they have done mischief;
And their sleep is taken away, unless they cause some to fall.
For they eat the bread of wickedness,
And drink the wine of violence.
But the Path of the Righteous is as the light of dawn,
That shineth more and more unto the perfect day.
The way of the wicked is as darkness:
They know not at what they stumble.

Enter not into the Path of the Wicked,
And walk not in the way of evil men.
Avoid it,
Pass not by it;
Turn from it,
And pass on.

Model Practice 1

Model Practice 2

Model Practice 3

The Vision of Belshazzar
died 539 BC
from <u>Journeys Through Bookland, Vol. 6</u>
by Lord Byron

The King was on his throne,
    The Satraps(153-1) throng'd the hall;
A thousand bright lamps shone
    O'er that high festival.
A thousand cups of gold,
    In Judah deem'd divine—
Jehovah's vessels hold(154-2)
    The godless Heathen's wine.

In that same hour and hall
    The fingers of a Hand
Came forth against the wall,
    And wrote as if on sand:
The fingers of a man;
    A solitary hand
Along the letters ran,
    And traced them like a wand.

The monarch saw, and shook,
    And bade no more rejoice;
All bloodless wax'd his look,
    And tremulous his voice:—
"Let the men of lore appear,
    The wisest of the earth,
And expound the words of fear,
    Which mar our royal mirth."

Chaldea's(154-3) seers are good,
    But here they have no skill;
And the unknown letters stood
    Untold and awful still.
And Babel's(154-4) men of age
    Are wise and deep in lore;
But now they were not sage,
    They saw—but knew no more.

A Captive in the land,
    A stranger and a youth,
He heard the king's command,
    He saw that writing's truth;
The lamps around were bright,
    The prophecy in view;
He read it on that night,—
    The morrow proved it true!

"Belshazzar's grave is made,
    His kingdom pass'd away,
He, in the balance weigh'd,
    Is light and worthless clay;
The shroud, his robe of state;
    His canopy, the stone:
The Mede is at his gate!
    The Persian on his throne!"

153-1 The satraps were the governors of the provinces, who ruled under the king and were accountable to him.
154-2 These were the sacred "vessels that were taken out of the temple of the house of God which was at Jerusalem."
154-3 The terms Chaldea and Babylonia were used practically synonymously.
154-4 Babel is a shortened form of Babylon.

Note.—According to the account given in the fifth chapter of *Daniel*, Belshazzar was the last king of Babylon, and the son of the great king Nebuchadnezzar, who had destroyed Jerusalem and taken the Jewish people captive to Babylon. The dramatic incident with which the second stanza of Byron's poem deals is thus described:
"In the same hour came forth fingers of a man's hand, and wrote over against the candlestick upon the plaister of the wall of the king's palace; and the king saw the part of the hand that wrote."
After all the Babylonian wise men had tried in vain to read the writing, the "captive in the land," Daniel, was sent for, and he interpreted the mystery.
"And this is the writing that was written, MENE, MENE, TEKEL, UPHARSIN.
"This is the interpretation of the thing: MENE; God hath numbered thy kingdom, and finished it.
"TEKEL; Thou art weighed in the balances, and art found wanting.
"PERES; Thy kingdom is divided, and given to the Medes and Persians."
The fulfillment of the prophecy thus declared by Daniel is described thus briefly: "In that night was Belshazzar the king of the Chaldeans slain. And Darius the Median took the kingdom."

In that same hour and hall
 The fingers of a Hand
Came forth against the wall,
 And wrote as if on sand:
The fingers of a man;
 A solitary hand
Along the letters ran,
 And traced them like a wand.

Model Practice 1

_____
_____
_____
_____
_____
_____
_____
_____
_____
_____
_____
_____
_____
_____

Model Practice 2

Model Practice 3

CHAPTER IV

Tales from Various Cultures

The Deluge of Ogyges
from The Story of the Greeks
by H. A. Guerber
the birth of Greece

The first Egyptian who thus settled in Greece was a prince called In´a-chus. Landing in that country, which has a most delightful climate, he taught the Pelasgians how to make fire and how to cook their meat. He also showed them how to build comfortable homes by piling up stones one on top of another, much in the same way as the farmer makes the stone walls around his fields.

The Pelasgians were intelligent, although so uncivilized; and they soon learned to build these walls higher, in order to keep the wild beasts away from their homes. Then, when they had learned the use of bronze and iron tools, they cut the stones into huge blocks of regular shape.

These stone blocks were piled one upon another so cleverly that some of the walls are still standing, although no mortar was used to hold the stones together. Such was the strength of the Pelasgians, that they raised huge blocks to great heights, and made walls which their descendants declared must have been built by giants.

As the Greeks called their giants Cy´clops, which means "round-eyed," they soon called these walls Cy-clo-pe´an; and, in pointing them out to their children, they told strange tales of the great giants who had built them, and always added that these huge builders had but one eye, which was in the middle of the forehead.

Some time after Inachus the Egyptian had thus taught the Pelasgians the art of building, and had founded a city called Ar´gos, there came a terrible earthquake. The ground under the people's feet heaved and cracked, the mountains shook, the waters flooded the dry land, and the people fled in terror to the hills.

In spite of the speed with which they ran, the waters soon overtook them. Many of the Pelasgians were thus drowned, while their terrified companions ran faster and faster up the mountain, never stopping to rest until they were quite safe.

Looking down upon the plains where they had once lived, they saw them all covered with water. They were now forced to build new homes; but when the waters little by little sank into the ground, or flowed back into the sea, they were very glad to find that some of their thickest walls had resisted the earthquake and flood, and were still standing firm.

The memory of the earthquake and flood was very clear, however. The poor Pelasgians could not forget their terror and the sudden death of so many friends, and they often talked about that horrible time. As this flood occurred in the days when Og´y-ges was king, it has generally been linked to his name, and called the Deluge (or flood) of Ogyges.

Written Summation

In spite of the speed with which they ran, the waters soon overtook them. Many of the Pelasgians were thus drowned, while their terrified companions ran faster and faster up the mountain, never stopping to rest until they were quite safe.

Model Practice 1

Model Practice 2

Model Practice 3

Story of Deucalion

from The Story of the Greeks
by H. A. Guerber
the birth of Greece

The Greeks used to tell their children that Deu-ca′li-on, the leader of the Thes-sa′li-ans, was a descendant of the gods, for each part of the country claimed that its first great man was the son of a god. It was under the reign of Deucalion that another flood took place. This was even more terrible than that of Ogyges; and all the people of the neighborhood fled in haste to the high mountains north of Thes′sa-ly, where they were kindly received by Deucalion.

When all danger was over, and the waters began to recede, they followed their leader down into the plains again. This soon gave rise to a wonderful story, which you will often hear. It was said that Deucalion and his wife Pyrrha were the only people left alive after the flood. When the waters had all gone, they went down the mountain and found that the temple at Del′phi, where they worshiped their gods, was still standing unharmed. They entered and, kneeling before the altar, prayed for help.

A mysterious voice then bade them go down the mountain, throwing their mother's bones behind them. They were very much troubled when they heard this, until Deucali-on said that a voice from heaven could not have meant them to do any harm. In thinking over the real meaning of the words he had heard, he told his wife that, as the Earth is the mother of all creatures, her bones must mean the stones.

Deucalion and Pyrrha, therefore, went slowly down the mountain, throwing the stones behind them. The Greeks used to tell that a sturdy race of men sprang up from the stones cast by Deucalion, while beautiful women came from those cast by Pyrrha.

The country was soon peopled by the children of these men, who always proudly declared that the story was true, and that they sprang from the race which owed its birth to this great miracle. Deucalion reigned over this people as long as he lived; and when he died, his two sons, Am-phic′ty-on and Hel′len, became kings in his stead. The former staid in Thessaly; and, hearing that some barbarians called Thra′cians were about to come over the mountains and drive his people away, he called the chiefs of all the different states to a council, to ask their advice about the best means of defense. All the chiefs obeyed the summons, and met at a place in Thessaly where the mountains approach the sea so closely as to leave but a narrow pass between. In the pass are hot springs, and so it was called Ther-mop′y-læ, or the Hot Gateway.

The chiefs thus gathered together called this assembly the Am-phic-ty-on′ic Council, in honor of Amphictyon. After making plans to drive back the Thracians, they decided to meet once a year, either at Thermopylæ or at the temple at Delphi, to talk over all important matters.

Written Summation

When all danger was over, and the waters began to recede, they followed their leader down into the plains again. This soon gave rise to a wonderful story, which you will often hear. It was said that Deucalion and his wife Pyrrha were the only people left alive after the flood. When the waters had all gone, they went down the mountain and found that the temple at Delphi, where they worshiped their gods, was still standing unharmed. They entered and, kneeling before the altar, prayed for help.

Model Practice 1

Model Practice 2

Model Practice 3

The Enchanted Waterfall
from Tales of Wonder Every Child Should Know
edited by Kate Douglas Wiggin and Nora Archibald Smith
a Japanese Tale

Once upon a time there lived alone with his father and mother a simple young woodcutter. He worked all day on the lonely hillside, or among the shady trees of the forest. But, work as hard as he might, he was still very poor and could bring home but little money to his old father and mother. This grieved him very much, for he was an affectionate and dutiful son.

For himself he had but few wants and was easily pleased. His mother, too, was always cheerful and contented. The old father, however, was of a selfish disposition and often grumbled at the poor supper of rice, washed down with weak tea, or, if times were very bad, with a cup of hot water.

"If we had but a little sake, now," he would say, "it would warm one up and do one's heart good." And then he would reproach the simple young fellow, vowing that in his young days he had always been able to afford a cup of sake for himself and his friends.

Grieved at heart, the young man would work harder than ever and think to himself: "How shall I earn some more money? How shall I get a little sake for my poor father, who really needs it in his weakness and old age?"

He was thinking in this way to himself one day as he was at work on the wooded hills, when the sound of rushing water caught his ear. He had often worked in the same spot before, and could not remember that there was any torrent or waterfall near. So, feeling rather surprised, he followed the sound, which got louder and louder until at last he came upon a beautiful little cascade.

The water looked so clear and cool that he stooped down where it was flowing away in a quiet stream, and, using his hand as a cup, drank a little of it. What was his amazement to find that instead of water it was the most excellent sake!

Overjoyed at this discovery, he quickly filled the gourd which was hanging at his girdle, and made the best of his way home, rejoicing that now at last he had something good to bring back to his poor old father. The old man was so delighted with the sake that he drank cup after cup. A neighbour happened to drop in, the story was told to him, and a cup of sake offered and drunk with many words of astonishment and gratitude.

Soon the news spread through the village, and before night there was hardly a man in the place who had not paid his visit of curiosity, been told the tale of the magic fountain, and smelt the gourd, which, alas! was now empty.

Next morning the young wood-cutter set off to work earlier even than usual, not forgetting to carry with him a large gourd, for of course the enchanted waterfall was to be visited again.

What was the surprise of the young man when he came to the spot, to find several of his neighbours already there, and all armed with buckets, jars, pitchers, anything that would carry a good supply of the coveted sake. Each man had come secretly, believing that he alone had found his way to the magic waterfall.

The young woodcutter was amused to see the looks of disappointment and anger upon the faces of those who already stood near the water, as they saw fresh arrivals every moment. Each one looked abashed and uncomfortable in the presence of his neighbours; but, at last, one bolder than the others broke the grim silence with a laugh, which soon the others were fain to join in.

"Here," said he, "we're all bent on the same errand. Let us fill our jars, pitchers, and gourds and go home. But first, I'll have just one more taste of the magic sake." He stooped down, filled his gourd, and put it to his lips. Once and yet again did he drink, with a face of astonishment, which soon gave place to anger.

"Water!" he shouted in a rage; "nothing but cold water! We have been tricked and deceived by a parcel of made-up stories—where is that young fellow? Let us duck him in his fine waterfall!"

But the young man had been wise enough to slip behind a big rock when he saw the turn things were taking and was nowhere to be found.

First one and then another tasted of the stream. It was but too true; no sake, but clear, cold water was there. Crestfallen and out of temper, the covetous band returned to their homes.

When they were fairly gone, the good young woodcutter crept from his hidingplace. "Could this be true," he thought, "or was it all a dream? At any rate," said he, "I must taste once more for myself." He stooped down, filled the gourd, and drank. Sure enough, there was the same fine flavored sake he had tasted yesterday. And so it remained. To the good, dutiful son the cascade flowed with the finest sake, while to all others it yielded only cold water.

The emperor, hearing this wonderful story, sent for the good young woodcutter, rewarded him for his kindness to his father, and even changed the name of the year in his honor as an encouragement to children in all future time to honor and obey their parents.

Written Summation

"Here," said he, "we're all bent on the same errand. Let us fill our jars, pitchers, and gourds and go home. But first, I'll have just one more taste of the magic sake." He stooped down and, filling his gourd, put it to his lips. Once and yet again did he drink, with a face of astonishment, which soon gave place to anger.

Model Practice 1

Model Practice 2

Model Practice 3

The Escape from the Burning City
from The Story of the Romans
by H. A. Guerber

In the days when the Greeks were fighting against Troy—that great city in Asia Minor which they besieged for ten years—the people in Italy were divided into several small kingdoms, among which were those of the Etruscans and the Latins.

The Etruscans occupied the northern part of Italy, or the top of the boot, and called their country Etruria, while the Latins dwelt farther south, in a province named Latium. Each of these kingdoms had its own leader or king, whom all the people obeyed.

Now the King of Latium in those days was Latinus. He had a beautiful daughter called Lavinia, and as soon as she was old enough to marry, he thought of getting her a good husband. One night King Latinus dreamed that the gods of his country came and spoke to him, telling him to be sure and give his daughter in marriage to a stranger whom they would send to Latium.

When Latinus awoke, he was very much troubled, because his wife was anxious that Lavinia should marry Turnus, a neighboring king. The queen soon persuaded Latinus to allow this engagement to take place, but he insisted that the marriage should be postponed for some time longer.

In the meanwhile the city of Troy had at last fallen into the hands of the Greeks. The brave Trojans were attacked by night, and only a few among them managed to escape death.

Among these few, however, there was a prince named Æneas. His father was Anchises, the cousin of the King of Troy, and his mother was Venus, the goddess of beauty. As Venus did not want her son to die with the rest of the Trojans, she appeared to him during the fatal night when the Greeks had secretly entered Troy and were plundering and burning the houses. She showed him that resistance would be useless and bade him flee from the city with all his family.

Æneas had been taught to obey every word the gods said; so he at once stopped fighting and hurried back to his house. Then he lifted his poor old father up on his back, took his little son Iulus by the hand, and called to his wife and servants to follow him.

This strange group of fugitives quickly passed out of the city, where the flames were now rising on all sides and, under cover of the darkness, made their way to a temple nearby. Here they paused to rest, and Æneas counted his followers to make sure that they were all there.

Imagine his sorrow when he found that his beloved wife was missing! He rushed back into the burning city and searched everywhere for her, calling her name aloud, in spite of the danger. At last he met someone who told him that his wife had been killed and that she wished him to escape to a better country where he should found a new kingdom and where a new wife should take her place and make him happy once more.

Æneas sorrowfully turned back and, at the temple, found that his followers had been joined by others who had managed to escape unseen amid the smoke and darkness. He led the way to a place of safety and, not long afterwards, set sail with his little band of faithful Trojans, who all promised to obey and follow him wherever he went.

The ships drifted aimlessly for a long time, because Æneas had no idea where he was to found his new kingdom. Twice he tried to settle down, but each time something happened to drive him away. Finally he asked the advice of his father, Anchises, a wise and pious old man, who had snatched up his gods when he left his house and had brought them with him on the ship.

The old man now said that he would consult these images, and he offered them a sacrifice. The next night Æneas dreamed that the gods spoke to him and told him that he should go to Italy, a land whence one of his ancestors had come to Troy.

The little band therefore sailed for the west, although it was foretold that they would have to suffer many hardships ere they could reach Italy and that they would not be able to settle until they had eaten the very boards upon which their food was served.

As Æneas was a brave man, the prospect of a terrible famine did not fill his heart with despair, and he calmly sailed on in search of a home. There are almost countless islands in that part of the Mediterranean, and thus the boats were seldom out of sight of land. They stopped from time to time, but Æneas did not dare to settle anywhere, because he thought the gods opposed it; and he always urged his people to embark again and sail on.

The Trojans were by this time very tired of sailing, but they loved Æneas so well that they gladly followed him, although they would have liked to make their homes in the islands they visited.

Written Summation

Among these few, however, there was a prince named Aeneas. His father was Anchises, the cousin of the King of Troy, and his mother was Venus, the goddess of beauty. As Venus did not want her son to die with the rest of the Trojans, she appeared to him during the fatal night when the Greeks had secretly entered Troy and were plundering and burning the houses. She showed him that resistance would be useless and bade him flee from the city with all his family.

Model Practice 1 (adapted from the original)

Model Practice 2

Model Practice 3

The Clever Trick
from The Story of the Romans
by H. A. Guerber

After many days of sailing thus on the blue waters of the Mediterranean and after much suffering in the different islands where they stopped to rest, Æneas and his companions came at last to the island of Sicily. This, as you will see on your maps, is a three-cornered piece of land, near the toe of the boot formed by the Italian peninsula. While the Trojans were resting here, poor old Anchises died and was buried by his sorrowing son. But as soon as the funeral rites were ended, Æneas prepared to sail away, for he knew that this was not the place where he was to make his new home.

Unfortunately for Æneas, some of the gods whom his people had so long worshiped had taken a dislike to all the Trojan race. It was these gods who made him suffer so much, and one of them now stirred up a terrible tempest.

The boats were tossed up and down on the waves and driven apart by the fierce winds, and some of them sank under the water. The other vessels would have been dashed to pieces and all the men on board would have perished had not a second god interfered in favor of Æneas and suddenly stilled the awful storm.

The wind was so high, the darkness so great, and the lightning flashes so blinding, that Æneas had lost his bearings. When the storm was over, he sailed for the nearest land and came to the coast of what is now Tunis; but he had no idea where he was. He therefore bade his companions remain on the ships, while he went ashore with only one man—the faithful Achates, who always went with him and was his devoted friend. So these two men started out and began cautiously to explore the country where they had landed, trying to find someone who could tell them where they were.

Before long they met a beautiful woman. This was Venus, the mother of Æneas, in disguise. She had come there to tell her son all about the place where he had landed and to give him some good advice; but she did not wish to have him know her at first.

Venus, therefore, began to speak to Æneas as if he were a stranger, and in answer to his questions said that he had landed in Africa, near the new city of Carthage. This town, she said, was ruled by Dido, a beautiful queen, who had also come from the coast of Asia, but from a spot southeast of the ruined city of Troy.

Dido's husband had been murdered by her brother, and she had fled in the night upon one of her vessels, carrying off all her treasures; for she knew that her brother would soon try to kill her also. Many of her faithful subjects followed her, swearing that they would settle wherever she wished and promising to help her found a new kingdom of which she should be queen.

When Dido reached the coast of Africa, near the present city of Tunis, and saw how beautiful the country seemed, she wished to settle there; but the people refused to sell her the land on which to build a city. She tried in vain to persuade them and finally made up her mind to secure the land by a clever trick. She therefore asked the people if they would be willing to sell her as much land as an oxhide would inclose. The rude people were quite ready to part with a few measures of dirt; so the bargain was at once made.

Imagine their surprise, however, when Dido had a large ox skin cut up into very narrow strips, drew these around a vast tract of land, and claimed it as her own! As the land had certainly been inclosed by an oxhide, they could not dispute her right to it, and Dido at once began to build a beautiful city, about which you will hear many tales.

Written Summation

The boats were tossed up and down on the waves and driven apart by the fierce winds, and some of them sank under the water. The other vessels would have been dashed to pieces and all the men on board would have perished had not a second god interfered in favor of Aeneas and suddenly stilled the awful storm.

Model Practice 1 (adapted from the original)

Model Practice 2

Model Practice 3

The Boards Are Eaten

from The Story of the Romans
by H. A. Guerber

Venus went away after telling her son the story of the oxhide and of the founding of Carthage; and Æneas, following her advice, then walked on to the city. Here he was kindly received by the beautiful queen, who made him and all his companions welcome in her palace. While there Æneas told her all about the long siege of Troy, the taking of the city, his escape by night, his long wanderings on the sea, and his shipwreck near her city.

These stories greatly interested Dido, and she kept Æneas in her palace almost a whole year. As she had fallen in love with him, she would have liked to keep him there always; but the gods had decided that Æneas should again set sail, and one day they sent him orders to depart at once.

Æneas knew that Dido would do her best to keep him in Carthage, so he stole away while she slept, without even bidding her good-by. When she awoke and asked for him, his ships were almost out of sight.

In her grief at his departure, Dido made up her mind to die. She gave orders that all the things he had used during his visit should be placed on a great pile of wood. Then she set fire to it with her own hand and, stabbing herself, sprang into the flames where she died.

Of course we know that such a deed is a crime; but in the days of Queen Dido, people had not learned many of the things that are now taught even to children, and they thought it was very brave to take one's own life.

Æneas and his companions, having left Carthage, now sailed back to Sicily, where they visited the tomb of Anchises just one year after his death. To show respect for his father's memory, Æneas ordered the celebration of games, as was the custom among the Trojans. The men strove with one another in a boat race, a foot race, in boxing and archery matches; and the boys took part in a drill and sham battle on horseback.

After the games were over, the Trojans coasted along the shore of Italy for some time and finally came to the mouth of the Tiber River. When Æneas saw the fair country that stretched out before him, he bade his men sail up the stream, and towards evening they all went ashore to cook their food. Some flat cakes were baked, and as they had no dishes with them, Iulus proposed that these should serve as plates.

The men all sat down around the fire; Iulus, who was very hungry indeed, quickly ate his share of meat and then devoured the cake on which it had been placed. As he swallowed the last mouthful he cried: "Just see how hungry I was! I have eaten even the board on which my meal was served!"

At these words Æneas sprang to his feet and cried that the prophecy was fulfilled at last and that now they could settle in the beautiful country they had reached. The next day they were welcomed by Latinus, King of Latium, who, after hearing their story, remembered his dream and promised that Æneas should have his daughter Lavinia in marriage.

Written Summation

The men all sat down around the fire; Iulus, who was very hungry indeed, quickly ate his share of meat and then devoured the cake on which it had been placed. As he swallowed the last mouthful he cried, "Just see how hungry I was! I've eaten even the board on which my meal was served!"

Model Practice 1 (adapted from the original)

Model Practice 2

Model Practice 3

The Golden Nugget
from A Chinese Wonder Book
by Norman Hinsdale Pitman

Once upon a time many, many years ago, there lived in China two friends named Ki-wu and Pao-shu. These two young men, like Damon and Pythias, loved each other and were always together. No cross words passed between them; no unkind thoughts marred their friendship. Many an interesting tale might be told of their unselfishness, and of how the good fairies gave them the true reward of virtue. One story alone, however, will be enough to show how strong was their affection and their goodness.

It was a bright beautiful day in early spring when Ki-wu and Pao-shu set out for a stroll together, for they were tired of the city and its noises.

"Let us go into the heart of the pine forest," said Ki-wu lightly. "There we can forget the cares that worry us; there we can breathe the sweetness of the flowers and lie on the moss-covered ground."

"Good!" said Pao-shu, "I, too, am tired. The forest is the place for rest."

So the two passed along the winding road, their eyes turned in longing toward the distant treetops. Their hearts beat fast in youthful pleasure as they drew nearer and nearer to the woods.

"For thirty days I have worked over my books," sighed Ki-wu. "For thirty days I have not had a rest. My head is stuffed so full of wisdom, that I am afraid it will burst. Oh, for a breath of the pure air blowing through the greenwood."

"And I," added Pao-shu sadly, "have worked like a slave at my counter and found it just as dull as you have found your books. My master treats me badly. It seems good, indeed, to get beyond his reach."

Now they came to the border of the grove, crossed a little stream, and plunged headlong among the trees and shrubs. For many an hour they rambled on, talking and laughing merrily; when suddenly on passing round a clump of flower-covered bushes, they saw shining in the pathway directly in front of them a lump of gold.

"See!" said both, speaking at the same time and pointing toward the treasure.

Ki-wu, stooping, picked up the nugget. It was nearly as large as a lemon and was very pretty. "It is yours, my dear friend," said he, at the same time handing it to Pao-shu; "yours because you saw it first."

"No, no," answered Pao-shu, "you are wrong, my brother, for you were first to speak. Now, you can never say hereafter that the good fairies have not rewarded you for all your faithful hours of study."

"Repaid me for my study! Why, that is impossible. Are not the wise men always saying that study brings its own reward? No, the gold is yours: I insist upon it. Think of your weeks of hard labour—of the masters that have ground you to the bone! Here is something far better. Take it," he laughed. "May it be the nest egg by means of which you may hatch out a great fortune."

Thus they joked for some minutes, each refusing to take the treasure for himself; each insisting that it belonged to the other. At last, the chunk of gold was dropped in the very spot where they had first spied it, and the two comrades went away, each happy because he loved his friend better than anything else in the world. Thus they turned their backs on any chance of quarrelling.

"It was not for gold that we left the city," exclaimed Ki-wu warmly.

"No," replied his friend, "One day in this forest is worth a thousand nuggets."

"Let us go to the spring and sit down on the rocks," suggested Ki-wu. "It is the coolest spot in the whole grove."

When they reached the spring, they were sorry to find the place already occupied. A countryman was stretched at full length on the ground.

"Wake up, fellow!" cried Pao-shu, "there is money for you near by. Up yonder path, a golden apple is waiting for some man to go and pick it up."

Then they described to the unwelcome stranger the exact spot where the treasure was and were delighted to see him set out in eager search.

For an hour they enjoyed each other's company, talking of all the hopes and ambitions of their future and listening to the music of the birds that hopped about on the branches overhead.

At last they were startled by the angry voice of the man who had gone after the nugget.

"What trick is this you have played on me, masters? Why do you make a poor man like me run his legs off for nothing on a hot day?"

"What do you mean, fellow?" asked Ki-wu, astonished. "Didn't you find the fruit we told you about?"

"No," he answered, in a tone of half-hidden rage, "but in its place, a monster snake, which I cut in two with my blade. Now, the gods will bring me bad luck for killing something in the woods. If you thought you could drive me from this place by such a trick, you'll soon find you were mistaken, for I was first upon this spot and you have no right to give me orders."

"Stop your chatter, bumpkin, and take this copper for your trouble. We thought we were doing you a favour. If you are blind, there's no one but yourself to blame. Come, Pao-shu, let us go back and have a look at this wonderful snake that has been hiding in a chunk of gold."

Laughing merrily, the two companions left the countryman and turned back in search of the nugget.

"If I am not mistaken," said the student, "the gold lies beyond that fallen tree."

"Quite true; we shall soon see the dead snake."

Quickly they crossed the remaining stretch of pathway, with their eyes fixed intently on the ground. Arriving at the spot where they had left the shining treasure, what was their surprise to see, not the lump of gold, not the dead snake described by the idler, but, instead, two beautiful golden nuggets, each larger than the one they had seen at first.

Each friend picked up one of these treasures and handed it joyfully to his companion.

"At last the fairies have rewarded you for your unselfishness!" said Ki-wu.

"Yes," answered Pao-shu, "by granting me a chance to give you your desserts."

Written Summation

"What trick is this you have played on me, masters? Why do you make a poor man like me run his legs off for nothing on a hot day?"

"What do you mean, fellow?" asked Ki-wu, astonished. "Didn't you find the fruit we told you about?"

Model Practice 1

Model Practice 2

Model Practice 3

The Lion and the Goat

by Ramaswami Raju
from the Junior Classics, vol. 1
a tale from India

A Lion was eating up one after another the animals of a certain country. One day an old Goat said, "We must put a stop to this. I have a plan by which he may be sent away from this part of the country."

"Pray act up to it at once," said the other animals.

The old Goat laid himself down in a cave on the roadside, with his flowing beard and long curved horns. The Lion, on his way to the village, saw him and stopped at the mouth of the cave.

"So you have come, after all," said the Goat.

"What do you mean?" said the Lion.

"Why, I have long been lying in this cave. I have eaten up one hundred elephants, a hundred tigers, a thousand wolves, and ninety-nine lions. One more lion has been wanting. I have waited long and patiently. Heaven has, after all, been kind to me," said the Goat, and shook his horns and his beard, and made a start as if he were about to spring upon the Lion.

The latter said to himself, "This animal looks like a Goat, but it does not talk like one. So it is very likely some wicked spirit in this shape. Prudence often serves us better than valor, so for the present I shall return to the wood," and he turned back.

The Goat rose up, advanced to the mouth of the cave, and said, "You'll come back tomorrow, won't you?"

"Never again," said the Lion.

"Do you think I'll be able to see you, at least, in the wood tomorrow?"

"Neither in the wood nor in this neighborhood any more," said the Lion, and running to the forest, soon left it with his kindred.

The animals in the country, not hearing him roar any more, gathered round the Goat and said, "The wisdom of one doth save a host."

Written Summation

The Goat rose up, advanced to the mouth of the cave, and said, "You'll come back tomorrow, won't you?"

"Never again," said the Lion.

"Do you think I'll be able to see you, at least, in the wood tomorrow?"

Model Practice 1 (adapted from the original)

Model Practice 2

Model Practice 3

The Penny-Wise Monkey
re-told by Ellen C. Babbitt
from More Jataka Tales

Once upon a time the king of a large and rich country gathered together his army to take a faraway little country. The king and his soldiers marched all morning long and then went into camp in the forest.

When they fed the horses, they gave them some peas to eat. One of the Monkeys living in the forest saw the peas and jumped down to get some of them. He filled his mouth and hands with them, and up into the tree he went again, and sat down to eat the peas.

As he sat there eating the peas, one pea fell from his hand to the ground. At once, the greedy Monkey dropped all the peas he had in his hands and ran down to hunt for the lost pea. But he could not find that one pea. He climbed up into his tree again and sat still looking very glum. "To get more, I threw away what I had," he said to himself.

The king had watched the Monkey, and he said to himself, "I will not be like this foolish Monkey, who lost much to gain a little. I will go back to my own country and enjoy what I now have."

So he and his men marched back home.

Written Summation

Once upon a time the king of a large and rich country gathered together his army to take a faraway little country. The king and his soldiers marched all morning long and then went into camp in the forest.

Model Practice 1

Model Practice 2

Model Practice 3

The Story of the Shipwrecked Sailor
from Peeps at Many Lands: Ancient Egypt,
by James Baikie

Chapter VIII
SOME FAIRY-TALES OF LONG AGO

Our next story belongs to a time several hundred years later, and I dare say it seemed as wonderful to the little Egyptians as the story of Sindbad the Sailor does to you. It is called "The Story of the Shipwrecked Sailor," and the sailor himself tells it to a noble Egyptian.

"I was going," he says, "to the mines of Pharaoh, and we set sail in a ship of 150 cubits long and 40 cubits wide (225 feet by 60 feet—quite a big ship for the time). We had a crew of 150 of the best sailors of Egypt, men whose hearts were as bold as lions. They all foretold a happy voyage, but as we came near the shore a great storm blew, the sea rose in terrible waves, and our ship was fairly overwhelmed. Clinging to a piece of wood, I was washed about for three days, and at last tossed up on an island; but not one was left of all my shipmates—all perished in the waves.

"I lay down in the shade of some bushes, and when I had recovered a little, I looked about me for food. There was plenty on every hand—figs and grapes, berries and corn, with all manner of birds. When my hunger was satisfied, I lit a fire and made an offering to the gods who had saved me. Suddenly I heard a noise like thunder; the trees shook, and the earth quaked. Looking round, I saw a great serpent approaching me. He was nearly 50 feet long, and had a beard 3 feet in length. His body shone in the sun like gold, and when he reared himself up from his coils before me, I fell upon my face.

"Then the serpent began to speak: 'What has brought thee, little one, what has brought thee? If thou dost not tell me quickly what has brought thee to this isle, I shall make thee vanish like a flame.' So saying, he took me up in his mouth, carried me gently to his lair, and laid me down unhurt; and again he said, 'What has brought thee, little one, what has brought thee to this isle of the sea?' So I told him the story of our shipwreck, and how I alone had escaped from the fury of the waves. Then said he to me: 'Fear not, little one, and let not thy face be sad. If thou hast come to me, it is God who has brought thee to this isle, which is filled with all good things. And now, see: thou shalt dwell for four months in this isle, and then a ship of thine own land shall come, and thou shalt go home to thy country and die in thine own town. As for me, I am here with my brethren and my children. There are seventy-five of us in all, besides a young girl, who came here by chance, and was burned by fire from heaven. But if thou art strong and patient, thou shalt yet embrace thy children and thy wife and return to thy home.'

"Then I bowed low before him and promised to tell of him to Pharaoh and to bring him ships full of all the treasures of Egypt; however, he only smiled at my speech and said, 'Thou hast nothing that I need, for I am Prince of the Land of Punt and all its perfumes are mine. Moreover, when thou departest, thou shall never again see this isle, for it shall be changed into waves.'

"Now, behold! when the time was come, as he had foretold, the ship drew near. And the good serpent said to me, 'Farewell, farewell! Go to thy home, little one, see again thy children, and let thy name be good in thy town; these are my wishes for thee.' So I bowed low before him, and he loaded me with precious gifts of perfume, cassia, sweet woods, ivory, baboons, and all kinds of precious things, and I embarked in the ship. And now, after a voyage of two months, we are coming to the house of Pharaoh, and I shall go in before Pharaoh, and offer the gifts which I have brought from this isle into Egypt, and Pharaoh shall thank me before the great ones of the land."

Written Summation

I bowed low before him and promised to tell of him to Pharaoh and to bring him ships full of all the treasures of Egypt; however, he only smiled at my speech and said, "Ah, little one, thou hast nothing that I need, for I am Prince of the Land of Punt and all its perfumes are mine. Moreover, when you depart, you shall never again see this isle, for it shall be changed into waves."

Model Practice 1 (adapted from the original)

Model Practice 2

Model Practice 3

The Tale of Ivan

from Celtic Fairy Tales
by Joseph Jacobs

There were formerly a man and a woman living in the parish of Llanlavan, in the place which is called wrdh. And work became scarce, so the man said to his wife, "I will go search for work, and you may live here." So he took fair leave, and travelled far toward the East, and at last came to the house of a farmer and asked for work.

"What work can ye do?" said the farmer. "I can do all kinds of work," said Ivan. Then they agreed upon three pounds for the year's wages.

When the end of the year came, his master showed him the three pounds. "See, Ivan," said he, "here's your wage; but if you will give it me back I'll give you a piece of advice instead."

"Give me my wage," said Ivan.

"No, I'll not," said the master; "I'll explain my advice."

"Tell it me, then," said Ivan.

Then said the master, "Never leave the old road for the sake of a new one."

After that they agreed for another year at the old wages, and at the end of it Ivan took instead a piece of advice, and this was it: "Never lodge where an old man is married to a young woman."

The same thing happened at the end of the third year, when the piece of advice was: "Honesty is the best policy."

But Ivan would not stay longer, but wanted to go back to his wife.

"Don't go today," said his master; "my wife bakes tomorrow, and she shall make thee a cake to take home to thy good woman."

And when Ivan was going to leave, "Here," said his master, "here is a cake for thee to take home to thy wife. And when ye are most joyous together, then break the cake, but not sooner."

So he took fair leave of them and travelled towards home, and at last he came to Wayn Her, and there he met three merchants from Tre Rhyn, of his own parish, coming home from Exeter Fair. "Oho! Ivan," said they, "come with us; glad are we to see you. Where have you been so long?"

"I have been in service," said Ivan, "and now I'm going home to my wife."

"Oh, come with us! you'll be right welcome." But when they took the new road, Ivan kept to the old one. And robbers fell upon them before they had gone far from Ivan as they were going by the fields of the houses in the meadow. They began to cry out, "Thieves!" and Ivan shouted out "Thieves!" too. And when the robbers heard Ivan's shout they ran away, and the merchants went by the new road and Ivan by the old one till they met again at Market.

"Oh, Ivan," said the merchants, "we are beholding to you; but for you we would have been lost men. Come lodge with us at our cost, and welcome."

When they came to the place where they used to lodge, Ivan said, "I must see the host."

"The host," they cried; "what do you want with the host? Here is the hostess, and she's young and pretty. If you want to see the host you'll find him in the kitchen."

So he went into the kitchen to see the host; he found him a weak old man turning the spit.

"Oh! Oh!" quoth Ivan, "I'll not lodge here, but will go next door."

"Not yet," said the merchants, "sup with us, and welcome."

Now it happened that the hostess had plotted with a certain monk in Market to murder the old man in his bed that night while the rest were asleep, and they agreed to lay it on the lodgers.

So while Ivan was in bed next door, there was a hole in the pine-end of the house, and he saw a light through it. So he got up and looked, and heard the monk speaking. "I had better cover this hole," said he, "or people in the next house may see our deeds." So he stood with his back against it while the hostess killed the old man.

But meanwhile Ivan out with his knife, and putting it through the hole, cut a round piece off the monk's robe. The very next morning the hostess raised the cry that her husband was murdered, and as there was neither man nor child in the house but the merchants, she declared they ought to be hanged for it.

So they were taken and carried to prison until at last Ivan came to them. "Alas! Alas! Ivan," cried they, "bad luck sticks to us; our host was killed last night, and we shall be hanged for it."

"Ah, tell the justices," said Ivan, "to summon the real murderers."

"Who knows," they replied, "who committed the crime?"

"Who committed the crime!" said Ivan. "If I cannot prove who committed the crime, hang me in your stead."

So he told all he knew and brought out the piece of cloth from the monk's robe. And with that, the merchants were set at liberty, and the hostess and the monk were seized and hanged.

Then they came all together out of Market, and they said to him, "Come as far as Coed Carrn y Wylfa, the Wood of the Heap of Stones of Watching, in the parish of Burman." Then their two roads separated, and though the merchants wished Ivan to go with them, he would not go with them, but went straight home to his wife.

And when his wife saw him she said, "Home in the nick of time. Here's a purse of gold that I've found; it has no name, but I'm sure it belongs to the great lord yonder. I was just thinking what to do when you came."

Then Ivan thought of the third counsel, and he said "Let us go and give it to the great lord."

So they went up to the castle, but the great lord was not in it, so they left the purse with the servant that minded the gate, and then they went home again and lived in quiet for a time.

But one day the great lord stopped at their house for a drink of water, and Ivan's wife said to him: "I hope your lordship found your lordship's purse quite safe with all its money in it."

"What purse is that you are talking about?" said the lord.

"Sure, it's your lordship's purse that I left at the castle," said Ivan.

"Come with me and we will see into the matter," said the lord.

So Ivan and his wife went up to the castle, and there they pointed out the man to whom they had given the purse, and he had to give it up and was sent away from the castle. And the lord was so pleased with Ivan that he made him his servant in the stead of the thief.

"Honesty's the best policy!" quoth Ivan, as he skipped about in his new quarters. "How joyful I am!"

Then he thought of his old master's cake that he was to eat when he was most joyful, and when he broke it, to and behold, inside it was his wages for the three years he had been with him.

Written Summation

"Don't go today," said his master; "my wife bakes tomorrow, and she shall make you a cake to take home to your good woman."

And when Ivan was going to leave, "Here," said his master, "here is a cake for you to take home to your wife. And, when you are most joyous together, then break the cake, but not sooner."

Model Practice 1 (adapted from the original)

Model Practice 2

Model Practice 3

The Two Melons

from Tales of Wonder Every Child Should Know
edited by Kate Douglas Wiggin and Nora Archibald Smith
a Chinese tale

An honest and poor old woman was washing clothes at a pool, when a bird that a hunter had disabled by a shot in the wing, fell down into the water before her. She gently took up the bird, carried it home with her, dressed its wound, and fed it until it was well, when it soared away. Some days later it returned, put before her an oval seed and departed again. The woman planted the seed in her yard and when it came up, she recognized the leaf as that of a melon. She made a trellis for it, and gradually a fruit formed on it, and grew larger and larger until it became very great in size.

Toward the end of the year, the old dame was unable to pay her debts, and her poverty so weighed upon her that she became ill. Sitting one day at her door, feverish and tired, she saw that the melon was ripe and looked luscious; so she determined to try its unknown quality. Taking a knife, she severed the melon from its stalk and was surprised to hear it chink in her hands. On cutting it in two, she found it full of silver and gold pieces, with which she paid her debts and bought supplies for many days.

Among her neighbors was a busybody who craftily found out how the old woman had so suddenly become rich. Thinking there was no good reason why she should not herself be equally fortunate, she washed clothes at the pool, keeping a sharp lookout for birds until she managed to hit and maim one of a flock that was flitting over the water. She then took the disabled bird home, and treated it with care till its wing healed and it flew away. Shortly afterward it came back with a seed in its beak, laid it before her, and again took flight. The woman quickly planted the seed, saw it come up and spread its leaves, made a trellis for it, and had the gratification of seeing a melon form on its stalk. In prospect of her future wealth, she ate rich food, bought fine garments, and got so deeply into debt that, before the end of the year, she was harried by duns. But the melon grew apace, and she was delighted to find that, as it ripened, it became of vast size, and that when she shook it there was a great rattling inside. At the end of the year she cut it down, and divided it, expecting it to be a coffer of coins; but there crawled out of it two old lame, hungry beggars, who told her they would remain and eat at her table as long as they lived.

Written Summation

In prospect of her future wealth, she ate richer foods, bought the finest garments, and got so deeply into debt that, before the end of the year, she was harried by duns. But the melon grew apace, and she was delighted to find that, as it ripened, it became of vast size, and that when she shook it there was a great rattling inside.

Model Practice 1 (adapted from the original)

Model Practice 2

Model Practice 3

The Wolf and the Twins
from the Story of the Romans
by H. A. Guerber

Although Æneas had been so kindly welcomed to Latium by the king, his troubles were not yet ended. Turnus, the young king who had been engaged to Lavinia, was angry at her being given to another, and, in the hope of winning her still, he declared war against the Trojan strangers.

During the war, Æneas and Turnus both won much glory by their courage. At last they met in single combat, in which Turnus was conquered and slain; and Æneas, having thus got rid of his rival, married the fair princess.

He then settled in Latium, where he built a city which was called Lavinium, in honor of his wife. Some time after, Æneas fell in battle and was succeeded by his sons. The Trojans and Latins were now united, and during the next four hundred years, the descendants of Æneas continued to rule over them; for this was the kingdom which the gods had promised him when he fled from Troy.

The throne of Latium finally came to Numitor, a good and wise monarch. He had a son and a daughter, and little suspected that any one would harm either of them.

Unfortunately for him, however, his brother Amulius was anxious to secure the throne. He took advantage of Numitor's confidence, and, having driven his brother away, killed his nephew, and forced his niece, Rhea Sylvia, to become a servant of the goddess Vesta.

The girls who served this goddess were called Vestal Virgins. They were obliged to remain in her temple for thirty years and were not allowed to marry until their time of service was ended. They watched over a sacred fire in the temple, to prevent its ever going out, because such an event was expected to bring misfortune upon the people.

If any Vestal Virgin proved careless, and allowed the sacred fire to go out, or if she failed to keep her vow to remain single, she was punished by being buried alive. With such a terrible fate in view, you can easily understand that the girls were very obedient, and Amulius thought that there was no danger of his niece's marrying as long as she served Vesta.

We are told, however, that Mars, the god of war, once came down upon earth. He saw the lovely Rhea Sylvia, fell in love with her, wooed her secretly, and finally persuaded her to marry him without telling any one about it.

For some time all went well, and no one suspected that Rhea Sylvia, the Vestal Virgin, had married the god of war. But one day a messenger came to tell Amulius that his niece was the mother of twin sons.

The king flew into a passion at this news and vainly tried to discover the name of Rhea Sylvia's husband. She refused to tell it, and Amulius gave orders that she should be buried alive. Her twin children, Romulus and Remus, were also condemned to die; but, instead of burying them alive with their mother, Amulius had them placed in their cradle and set adrift on the Tiber River.

The king thought that the babes would float out to sea, where they would surely perish; but the cradle drifted ashore before it had gone far. There the cries of the hungry children were heard by a she-wolf. This poor beast had just lost her cubs, which a cruel hunter had killed. So instead of devouring the babies, the she-wolf suckled them as if they were the cubs she had lost; and the Romans used to tell their children that a woodpecker brought the twins fresh berries to eat.

Thus kept alive by the care of a wolf and a bird, the children remained on the edge of the river, until a shepherd passed that way. He heard a strange noise in a thicket and, on going there to see what was the matter, found the children with the wolf. Of course the shepherd was greatly surprised at this sight; but he took pity on the poor babies and carried them home to his wife, who brought them up.

Written Summation

During the war, Aeneas and Turnus both won much glory by their courage. At last they met in single combat, in which Turnus was conquered and slain; and Aeneas, having thus got rid of his rival, married the fair princess.

Model Practice 1 (adapted from the original)

Model Practice 2

Model Practice 3

Romulus Builds Rome
from the Story of the Romans
by H. A. Guerber

Remus and Romulus, the twins who had been nursed by the she-wolf, grew up among the shepherds. They were tall and strong and so brave that all their companions were ready to follow them anywhere. One day, when they were watching their flocks on the hillside, their pasture was claimed by the shepherds who were working for Numitor.

The young men were angry at this, and as the shepherds would not go away, they began to fight. As they were only two against many, they were soon made prisoners, and were led before Numitor.

Their strong resemblance to the royal family roused the old man's suspicions. He began to question them, and soon the young men found out who they were. Then they called together a few of their bravest companions and entered the city of Alba, where Amulius dwelt. The unjust king, taken by surprise, was easily killed; and the brothers made haste to place their grandfather, Numitor, again on the throne.

Remus and Romulus were too restless and fond of adventure to enjoy the quiet life at Alba, so they soon left their grandfather's court to found a kingdom of their own. They had decided that they would settle in the northern part of Latium, on the banks of the Tiber, in a place where seven hills rose above the surrounding plain. Here the two brothers said that they would build their future city.

Before beginning, however, they thought it would be well to give the city a name. Each wanted the honor of naming it, and each wanted to rule over it when it was built. As they were twins, neither was willing to give up to the other, and as they were both hot-tempered and obstinate, they soon began to quarrel.

Their companions then suggested that they should stand on separate hills the next day and let the gods decide the question by a sign from the heavens. Remus, watching the sky carefully, suddenly cried that he saw six vultures; Romulus, a moment later, exclaimed that he could see twelve. So the naming of the city was awarded to him, and he said that it should be called Rome.

The next thing was to draw a furrow all around the hill chosen as the most favorable site. The name of this hill was the Palatine. Romulus, therefore, harnessed a bullock and a heifer together, and began to plow the place where the wall of the town was to be built. Remus, disappointed in his hopes of claiming the city, began to taunt his brother, and, in a fit of anger, Romulus killed him.

Although this was a horrible crime, Romulus felt no remorse and went on building his capital. All the hotheaded and discontented men of the neighboring kingdoms soon joined him; and the new city, which was founded seven hundred and fifty-three years before Christ, thus became the home of lawless men.

The city of Rome was at first composed of a series of mud huts, and, as Romulus had been brought up among shepherds, he was quite satisfied with a palace thatched with rushes. As the number of his subjects increased, however, the town grew larger and richer, and before long it became a prosperous city, covering two hills instead of one. On the second hill the Romans built a fortress, or citadel, which was perched on top of great rocks, and was the safest place in case of an attack by an enemy.

Written Summation

The city of Rome was at first composed of a series of mud huts. Soon the town grew larger and richer, and before long it became a prosperous city, covering two hills instead of one. On the second hill the Romans built a fortress, or citadel, which was perched on top of great rocks, and was the safest place in case of an attack by an enemy.

Model Practice 1 (adapted from the original)

Model Practice 2

Model Practice 3

APPENDIX

Models Only

For Teacher Use

Note: Paragraph-sized models from Chapters I and IV are treated as independent models and are indented.

Oral Narration Questions
(Your student may not need these questions, if he can retell the story easily.)

Questions for Chapter I, historical narratives, or Chapter IV, cultural tales.

1. Who was the main character?
2. What was the character like?
3. Where was the character?
4. What time was it in the story? Time of day? Time of year?
5. Who else was in the story?
6. Does the main character have an enemy? What is the enemy's name?
   (The enemy may also be self or nature.)
7. Does the main character want something? If not, does the main character have a problem?
8. What does the main character do? What does he say? If there are others, what do they do or say?
9. Why does the character do what he does?
10. What happens to the character as he tries to solve his problem?
11. Does the main character solve his problem? How does he solve his problem?
12. What happens at the end of the story?
13. Is there a moral to the story? If so, what was it?

Questions for Chapter II, primary source documents.
(This may be difficult for grammar stage students, help them to answer the questions. Over time, it will become easier.)

1. Who is speaking?
2. To whom is he speaking?
3. What is the main idea from the speaker?
4. Does he give facts to support his message?
5. Why is he telling this information?

Questions for Chapter III, poetry.

1. Is the poem about a character, an event, or an idea?
2. Does this poem express a feeling of happiness, sadness, anger, excitement, joy, hope, determination, or fear?
3. How does the poem make you feel?
4. Do you think the author of the poem had a message?
5. What do you think the message of the poem is?

Written Summations
(Have your student sum up the story in no more than six sentences—two for each question.)

1. What happened at the beginning of the story?
2. What happened at the middle of the story?
3. What happened at the end of the story?

Principle of Praise
Encourage, build up, praise, and celebrate your student's successes.

*Let no corrupt communication
proceed out of your mouth, but
that which is good to the use of edifying,
that it may minister grace
unto the hearers*

Using the Grammar Guide

The Grammar Guide only provides an overview with definitions and a few examples of the grammar concepts. For 3rd – 5th graders, this will more than likely be enough, since the students are working with the grammar in context. But for some, this may not be enough. To supplement, you may use a separate yearlong grammar curriculum, or you, as the teacher, may purchase a guide to provide you with further explanations to pass on to your student. If you use the guide in this book, please note that the guide is not all inclusive. More advanced grammar terms, such as relative pronouns and indefinite adjectives, are not included.

1. Have your student read the model.
2. Have your student copy the selection before he marks up the model.
3. Return to the model and circle the part of speech being learned in the proper color. See page 4.
4. **For older students, have them label the parts of speech according to the definitions and abbreviations below.**
5. For adjectives, adverbs, and prepositional phrases, have your student draw an arrow to the word being modified.

Label   Definition

nouns   DO, IO, PN   **direct object, indirect object, or predicate nominative**

Subject is the noun that is or does something. (Who ran? What stinks?)	I ran. The **dog** stinks.
Direct objects answers what. (I ate what?)	I ate **the cookie**.
Indirect objects tell for whom the action of the verb was done.	I gave **her** the cookie.
Predicate Nominative (Noun Linking Verb Noun.)	John is my **dad**.

verbs   AV, SB, LV   **action verb, state of being, or linking verb**

Action verbs with a direct object are transitive verbs.	(He kicked the ball.)
Action verbs without a direct object are intransitive.	(He kicked.)
State of being verbs are the "to be" verbs.	(am, are, is, was, were, be, being, been)
Helping verbs help the main verb express time and mood.	(do run, can clean, am eating, might hit)
Linking verbs link the subject to the predicate.	(The wind grew chilly. The wind was chilly.)
	(If I can replace grew with was, it is a LV.)

pronouns   SP, OP, PP, DP   **Subject, Object, Possessive, Demonstrative**

Subject Pronouns	I, you, he, she, it, we, they	We love to read. It was outside.
Object Pronouns	me, you, him, her, it, us, them	She took it. I handed them the candy.
Possessive Pronouns	mine, yours, his, hers, theirs, ours, its, whose	That is **mine**! Ours is blue.
Demonstrative Pronouns	this, that, these, those	**That** is mine! We love that.

adjectives   AA, PA, DA   **Attributive, Predicate, or Demonstrative Adjectives**

Attributive Adjectives modify the noun and are right next to it.	(The **big** car.)
Predicate Adjectives follow linking verbs.	(The car is **big**.)
Demonstrative Adjectives (This, that, these, those)	**That** flower grew.

adverbs   **where, how, when, extent**

Adverbs that tell where, how, and when modify an adverb.	(up, down, quickly, softly, yesterday, now)
Adverbs that tell extent modify an adverb or adjective.	(almost, also, only, very, enough, rather, too)

prepositions   OP   **object of the preposition**

GRAMMAR GUIDE
Month 1
Memorize the definitions for each part of speech. Review Weekly.
Teach the following with copywork. Circle the nouns in the copywork.

Nouns <u>**circle blue**</u>   a word that names a person, place, thing, or idea

Common nouns	**man, city, car, happiness**	
Proper nouns	**David, Lake Charles, Mustang**	
Subject	**Children** should appreciate their pastor.	
Direct object	My parents bought **a birthday present**.	(noun phrase)
Indirect object	My parents gave **the pastor** the present.	(noun phrase)
Predicate Nominative	The queen is a **pilot**.	(A noun that renames a noun, queen = **pilot**.)

Capitalization   Beginning of a sentence, I, proper nouns.

Month 2
Teach everything in month one and the following. Color-code the nouns and verbs in the copywork.

Verbs <u>**circle red**</u>   a word that expresses action, state of being, or links two words together

Action verbs	**jump, run, think, have, skip, throw, say, dance, smell**
State of being	any form of to be = **am, are, is, was, were, be, being, been**
Linking verbs	**any "to be" verb** and any verb that can logically be replaced by a "to be" verb
	She **seems** nice. She is nice. The flower **smells** stinky. The flower is stinky.
Helping verbs	am, are, is, was, were, be, being, been, do, does, did, has, have, had, may, might, must shall, will, can, should, would, could

Month 3
Teach everything previous and the following.

Pronouns <u>**circle green**</u>   a word that replaces the noun

Jack ran.	**He** ran.
Ike hit Al and Mary.	Ike hit **them**.
The car is very nice.	**That** is very nice.

Types of sentences and punctuation

Declarative or statement	I have a blue dress. The ground is wet from the rain.
Interrogative or question	Will we have dessert today? What time is it?
Imperative or demand	Come here. Sit down. Mop the floor at 2:00.
Exclamation	I sold my painting for ten million dollars!

Month 4
Teach everything previous and the following.

Adjectives <u>**circle yellow**</u>   a word that describes a noun or a pronoun
(When studying adverbs, you may have your student draw an arrow to the word being modified.)

I want candy.	I want **five** candies.	
the car	the **red** car	
I like shoes.	I like **those** shoes.	
The tall girl	The girl is **tall**.	Predicate adjectives (tall, stinky, angry)
The stinky dog	The dog smells **stinky**.	
The angry man	The man appeared **angry**.	

Month 5

Adverbs <u>circle orange</u> a word that describes a verb, another adverb, or an adjective

		Modifies the verb
Don't run.	Don't run **inside**.	tells where
The man ran.	The man ran **swiftly**.	tells how
It will rain.	It will rain **soon**.	tells when

		Modifies adjectives or other adverbs
The dog is hairy.	The dog is **very** hairy.	tells extent (modifies hairy)

Possessives   words that show ownership

Mine, yours, his, hers, ours, theirs, whose	possessive pronouns (used alone)
My car, **your** house, **his** shirt, **her** computer	possessive pronouns (used with a noun)
Jane's car, Mike's shoes, Jesus' parables,	singular possessive nouns
Mom and Dad's sons, my sisters' names, children's books	plural possessive nouns

Month 6

Preposition <u>circle purple</u> a word that shows relationship between one noun and another word in the sentence
(Prepositional phrases are to be underlined)

He is <u>**on** the box</u>.   He is <u>**under** the box</u>.   He went <u>**around** the box</u>.   He is <u>**in** the box</u>.

Commas   3 items or more in a series

The elephant**,** the mouse**,** and the gnat are best friends.
I like red**,** green**,** and orange vegetables.

Month 7

Conjunction <u>circle brown</u> a word that links words, phrases, or clauses (and, but, or, nor, so, for, yet)

Jamie **and** I left.
        (words)
The blue sky, the warm sun, **and** the rainbow of flowers brightened my spirits.
        (phrases)
He is tall**, for** both of his parents are tall.
        (independent clauses, must have a comma when combining main clauses)

Quotation Marks   Use quotation marks to set off direct quotations.

"No, I don't like peas," answered the little boy.	beginning of a sentence
The little boy answered, "I don't like peas."	end of a sentence
"No," answered the little boy, "I don't like peas."	middle of a sentence

Month 8

Interjection <u>circle black</u> a word that expresses emotion, sometimes but not always, sudden or intense.

Yes! I want ice cream too! **Well**, we're late because the car broke down.

Semi-colons   replace commas and conjunction when combining two independent clauses

My family is going to the farm**, and** we are going to have a grand time riding horses.
My family is going to the farm**;** we are going to have a grand time riding horses.

Models from Chapter I

from **The Goddess of the Silkworm**
from A Child's World Reader
    by Hetty Browne, Sarah Withers, and W K. Tate

"This is indeed a wonderful, wonderful thing!" said Si-ling. "Why, the worms have threads on their bodies. Each worm has a thread long enough to make a house for itself!"

She put the cocoons in a hot place, and the little sleepers soon died. Then the cocoons were thrown into boiling water to make the threads soft. After that. the long threads could be easily unwound from the bodies of the worms.

from **Early Inhabitants of Greece**
from The Story of the Greeks
    by H. A. Guerber

About two thousand years before the birth of Christ, Greece was inhabited by a savage race of men called the Pelasgians. They lived in the forests or in caves hollowed out of the mountainside and hunted wild beasts with great clubs and stone-tipped arrows and spears. They were so rude and wild that they ate nothing but raw meat, berries, and roots.

In Egypt, there were at that time a number of learned men. They were acquainted with many of the arts and sciences and recorded all they knew in a peculiar writing of their own invention. Their neighbors, the Phœnicians whose land also bordered on the Mediterranean Sea, were quite civilized too; and as both of these nations had ships, they soon began to sail all around that great inland sea.

from **The Story of Joseph and His Coat of Many Colors**
from The Wonder Book of Bible Stories
    by Logan Marshall

Of all his children, Jacob loved Joseph the best. Jacob gave to Joseph a robe or coat of bright colors, made somewhat like a long cloak with wide sleeves. This was a special mark of Jacob's favor to Joseph, and it made his older brothers envious of him.

He said one day, "Listen to this dream that I have dreamed. I dreamed that we were out in the field binding sheaves, when suddenly my sheaf stood up, and all your sheaves came around it and bowed down to my sheaf!"

from The Story of the Grapes from Canaan
from <u>The Wonder Book of Bible Stories</u>
   by Logan Marshall

But all the other spies, except Joshua, said, "No, there is no use in trying to make war upon such strong people. We can never take those walled cities, and we dare not fight those tall giants."

But Caleb and Joshua, two of the spies, said, "Why should we fear? The land of Canaan is a good land; it is rich with milk and honey. If God is our friend and is with us, we can easily conquer the people who live there. Above all things, let us not rebel against the Lord, or disobey him, and make him our enemy."

from The Story of Gideon and His Three Hundred Soldiers
from <u>The Wonder Book of Bible Stories</u>
   by Logan Marshall

And Joash, Gideon's father, said, "If Baal is a god, he can take care of himself and punish the man who has destroyed his image. Why should you help Baal? Let Baal help himself."

And when they saw that Baal could not harm the man who had broken down his altar and his image, the people turned from Baal, back to their own Lord God.

The next morning, Gideon found the grass and the bushes wet with dew, while the fleece of wool was dry. And Gideon was now sure that God had called him, and that God would give him victory over the enemies of Israel.

from The Story of Samson, the Strong Man
from <u>The Wonder Book of Bible Stories</u>
   by Logan Marshall

As Samson was going down to Timnath to see this young woman, a hungry lion came out of the mountain, roaring against him. Samson seized the lion and tore him in pieces as easily as another man would have killed a little kid of the goats, and then went on his way. He made his visit and came home, but said nothing to any one about the lion.

Then, while he was asleep, she wove his hair in the loom and fastened it with a large pin to the weaving frame. But when he awoke, he rose up and carried away the pin and the beam of the weaving frame; for he was as strong as before.

from **Ruth**
from Journeys Through Bookland, Vol. 6
  by Charles H. Sylvester

And Ruth said unto Naomi, "Let me now go to the field and glean ears of corn after him in whose sight I shall find grace."

And Naomi answered, "Go, my daughter.

And Ruth said, "Ask me not to leave you, or to return from following after you. For where you go, I will go; and where you stay, I will stay. Your people shall be my people, and your God my God. Where you die, I will die, and there I will be buried. The Lord do so to me, and more also, if anything but death part you and me."

from **The Story of the Fight with the Giant**
from The Wonder Book of Bible Stories
  by Logan Marshall

You come against me with a sword and a spear and a dart; but I come to you in the name of the Lord of hosts, the God of the armies of Israel. This day will the Lord give you into my hand. I will strike you down and take off your head, and the host of the Philistines shall be dead bodies, to be eaten by the birds and the beasts.

While the two armies stood wondering and scarcely knowing what had caused the giant to fall so suddenly, David ran forward, drew out the giant's own sword, and cut off his head. David won a great victory and stood before all the land as the one who had saved his people from their enemies.

from **The Story of the Cave of Adullam**
from The Wonder Book of Bible Stories
  by Logan Marshall

From his meeting with Jonathan, David went forth to be a wanderer, having no home as long as Saul lived. He found a great cave, called the cave of Adullam, and hid in it. Soon people heard where he was, and men from his own tribe and from all parts of the land who were not satisfied with the rule of King Saul gathered around David.

When Saul died, he was followed by David, the shepherd boy, now grown to manhood and greatly loved by the people. He had many battles to fight with the Philistines and was nearly always victorious. He was a warrior king, but he was more than a warrior. He played on his harp and composed many beautiful hymns and songs, which are collected in the book of Psalms.

from **The Blind Poet**
from The Story of the Greeks
by H. A. Guerber

Homer's two great heroic poems were the Iliad, telling all about the Trojan War, and the Odyssey, relating how Ulysses sailed about for ten years on his way home from Troy. Such was the admiration felt for these poems that years after Homer's death an attempt was made to find out more about him and about the place where he was born.

By some happy chance, poor blind Homer found his way to the inhabited parts of the country, where he soon won many friends. Instead of spending all his time in weeping over his troubles, Homer tried to think of some way in which he could earn his living and at the same time give pleasure to others. He soon found such a way in telling the stories of the past to all who cared to listen to them.

from **Death of Romulus**
from The Story of the Romans
by H. A. Guerber

In The Story of the Romans, we are told that Romulus reigned over the Romans for thirty-seven years. Although he was at first a very good ruler, he soon grew proud and cruel. As he was king, he wanted to have his own way in everything; and as he ceased to care whether what he wished would be good for the Romans, they began to dislike him.

As soon as he could make himself heard, this man told the assembled Romans that he had seen Romulus being carried up to heaven. The king, he said, had called out that he was going to live with the gods and wished his people to worship him under the name of Quirinus.

from **Laws of Lycurgus**
from The Story of the Greeks
by H. A. Guerber

Then, knowing that great wealth is not desirable, Lycurgus said that the Spartans should use only iron money. All the Spartan coins were therefore bars of iron. This made the money so heavy that a yoke of oxen and a strong cart were needed to carry a sum equal to one hundred dollars from one spot to another.

The Spartans were very grateful for all he had done for them, so they gladly took this oath, and Lycurgus left the place. Some time after, he came back to Greece; but, hearing that the Spartans were thriving under the rules he had laid down, he made up his mind never to visit Sparta again.

from **The Laws of Solon**
from The Story of the Greeks
by H. A. Guerber

This report spread quickly throughout the city. The terrified people assembled and voted to exile Megacles and all his family. Such was the fury of the Athenians against the archon whose crime had brought misfortunes upon them that they even dug up the bones of his ancestors and had them carried away beyond the boundary of Attica.

When a man was accused of any wrongdoing, he was brought before this jury, who sat under the open sky at night. No light was provided, and the whole trial was carried on in the dark, so that the jury should not be influenced by the good or bad looks of the prisoner, but should judge merely from what was proved about him.

from **The Story of the Fiery Furnace**
from The Wonder Book of Bible Stories
by Logan Marshall

But while the people were kneeling, there were three men who stood up and would not bow down. These were the three young Jewish men called Shadrach, Meshach, and Abednego. They knelt down before the Lord God only.

O King Nebuchadnezzar, we are ready to answer you at once. The God whom we serve is able to save us from the fiery furnace, and we know that he will save us. But if it is God's will that we should die, even then you may understand, O king, that we will not serve your gods, nor worship the golden image.

from **Aesop**
from Journeys Through Bookland, Vol. 2
by Charles H. Sylvester

The next day, when dinnertime came, the guests were assembled. Great was their astonishment and great the anger of Xanthus at finding that again nothing but tongue was put upon the table.

"Tongue again! How, sir," asked Xanthus, "should tongues be the best of meat one day, and the worst another?"

"But what can you do?" said Xanthus, turning to Aesop.

"Nothing at all. The others can do so much and so well," said Aesop, "that there's nothing left for me to do."

"Will you be honest and faithful if I buy you?"

"I shall be that whether you buy me or not."

from Death of Pericles
from The Story of the Greeks
by H. A. Guerber

Although the Athenian fleet had caused much damage and had come home victorious, the Spartan army was still in Attica. The Spartans had been awed and frightened by the eclipse, but they did not give up their purpose and continued the war.

His care and skill restored many sufferers; and although thousands died of the plague, the remaining Athenians knew that they owed him their lives. When the danger was over, they all voted that Hippocrates should have a golden crown and said he should be called an Athenian citizen.

from The Philosopher Socrates
from The Story of the Greeks
by H. A. Guerber

The philosopher Socrates not only taught this gentleness, but also practiced it carefully at home and abroad. He had plenty of opportunity to make use of it, for he had such a cross wife that her name, Xanthippe, is still used to describe a scolding and bad-tempered woman.

Socrates was a poor man, a stonecutter by trade; but he spent every moment he could spare from his work in thinking, studying, and questioning others. Little by little, in spite of the contrary opinion of his fellow citizens, he began to understand that the stories of the Greek gods and goddesses could not be true.

from Accusation of Socrates
from The Story of the Greeks
by H. A. Guerber

Socrates was one of the best and gentlest of men, yet he had many enemies. These were principally the people who were jealous of him and of his renown for great wisdom; for his reputation was so well established that the oracle at Delphi, when consulted, replied that the most learned man in Greece was Socrates.

Everybody talked about it, repeated the best jokes, and went again and again to see and laugh over it. We are told that Socrates went there himself one day; and when asked why he had come, he quietly said, "I came to find out whether, among all the faults of which I am accused, there may not be some that I can correct."

from **Pythagoras**
from <u>Little Journeys To The Homes Of Great Teachers</u>
   by Elbert Hubbard

The wind sprang up fresh and cold. The young man was chilled to the bone, but still he pounded and then called aloud, demanding admittance. His answer now was the growling and barking of dogs within.

But Samos soon tired of Pythagoras. He was too austere, too severe. And when he began to rebuke the officials for their sloth and indifference, he was invited to go elsewhere and teach others his science of life. And so he journeyed into Southern Italy, and at Crotona built his Temple to the Muses and founded the Pythagorean School. He was the wisest as well as the most learned man of his time.

from **Birth of Alexander**
from <u>The Story of the Greeks</u>
   by H. A. Guerber

Philip was so delighted with the coolness, courage, and good horsemanship that Alexander had shown on this occasion that he made him a present of the steed. Bucephalus became Alexander's favorite mount, and while he would allow no one else to ride him, he obeyed his master perfectly.

But although Alexander did not always practice the virtues which Aristotle had tried to teach him, he never forgot his old tutor. He gave him large sums of money, so that the philosopher could continue his studies and find out new things. And during his journeys, he always sent him complete collections of the animals and plants of the regions he visited.

from **Alexander and Diogenes**
from <u>The Story of the Greeks</u>
   by H. A. Guerber

As he could win nothing but short or rude answers, Alexander was about to go away, but he first asked the sage a question. He wanted to know whether or not there was anything he could do for him. "Yes!" snapped Diogenes. "Stand out of my sunshine!"

Strange to relate, Alexander the king and Diogenes the cynic died on the same night and from the same cause. Diogenes died in his tub after a too plentiful supper from the raw leg of an ox; while Alexander breathed his last in a Babylonian palace after having eaten and drunk to excess at a rich banquet.

from **A Roman's Honor**
from The Ontario Readers, by Ontario Ministry of Education
adapted from The Book of Golden Deeds by Charlotte M. Yonge

"Have you resolved to dishonor me?" he said. "I am not ignorant that death and the most extreme tortures are preparing for me; but what are these to the shame of an infamous action, or the wounds of a guilty mind? Slave as I am to Carthage, I have still the spirit of a Roman. I have sworn to return. It is my duty to go. Let the gods take care of the rest."

Worn and dejected, the captive warrior came to the outside of the gates of his own city and there paused, refusing to enter. "I am no longer a Roman citizen," he said. "I am but the barbarian's slave, and the Senate may not give audience to strangers within the walls."

from **The Story of the Empty Tomb**
from The Wonder Book of Bible Stories
by Logan Marshall

But the other robber said to him, "Have you no fear of God, to speak thus, while you are suffering the same fate with this man? And we deserve to die, but this man has done nothing wrong."

Then this man said to Jesus, "Lord, remember me when you come into thy kingdom!"

At about noon, a sudden darkness came over the land and lasted for three hours. And in the middle of the afternoon, when Jesus had been on the cross six hours of terrible pain, he cried out aloud, "My God, my God, why have you forsaken me?"

from **The Wild Caligula**
from The Story of the Romans
by H. A. Guerber

An ordinary boat to travel about in would not have suited Caligula, so he had a galley built of cedar wood. The oars were gilded, the sails were made of silk, and on the deck was a pleasure garden with real plants and trees bearing fruit of all kinds.

Before going back home, however, he started out to conquer Britain. But when he came to the sea, he directed his soldiers to pick up a lot of shells on the shore. These he brought back to Rome as booty, and he pompously called them the spoils of the ocean.

from **Nero's First Crimes**
from The Story of the Romans
   by H. A. Guerber

Nero was only about seventeen years of age when he began his reign. He was handsome, well educated, and pleasant-mannered, but unfortunately he, too, was a hypocrite. Although he pretended to admire all that was good, he was in reality very wicked.

His mother, Agrippina, had set him on the throne only that she herself might reign, and she was very angry at being sent away from court. However, she did not give up all hopes of ruling, but made several attempts to win her son's confidence once more, and to get back her place at court.

from **The Christians Persecuted**
from The Story of the Romans
   by H. A. Guerber

During this first Roman persecution, St. Paul was beheaded and St. Peter was crucified. St. Peter was placed on the cross head downward, at his own request, because he did not consider himself worthy to die as his beloved master had died.

The Christians, who had been taught to love one another and to be good, could not of course approve of the wicked Nero's conduct. They boldly reproved him for his vices, and Nero soon took his revenge by accusing them of having set fire to Rome and by having them seized and tortured in many ways.

from **The Siege of Jerusalem**
from The Story of the Romans
   by H. A. Guerber

All his thoughts were about eating and drinking. He lived in great luxury at home; but he often invited himself out to dinner, breakfast, or supper at the house of one of his courtiers, where he expected to be treated to the most exquisite viands.

In spite of all these signs, Titus battered down the heavy walls, scaled the ramparts, and finally took the city where famine and pestilence now reigned. The Roman soldiers robbed the houses and then set fire to them. The flames, thus started, soon reached the beautiful temple built by Herod, and in spite of all that Titus could do to save it, this great building was burned to the ground.

from **A Prophecy Fulfilled**
from The Story of the Romans
by H. A. Guerber

Diocletian, however, found that the Roman Empire was too large and hard to govern for a single ruler. He therefore made his friend Maximian associate emperor. Then he said that Galerius and Constantius should be called Caesars, and gave them also a portion of the empire to govern.

At noontide, on the day before his battle with Maxentius, Constantine and his army were startled by a brilliant cross which suddenly appeared in the sky. Around the cross were the Greek words meaning, "By this sign conquer."

Models from Chapter II

The Babylonian Story of the Deluge as Told by Assyrian Tablets *from* **from Nineveh (excerpt)**
by E. A. Wallis Budge

With everything that I possessed, I loaded it.
With everything that I possessed of silver, I loaded it.
With everything that I possessed of gold, I loaded it.
With all that I possessed of living grain, I loaded it.

I brought out a swallow and let her go free.
The swallow flew away and then came back;
Because she had no place to alight on, she came back.
I brought out a raven and let her go free.
The raven flew away; she saw the sinking waters.
She ate, she pecked in the ground, she croaked, she came not back.

from **The Oldest Code of Laws in the World, by Hammurabi, King of Babylon**
by C. H. W. JOHNS, M.A.

If a man has harbored in his house a manservant or a maidservant, fugitive from the palace, or a poor man, and has not produced them at the demand of the commandant, the owner of that house shall be put to death.

If a man has stolen ox or sheep or donkey or pig or ship, whether from the temple or the palace, he shall pay thirty fold. If he be a poor man, he shall render tenfold. If the thief has nought to pay, he shall be put to death.

from **The Babylonian Legends of the Creation**
by British Museum
FIRST TABLET (lines 1-61)

By day I find no peace; by night I have no rest.
Verily I will make an end of their way; I will sweep them away.
There shall be a sound of lamentation; lo, then we shall rest.

When the heavens above were yet unnamed,
And the name of the earth beneath had not been recorded,
Their waters were merged into a single mass.
A field had not been measured, a marsh had not been searched out,

from The Shih King or Book of Poetry (excerpt)
from <u>The Sacred Books of the East, Vol. 3</u>
by James Legge

The large bells and drums fill the ear. The various dances are grandly performed. We have the admirable visitors, who are pleased and delighted.

From of old, before our time, the former men set us the example how to be mild and humble from morning to night and to be reverent in discharging the service.

He received the tribute of the states, small and large,
And he supported them as a strong steed does its burden
So did he receive the favour of Heaven.
He displayed everywhere his valour,
Unshaken, unmoved, Unterrified, unscared
All dignities were united in him.

from The Literature of the Ancient Egyptians (excerpt)
by E. A. Wallis Budge

"I have come, making thee to trample under foot the uttermost ends of the earth. The Circuit of the Great Circuit is in thy grasp. I have made them to see Thy Majesty as the hawk, which seizeth what it seeth when it pleaseth."

"I have come, making thee to trample under foot those who dwell in the Islands, those who live in the Great Green hear thy roarings. I have made them to see Thy Majesty as the slayer when he mounteth on the back of his sacrificial animal.

from David and Goliath
from The King James Bible

And David said to Saul, "Let no man's heart fail because of him; thy servant will go and fight with this Philistine."

And Saul said to David, "Thou art not able to go against this Philistine to fight with him; for thou art but a youth, and he a man of war from his youth."

Then said David to the Philistine, "Thou comest to me with a sword and with a spear and with a shield, but I come to thee in the name of the LORD of hosts, the God of the armies of Israel, whom thou hast defied."

from **Works And Days (excerpt)**
from by Hesiod
translated by Hugh G. Evelyn-White

Do not get base gain: base gain is as bad as ruin. Be friends with the friendly and visit him who visits you. Give to one who gives, but do not give to one who does not give. A man gives to the freehanded, but no one gives to the close-fisted.

He who adds to what he has will keep off bright-eyed hunger; for if you add only a little to a little and do this often, soon that little will become great. What a man has by him at home does not trouble him; it is better to have your stuff at home, for whatever is abroad may mean loss.

from **Apocryphal Life of Esop, the Fabulist (excerpt)**
from Flowers from a Persian Garden and Other Papers
by W. A. Clouston

The merchant sets out for Asia with all his house-hold. Esop is offered the lightest load, as being a raw recruit. From among the bags, beds, and baskets, he chooses a basket full of bread—a load for two men. They laugh at his folly, but let him have his will, and he staggers under the burden to the wonder of his master.

A party of guests are coming to dinner one day, and Esop is set just within the door to keep out all but the wise. When there is a knock at the door Esop shouts, "What does the dog shake?" All but one go away, thinking he means them. The last answers, "His tail," and is admitted.

from **The Tao Teh King, or the Tao and its Characteristics**
by Lao-Tse
translated by James Legge

All in the world know the beauty of the beautiful, and in doing this they have the idea of what ugliness is. They all know the skill of the skillful, and in doing this they have the idea of what the want of skill is.

Not to value and employ men of superior ability is the way to keep the people from rivalry among themselves. Not to prize articles which are difficult to obtain is the way to keep them from becoming thieves. Not to show them what is likely to excite their desires is the way to keep their minds from disorder.

from The Sayings of Confucius (excerpt)
by Confucius
translated by Leonard A. Lyall

13. Tzu-kung asked, What is a gentleman?
The Master said, He puts words into deeds first, and follows these up with words.
14. The Master said, "A gentleman is broad and fair; the small man takes sides and is narrow."
15. The Master said, "Learning without thought is naught; thought without learning is dangerous."

The Master said, "Hear much, leave all that is doubtful alone, speak warily of everything else, and few will be offended. See much, leave all that is dangerous alone, deal warily with everything else, and thou wilt have little to rue. If thy words seldom give offence, and thy deeds leave little to rue, pay will follow.   (rue = regret)

from An Account of Egypt (excerpt)
by Herodotus
translated by G. C. Macaulay

The priests of the gods in other lands wear long hair, but in Egypt they shave their heads. Among other men, the custom is that in mourning, those whom the matter concerns most nearly, have their hair cut short, but the Egyptians, when deaths occur, let their hair grow long.

They drink from cups of bronze and rinse them out every day, and not some only do this but all. They wear garments of linen always newly washed, and this they make a special point of practice. The priests shave themselves all over their bodies every other day, so that no lice or any other foul thing may come to be upon them when they minister to the gods.

from The Apology (excerpt)
by Xenophon
translation by H. G. Dakyns

He exclaimed very innocently, "But the hardest thing of all to bear, Socrates, is to see you put to death unjustly."

Whereupon Socrates, it is said, gently stroked the young man's head. "Would you have been better pleased, my dear one, to see me put to death for some just reason rather than unjustly?"

When once he had decided that death was better for him than life, just as in the old days he had never harshly opposed himself to the good things of life, so even in the face of death he showed no touch of weakness. But with gaiety, he welcomed death's embrace and discharged life's debt.

from **The Categories (excerpt)**
by Aristotle
translated by E. M. Edghill

Things are said to be named 'derivatively', which derive their name from some other name, but differ from it in termination. Thus, the grammarian derives his name from the word 'grammar', and the courageous man from the word 'courage'.

For every assertion must, as is admitted, be either true or false. Whereas expressions which are not in any way composite such as man, white, runs, or wins cannot be either true or false.
(composite = statements)

from **On Old Age (excerpt)**
by Marcus Tullius Cicero January 3
translated by E. S. Shuckburgh

Bodily strength is wanting to old age; but neither is bodily strength demanded from old men. Therefore, both by law and custom, men of my time of life are exempt from those duties which cannot be supported without bodily strength. Accordingly, not only are we not forced to do what we cannot do; we are not even obliged to do as much as we can.

The fact is that old age is respectable just as long as it asserts itself, maintains its proper rights, and is not enslaved to any one. For as I admire a young man who has something of the old man in him, so do I an old one who has something of a young man. The man who aims at this may possibly become old in body, but in mind he never will.

from **The Crucifixion of Christ**
from The King James Bible

And Jesus stood before the governor. And the governor asked him, saying, "Art thou the King of the Jews?" And Jesus said unto him, "Thou sayest."

And when he was accused of the chief priests and elders, he answered nothing.

When he was set down on the judgment seat, his wife sent unto him, saying, "Have thou nothing to do with that just man; for I have suffered many things this day in a dream because of him."

from **Marcus Aurelius Antoninus (excerpt)**
from The Library of the World's Best Literature, Ancient and Modern—Vol. 3
edited by Charles Dudley Warner

In the mind of him who is pure and good will be found neither corruption nor defilement nor any malignant taint. Unlike the actor who leaves the stage before his part is played, the life of such a man is complete whenever death may come.

If it be in thy power, teach men to do better. If not, remember it is always in thy power to forgive. The gods are so merciful to those who err, that for some purposes they grant their aid to such men by conferring upon them health, riches, and honor. What prevents thee from doing likewise?

from **The Nicene Creed**
from The second Ecumenical Council
notes from The Exposition of the Apostles' Creed
by Rev. James Dodds, D.D.

He suffered and was buried, and the third day He rose again according to the Scriptures and ascended into heaven and sitteth on the right hand of the Father. And He shall come again with glory to judge the quick and the dead, whose kingdom shall have no end.

And I believe in one holy Catholic and Apostolic Church. I acknowledge one Baptism for the remission of sins; and I look for the resurrection of the dead, and the life of the world to come.

Models from Chapter III

from **Age**
from The Library of the World's Best Literature, Ancient and Modern—Vol. 2
by Anacreon
by Charles Dudley Warner

Whether I grow old or no,
By th' effects I do not know;
This I know, without being told,
'Tis time to live, if I grow old;

Oft am I by the women told,
Poor Anacreon, thou grow'st old!
Look how thy hairs are falling all;
Poor Anacreon, how they fall!

from **The Boaster**
from Baby's Own Aesop 1887
by Aesop, W. J. Linton, and Walter Crane

In the house, in the market, the streets,
Everywhere he was boasting his feats;
Till one said, with a sneer,
"Let us see it done here!
What's so oft done with ease, one repeats."

How the cunning old Crow got his drink
When 'twas low in the pitcher, just think!
Don't say that he spilled it!
With pebbles he filled it,
Till the water rose up to the brink.
From "The Crow and the Pitcher"

from **The Cloud Chorus (excerpt)**
from 'The Clouds'
  by Aristophanes
from The Library of the World's Best Literature, Ancient and Modern, Vol. 2
translation by Andrew Lang
  edited by Charles Dudley Warner

Immortal Clouds from the echoing shore
    Of the father of streams from the sounding sea,
Dewy and fleet, let us rise and soar;
    Dewy and gleaming and fleet are we!

Let us look on the tree-clad mountain-crest,
    On the sacred earth where the fruits rejoice,
On the waters that murmur east and west,
    On the tumbling sea with his moaning voice.

from **The Destruction of Sennacherib**
  by Lord Byron
  from Children's Literature
edited by Charles Madison Curry and Erle Elsworth Clippinger

Like the leaves of the forest when summer is green,
That host with their banners at sunset were seen:
Like the leaves of the forest when autumn hath blown,
The host on the morrow lay wither'd and strown.

And the widows of Ashur are loud in their wail,
And the idols are broke in the temple of Baal;
And the might of the Gentile, unsmote by the sword,
Hath melted like snow in the glance of the Lord.

from **Horatius (excerpt)**
from Lays of Ancient Rome
by Thomas Babbington Macaulay

But friends and foes in dumb surprise,
With parted lips and straining eyes,
   Stood gazing where he sank;
And when above the surges,
   They saw his crest appear,
All Rome sent forth a rapturous cry,
And even the ranks of Tuscany
   Could scarce forbear to cheer.

"Haul down the bridge, Sir Consul,
   With all the speed ye may;
I, with two more to help me,
   Will hold the foe in play.
In yon strait path a thousand
   May well be stopped by three.
Now who will stand on either hand,
   And keep the bridge with me?"

from **Hymn to the Nile**
from Ancient Egypt
by George Rawlinson and Arthur Gilman by

O inundation of Nile, offerings are made to thee;
Oxen are slain to thee;
Great festivals are kept for thee;
Fowls are sacrificed to thee;
Beasts of the field are caught for thee;
Pure flames are offered to thee;

Watering the land without ceasing:
The way of heaven descending:
Lover of food, bestower of corn,
Giving life to every home!...

from **Moderation**
from World's Best Poetry, Vol. 10
   translation of Horace, Bk. II. Ode X_. W. COWPER.
edited by Bliss Carman

He that holds fast the golden mean,
 And lives contentedly between
  The little and the great,
Feels not the wants that pinch the poor,
Nor plagues that haunt the rich man's door.

   (complete poem)

from **The Mouse and the Lion**
from Baby's Own Aesop 1887
by Aesop, W. J. Linton, and Walter Crane

A poor thing the Mouse was, and yet,
When the Lion got caught in a net,
All his strength was no use
'Twas the poor little Mouse
Who nibbled him out of the net.

(complete poem)

from **Night**
by Alcman
translation by Colonel Mure
edited by Charles Dudley Warner

Over the drowsy earth still night prevails;
    Calm sleep the mountain tops and shady vales,
        The rugged cliffs and hollow glens;
The cattle on the hill. Deep in the sea,
    The countless finny race and monster brood
  Tranquil repose. Even the busy bee
    Forgets her daily toil. The silent wood
No more with noisy hum of insect rings;

(most of poem)

from **The People Who Are Really Happy**
from The Children's Bible
translated, arranged by Henry A. Sherman

"Blessed are the poor in spirit,
For theirs is the Kingdom of Heaven.
Blessed are the meek,
For they shall inherit the earth.
Blessed are they who mourn,
For they shall be comforted.

Blessed are they who hunger and thirst for righteousness,
For they shall be satisfied.
Blessed are the merciful,
For they shall receive mercy.
Blessed are the pure in heart,
For they shall see God.
Blessed are the peacemakers,
For they shall be called the sons of God.

from **Psalms 23 and 121**
from The King James Bible

The LORD is my shepherd; I shall not want.

He maketh me to lie down in green pastures: he leadeth me beside the still waters.

He restoreth my soul: he leadeth me in the paths of righteousness for his name's sake.

Yea, though I walk through the valley of the shadow of death, I will fear no evil; for thou art with me.
Thy rod and thy staff, they comfort me.
Thou preparest a table before me in the presence of mine enemies. Thou anointest my head with oil.
My cup runneth over.

from **The Two Paths**
from Ontario Reader
by Solomon

Enter not into the Path of the Wicked,
And walk not in the way of evil men.
        Avoid it,
           Pass not by it;
        Turn from it,
        And pass on.

When thou goest, thy steps shall not be straitened;
And if thou runnest, thou shalt not stumble.
        Take fast hold of instruction;
        Let her not go:
        Keep her;
        For she is thy life.

from **The Vision of Belshazzar**
   by Lord Byron
  from Journeys Through Bookland, Vol. 6

In that same hour and hall
   The fingers of a Hand
Came forth against the wall,
   And wrote as if on sand:
The fingers of a man;—
   A solitary hand
Along the letters ran,
   And traced them like a wand.

A Captive in the land,
   A stranger and a youth,
He heard the king's command,
   He saw that writing's truth;
The lamps around were bright,
   The prophecy in view;
He read it on that night,—
   The morrow proved it true!

Models from Chapter IV

from The Deluge of Ogyges
from The Story of the Greeks
   by H. A. Guerber

    In spite of the speed with which they ran, the waters soon overtook them. Many of the Pelasgians were thus drowned, while their terrified companions ran faster and faster up the mountain, never stopping to rest until they were quite safe.

    The memory of the earthquake and flood was very clear, however. The poor Pelasgians could not forget their terror and the sudden death of so many friends, and they often talked about that horrible time. As this flood occurred in the days when Ogyges was king, it has generally been linked to his name, and called the Deluge (or flood) of Ogyges.

Story of Deucalion
   from The Story of the Greeks
     by H. A. Guerber

   When all danger was over, and the waters began to recede, they followed their leader down into the plains again. This soon gave rise to a wonderful story, which you will often hear. It was said that Deucalion and his wife Pyrrha were the only people left alive after the flood. When the waters had all gone, they went down the mountain and found that the temple at Delphi, where they worshiped their gods, was still standing unharmed. They entered and, kneeling before the altar, prayed for help.

    A mysterious voice then bade them go down the mountain, throwing their mother's bones behind them. They were very much troubled when they heard this, until Deucalion said that a voice from heaven could not have meant them to do any harm. In thinking over the real meaning of the words he had heard, he told his wife that, as the Earth is the mother of all creatures, her bones must mean the stones.

from The Enchanted Waterfall
   from Tales of Wonder Every Child Should Know
    edited by Kate Douglas Wiggin and Nora Archibald Smith

   "Here," said he, "we're all bent on the same errand. Let us fill our jars, pitchers, and gourds and go home. But first, I'll have just one more taste of the magic sake." He stooped down and, filling his gourd, put it to his lips. Once and yet again did he drink, with a face of astonishment, which soon gave place to anger.

    When they were fairly gone, the good young woodcutter crept from his hiding place. "This can't be true," he thought, "or was it all a dream? At any rate," said he, "I must taste once more for myself." He stooped down, filled the gourd, and drank. Sure enough, there was the same fine flavored sake he had tasted yesterday. And so it remained.

from **The Escape from the Burning City**
from The Story of the Romans
by H. A. Guerber

Among these few, however, there was a prince named Aeneas. His father was Anchises, the cousin of the King of Troy, and his mother was Venus, the goddess of beauty. As Venus did not want her son to die with the rest of the Trojans, she appeared to him during the fatal night when the Greeks had secretly entered Troy and were plundering and burning the houses. She showed him that resistance would be useless and bade him flee from the city with all his family.

Æneas had been taught to obey every word the gods said; so he at once stopped fighting and hurried back to his house. Then he lifted his poor old father up on his back, took his little son Iulus by the hand, and called to his wife and servants to follow him.

The Clever Trick
from The Story of the Romans
by H. A. Guerber

The boats were tossed up and down on the waves and driven apart by the fierce winds, and some of them sank under the water. The other vessels would have been dashed to pieces and all the men on board would have perished had not a second god interfered in favor of Æneas and suddenly stilled the awful storm.

The wind was so high, the darkness so great, and the lightning flashes so blinding, that Æneas had lost his bearings. When the storm was over, he sailed for the nearest land and came to the coast of what is now Tunis; but he had no idea where he was. He therefore bade his companions remain on the ships, while he and his devoted friend, Achates, went ashore. The two men started out and began cautiously to explore the country where they had landed, trying to find someone who could tell them where they were. (adapted from the original)

The Boards Are Eaten
from The Story of the Romans
by H. A. Guerber

The men all sat down around the fire. Iulus, who was very hungry indeed, quickly ate his share of meat and then devoured the cake on which it had been placed. As he swallowed the last mouthful he cried, "Just see how hungry I was! I've eaten even the board on which my meal was served!"

Aeneas knew that Dido would do her best to keep him in Carthage, so he stole away while she slept, without even bidding her good-by. When she awoke and asked for him, his ships were almost out of sight.

from **The Golden Nugget**
from A Chinese Wonder Book
    by Norman Hinsdale Pitman

"What trick is this you have played on me, masters? Why do you make a poor man like me run his legs off for nothing on a hot day?"

"What do you mean, fellow?" asked Ki-wu, astonished. "Didn't you find the fruit we told you about?"

"No," he answered, in a tone of half-hidden rage, "but in its place, a monster snake, which I cut in two with my blade. Now, the gods will bring me bad luck for killing something in the woods. If you thought you could drive me from this place by such a trick, you'll soon find you were mistaken."

from **The Lion and the Goat**
from Junior Classics, Vol. 1
    by Ramaswami Raju

The Goat rose up, advanced to the mouth of the cave, and said, "You'll come back tomorrow, won't you?"

"Never again," said the Lion.

"Do you think I'll be able to see you, at least, in the wood tomorrow?"

The latter said to himself, "This animal looks like a Goat, but it doesn't talk like one. So it is very likely some wicked spirit in this shape. Prudence often serves us better than valor, so for the present I'll return to the wood," and he turned back.

from **The Penny-Wise Monkey**
from More Jataka Tales
re-told by Ellen C. Babbitt

Once upon a time the king of a large and rich country gathered together his army to take a faraway little country. The king and his soldiers marched all morning long and then went into camp in the forest.

The king had watched the Monkey, and he said to himself, "I will not be like this foolish Monkey, who lost much to gain a little. I will go back to my own country and enjoy what I now have."

from **The Story of the Shipwrecked Sailor**
from Peeps at Many Lands: Ancient Egypt,
   by James Baikie

I bowed low before him and promised to tell of him to Pharaoh and to bring him ships full of all the treasures of Egypt; however, he only smiled at my speech and said, "Ah, little one, thou hast nothing that I need, for I am Prince of the Land of Punt and all its perfumes are mine. Moreover, when you depart, you shall never again see this isle, for it shall be changed into waves."

Now, behold! When the time was come, as he had foretold, the ship drew near. And the good serpent said to me, "Farewell, farewell! Go to thy home, little one, see again thy children and let thy name be good in thy town; these are my wishes for thee." So I bowed low before him, and he loaded me with precious gifts.

from **The Tale of Ivan**
from Celtic Fairy Tales
   by Joseph Jacobs

"Don't go today," said his master; "my wife bakes tomorrow, and she shall make you a cake to take home to your good woman."

And when Ivan was going to leave, "Here," said his master, "here is a cake for you to take home to your wife. And when you are most joyous together, then break the cake, but not sooner."

So they were taken and carried to prison until at last Ivan came to them. "Alas! Alas! Ivan," cried they, "bad luck sticks to us; our host was killed last night, and we shall be hanged for it."

"Ah, tell the justices," said Ivan, "to summon the real murderers."

"Who knows," they replied, "who committed the crime?"

from **The Two Melons**
from Tales of Wonder Every Child Should Know
edited by Kate Douglas Wiggin and Nora Archibald Smith

In prospect of her future wealth, she ate richer foods, bought the finest garments, and got so deeply into debt that, before the end of the year, she was harried by duns. But the melon grew rapidly, and she was delighted to find that, as it ripened, it became of vast size, and that when she shook it there was a great rattling inside.   (duns = those asking for payment)

Among her neighbors was a busybody who craftily found out how the old woman had so suddenly become rich. Thinking there was no good reason why she should not herself be equally fortunate, she washed clothes at the pool, keeping a sharp lookout for birds until she managed to hit and maim one of a flock that was flitting over the water.

from **The Wolf and the Twins**
from The Story of the Romans
by H. A. Guerber

During the war, Æneas and Turnus both won much glory by their courage. At last they met in single combat, in which Turnus was conquered and slain; and Æneas, having thus got rid of his rival, married the fair princess.

The king flew into a passion at this news and vainly tried to discover the name of Rhea Sylvia's husband. She refused to tell it, and Amulius gave orders that she should be buried alive. Her twin children, Romulus and Remus, were also condemned to die; but, instead of burying them alive with their mother, Amulius had them placed in their cradle and set adrift on the Tiber River.

from **Romulus Builds Rome**
from The Story of the Romans
by H. A. Guerber

Before beginning, however, they thought it would be well to give the city a name. Each wanted the honor of naming it, and each wanted to rule over it when it was built. As they were twins, neither was willing to give up to the other, and as they were both hot-tempered and obstinate, they soon began to quarrel.

The city of Rome was at first composed of a series of mud huts, and, as Romulus had been brought up among shepherds, he was quite satisfied with a palace thatched with rushes. As the number of his subjects increased, however, the town grew larger and richer, and before long it became a prosperous city, covering two hills instead of one. On the second hill the Romans built a fortress, or citadel, which was perched on top of great rocks, and was the safest place in case of an attack by an enemy.

Models from The King James Bible

For parents sensitive to models that reference pagan gods, extra passages are listed below. These can be used for copywork or studied dictation.

Psalms 121

01 I will lift up mine eyes unto the hills, from whence cometh my help.
02 My help cometh from the LORD, which made heaven and earth.
03 He will not suffer thy foot to be moved: he that keepeth thee will not slumber.
04 Behold, he that keepeth Israel shall neither slumber nor sleep.
05 The LORD is thy keeper: the LORD is thy shade upon thy right hand.
06 The sun shall not smite thee by day, nor the moon by night.
07 The LORD shall preserve thee from all evil: he shall preserve thy soul.
08 The LORD shall preserve thy going out and thy coming in from this time forth and even for evermore.

The Ten Commandments
Exodus 20:1-17

And God spake all these words, saying, I am the LORD thy God, which have brought thee out of the land of Egypt, out of the house of bondage.

Thou shalt have no other gods before me.

Thou shalt not make unto thee any graven image, or any likeness of any thing that is in heaven above, or that is in the earth beneath, or that is in the water under the earth. Thou shalt not bow down thyself to them, nor serve them. For I the LORD thy God am a jealous God, visiting the iniquity of the fathers upon the children unto the third and fourth generation of them that hate me; and showing mercy unto thousands of them that love me, and keep my commandments.

Thou shalt not take the name of the LORD thy God in vain, for the LORD will not hold him guiltless that taketh his name in vain.

Remember the sabbath day, to keep it holy. Six days shalt thou labour, and do all thy work.
But the seventh day is the sabbath of the LORD thy God. In it thou shalt not do any work—thou, nor thy son, nor thy daughter, thy manservant, nor thy maidservant, nor thy cattle, nor thy stranger that is within thy gates. For in six days the LORD made heaven and earth, the sea, and all that in them is, and rested the seventh day. Wherefore the LORD blessed the sabbath day, and hallowed it.

Honour thy father and thy mother that thy days may be long upon the land which the LORD thy God giveth thee.

Thou shalt not kill.
Thou shalt not commit adultery.
Thou shalt not steal.
Thou shalt not bear false witness against thy neighbor.

Thou shalt not covet thy neighbor's house. Thou shalt not covet thy neighbor's wife, nor his manservant, nor his maidservant, nor his ox, nor his ass, nor any thing that is thy neighbor's.

Hebrews 13:5,6

Let your conduct be without covetousness; be content with such things as you have. For He Himself has said, "I will never leave you nor forsake you." 6 So we may boldly say:

> " The LORD is my helper;
> I will not fear.
> What can man do to me?"

Romans 12:1,2

1 I beseech you therefore, brethren, by the mercies of God, that you present your bodies a living sacrifice, holy, acceptable to God, which is your reasonable service. 2 And do not be conformed to this world, but be transformed by the renewing of your mind, that you may prove what *is* that good and acceptable and perfect will of God.

1 Corinthians 10:13

13There hath no temptation taken you but such as is common to man: but God is faithful, who will not suffer you to be tempted above that ye are able; but will with the temptation also make a way to escape, that ye may be able to bear it.

Deuteronomy 31:8

8And the LORD, he it is that doth go before thee; he will be with thee, he will not fail thee, neither forsake thee: fear not, neither be dismayed.

James 1:5

My brethren, count it all joy when ye fall into divers temptations; 3Knowing this, that the trying of your faith worketh patience. 4But let patience have her perfect work, that ye may be perfect and entire, wanting nothing. 5If any of you lack wisdom, let him ask of God, that giveth to all men liberally, and upbraideth not; and it shall be given him. 11Believe me that I am in the Father, and the Father in me: or else believe me for the very works' sake.

John 14:12-15

12Verily, verily, I say unto you, He that believeth on me, the works that I do shall he do also; and greater works than these shall he do; because I go unto my Father. 13And whatsoever ye shall ask in my name, that will I do, that the Father may be glorified in the Son. 14If ye shall ask any thing in my name, I will do it. 15If ye love me, keep my commandments.

John 14: 26,27

26But the Comforter, which is the Holy Ghost, whom the Father will send in my name, he shall teach you all things, and bring all things to your remembrance, whatsoever I have said unto you. 27Peace I leave with you, my peace I give unto you: not as the world giveth, give I unto you. Let not your heart be troubled, neither let it be afraid.

1 John 5:14-15

14And this is the confidence that we have in him, that, if we ask any thing according to his will, he heareth us: 15And if we know that he hear us, whatsoever we ask, we know that we have the petitions that we desired of him.

Made in the USA
Columbia, SC
03 November 2024